Lecture Notes in Computer Science 12443

More information about this series at http://www.springer.com/series/7412

Carole H. Sudre · Hamid Fehri et al. (Eds.)

Uncertainty for Safe Utilization of Machine Learning in Medical Imaging, and Graphs in Biomedical Image Analysis

Second International Workshop, UNSURE 2020
and Third International Workshop, GRAIL 2020
Held in Conjunction with MICCAI 2020
Lima, Peru, October 8, 2020
Proceedings

Springer

Editors
Carole H. Sudre 🅿
University College London
London, UK

Hamid Fehri 🅿
University of Oxford
Oxford, UK

Additional Volume Editors *see next page*

ISSN 0302-9743   ISSN 1611-3349   (electronic)
Lecture Notes in Computer Science
ISBN 978-3-030-60364-9   ISBN 978-3-030-60365-6   (eBook)
https://doi.org/10.1007/978-3-030-60365-6

LNCS Sublibrary: SL6 – Image Processing, Computer Vision, Pattern Recognition, and Graphics

This Springer imprint is published by the registered company Springer Nature Switzerland AG
The registered company address is: Gewerbestrasse 11, 6330 Cham, Switzerland

Additional Volume Editors

UNSURE 2020 Editors

Tal Arbel (iD)
McGill University
Montreal, QC, Canada

Adrian Dalca (iD)
Massachusetts General Hospital
Charlestown, MA, USA

Koen Van Leemput (iD)
Technical University of Denmark
Kongens Lyngby, Denmark

Christian F. Baumgartner (iD)
ETH Zurich
Zürich, Switzerland

Ryutaro Tanno
University College London
London, UK

William M. Wells
Harvard Medical School
Boston, MA, USA

GRAIL 2020 Editors

Aristeidis Sotiras (iD)
Washington University School
of Medicine
St. Louis, MO, USA

Enzo Ferrante (iD)
Ciudad Universitaria UNL
Santa Fe, Argentina

Bartlomiej Papiez (iD)
University of Oxford
Oxford, UK

Sarah Parisot (iD)
Huawei Noah's Ark Lab
London, UK

Preface UNSURE 2020

The Second Workshop on UNcertainty for Safe Utilization of machine lEarning in mEdical imaging (UNSURE 2020), was organized as a satellite event of the 23rd International Conference on Medical Image Computing and Computer Assisted Intervention (MICCAI 2020).

Given the ever-increasing diversity of machine learning techniques in medical imaging applications, the need to quantify and acknowledge the limitations of a given technique has been a growing topic of interest of the MICCAI community. The purpose of this workshop is to develop awareness and encourage research in the field of uncertainty modeling to enable safe implementation of machine learning tools in the clinical world.

This year, the proceedings of UNSURE 2020 include 10 high-quality papers that have been selected among 18 submissions following a double-blind review process. Each submission of 8 to 10 pages was reviewed by 3 members of the Program Committee, formed by 26 experts in the field of deep learning, Bayesian modeling, and Gaussian processes.

The accepted papers cover the fields of uncertainty quantification and modeling, as well as application to clinical pipelines, with applications ranging from multi-label segmentation to landmark detection and classification to registration, including image quality evaluation.

Two keynote presentations, from experts Dr. Yarin Gal, University of Oxford, UK, and Dr. Herve Delingette, Inria Asclepios, France, further enriched the workshop.

We hope this workshop highlighted both theoretical and practical challenges in communicating uncertainties, and further encourages research to (a) improve safety in the application of machine learning tools and (b) assist in the translation of such tools to clinical practice.

We would like to thank all the authors for submitting their manuscripts to UNSURE, as well as the Program Committee members for the quality of their feedback and dedication to the review process.

August 2020

Carole H. Sudre
Tal Arbel
Christian F. Baumgartner
Adrian Dalca
Ryutaro Tanno
Koen Van Leemput
William M. Wells

Organization

Program Committee Chairs UNSURE 2020

Tal Arbel	McGill University, Canada
Christian Baumgartner	ETH Zurich, Switzerland
Adrian Dalca	Harvard Medical School and Massachusetts Institute of Technology, USA
Carole H. Sudre	University College London and King's College London, UK
Ryutaro Tanno	University College London, UK
Koen Van Leemput	Harvard Medical School, USA and Technical University of Denmark, Denmark
William M. Wells	Harvard Medical School, USA

Program Committee UNSURE 2020

Alejandro Granados	King's College London, UK
Alireza Sedghi	Queen's University, Canada
Daniel Coelho	Imperial College London, UK
Dennis Madsen	University of Basel, Switzerland
Evan Yu	Cornell University, USA
Felix Bragman	King's College London, UK
Hongxiang Lin	University College London, UK
Ivor Simpson	University of Sussex, UK
Jinwei Zhang	Cornell University, USA
Jorge Cardoso	King's College London, UK
Kerem Can Tezcan	ETH Zurich, Switzerland
Leo Joskowicz	Hebrew University of Jerusalem, Israel
Liane Canas	King's College London, UK
Lucas Fidon	King's College London, UK
Mark Graham	King's College London, UK
Max-Heinrich Laves	Leibniz Universitat Hannover, Germany
Nalini Singh	Massachusetts Institute of Technology, USA
Pedro Borges	King's College London, UK
Pieter Van Molle	Ghent University, Belgium
Raghav Mehta	McGill University, Canada
Richard Shaw	King's College London, UK
Roger Soberanis-Mukul	Technische Universitat Munchen, Germany
Tanya Nair	Imagia, Canada
Thomas Varsavsky	King's College London, UK
Tim Adler	DKFZ, Germany

Preface GRAIL 2020

The Third International Workshop on Graphs in Biomedical Image Analysis (GRAIL 2020), was organized as a satellite event of the 23rd International Conference on Medical Image Computing and Computer Assisted Intervention (MICCAI 2020) in Lima, Peru, which was held completely virtually due to the COVID-19 pandemic. After the success and positive feedback obtained through previous years, GRAIL had its third presence at MICCAI 2020, in the spirit of strengthening the links between graphs and biomedical imaging.

This workshop provides a unique opportunity to meet and discuss both theoretical advances in graphical methods, as well as the practicality of such methods when applied to complex biomedical imaging problems. Simultaneously, the workshop seeks to be an interface to foster future interdisciplinary research, including signal processing and machine learning on graphs.

Graphs and related graph-based modeling have attracted significant research focus as they enable us to represent complex data and their interactions in a perceptually meaningful way. With the emergence of big data in the medical imaging community, the relevance of graphs as a means to represent data sampled from irregular and non-Euclidean domains is increasing, together with the development of new inference and learning methods that operate on such structures. There is a wide range of well-established and emerging biomedical imaging problems that can benefit from these advances; we believe that the research presented at this workshop constitutes a clear example of that.

The GRAIL 2020 proceedings contain 10 high-quality papers of 8 to 12 pages that were pre-selected through a rigorous peer-review process. All submissions were peer-reviewed through a double-blind process by at least 3 members of the Program Committee, comprising 15 experts on graphs in biomedical image analysis, each doing at least 1 review. The accepted manuscripts cover a wide set of graph-based medical image analysis methods and applications, including brain connectomics analysis for anomaly detection, disease diagnosis, and progression modeling through graph matching, graph-cuts, multi-scale profiling, hierarchical graphs and generating connectivity maps, classification of chest X-ray, mammography and histology images when limited training data is available using deep graphical models, and data augmentation for laparoscopic procedures, organ surface modeling, and segmentation using geometric deep networks and graph domain adaptation.

In addition to the papers presented in this LNCS volume, the workshop included short abstracts and three keynote presentations from world-renowned experts: Prof. Herve Lombaert, Dr. Ahmad Ahmadi, and Prof. Xavier Bresson, in addition to a tutorial by Jonny Hancox from NVIDIA. The keynotes and the tutorial were designed to facilitate the development of new multidisciplinary ideas by introducing ongoing cutting-edge research in graph-based models within the biomedical image analysis domain.

We wish to thank all the GRAIL 2020 authors for their participation, and the members of the Program Committee for their feedback and commitment to the workshop. We are very grateful to our sponsor NVIDIA for their valuable support and awarding a GPU to the best workshop presentation.

The proceedings of the workshop are published as a joint LNCS volume alongside other satellite events organized in conjunction with MICCAI. In addition to the papers, abstracts and slides presented during the workshop will be made publicly available on the GRAIL website (http://grail-miccai.github.io/).

August 2020   Hamid Fehri
                                                         Aristeidis Sotiras
                                                        Bartlomiej Papiez
                                                           Enzo Ferrante
                                                           Sarah Parisot

Organization

Organizing Committee GRAIL 2020

Hamid Fehri	University of Oxford, UK
Bartlomiej Papiez	University of Oxford, UK
Enzo Ferrante	CONICET, Universidad Nacional del Litoral, Argentina
Sarah Parisot	Huawei Noah's Ark Lab, Canada
Aristeidis Sotiras	Washington University in St Louis, USA

Scientific Committee GRAIL 2020

Angelica Aviles-Rivero	University of Cambridge, UK
Mariusz Bajger	Flinders University, Australia
Matthew Clarkson	University College London, UK
Mariia Dmitrieva	Oxford University, UK
Rodrigo Echeveste	CONICET, Universidad Nacional del Litoral, Argentina
Zhenghan Fang	University of North Carolina at Chapel Hill, USA
Evgenios Kornaropoulous	University of Cambridge, UK
Gobert Lee	Flinders University, Australia
Gang Li	University of North Carolina at Chapel Hill, USA
Mingxia Liu	University of North Carolina at Chapel Hill, USA
Andrew Melbourne	Kings College London, UK
Yusuf Osmanlioglu	University of Pennsylvania, USA
Raghavendra Selvan	University of Copenhagen, Denmark
Yalin Wang	Arizona State University, USA
Zhiwei Zhai	Leiden University Medical Center, The Netherlands

Contents

UNSURE 2020

Image Registration via Stochastic Gradient Markov Chain Monte Carlo 3
  Daniel Grzech, Bernhard Kainz, Ben Glocker, and Loïc le Folgoc

RevPHiSeg: A Memory-Efficient Neural Network for Uncertainty
Quantification in Medical Image Segmentation 13
  Marc Gantenbein, Ertunc Erdil, and Ender Konukoglu

Hierarchical Brain Parcellation with Uncertainty 23
  Mark S. Graham, Carole H. Sudre, Thomas Varsavsky,
  Petru-Daniel Tudosiu, Parashkev Nachev, Sebastien Ourselin,
  and M. Jorge Cardoso

Quantitative Comparison of Monte-Carlo Dropout Uncertainty Measures
for Multi-class Segmentation 32
  Robin Camarasa, Daniel Bos, Jeroen Hendrikse, Paul Nederkoorn,
  Eline Kooi, Aad van der Lugt, and Marleen de Bruijne

Uncertainty Estimation in Landmark Localization Based
on Gaussian Heatmaps 42
  Christian Payer, Martin Urschler, Horst Bischof, and Darko Štern

Weight Averaging Impact on the Uncertainty of Retinal
Artery-Venous Segmentation 52
  Markus Lindén, Azat Garifullin, and Lasse Lensu

Improving Pathological Distribution Measurements
with Bayesian Uncertainty 61
  Ka Ho Tam, Korsuk Sirinukunwattana, Maria F. Soares, Maria Kaisar,
  Rutger Ploeg, and Jens Rittscher

Improving Reliability of Clinical Models Using Prediction Calibration 71
  Jayaraman J. Thiagarajan, Bindya Venkatesh, Deepta Rajan,
  and Prasanna Sattigeri

Uncertainty Estimation in Medical Image Denoising with Bayesian Deep
Image Prior 81
  Max-Heinrich Laves, Malte Tölle, and Tobias Ortmaier

Uncertainty Estimation for Assessment of 3D US Scan Adequacy
and DDH Metric Reliability 97
   Arunkumar Kannan, Antony Hodgson, Kishore Mulpuri,
   and Rafeef Garbi

GRAIL 2020

Clustering-Based Deep Brain MultiGraph Integrator Network for Learning
Connectional Brain Templates 109
   Uğur Demir, Mohammed Amine Gharsallaoui, and Islem Rekik

Detection of Discriminative Neurological Circuits Using Hierarchical
Graph Convolutional Networks in fMRI Sequences.................. 121
   Xiaodan Xing, Lili Jin, Qinfeng Li, Lei Chen, Zhong Xue, Ziwen Peng,
   Feng Shi, and Dinggang Shen

Graph Matching Based Connectomic Biomarker with Learning
for Brain Disorders 131
   Rui Sherry Shen, Jacob A. Alappatt, Drew Parker, Junghoon Kim,
   Ragini Verma, and Yusuf Osmanlıoğlu

Multi-scale Profiling of Brain Multigraphs by Eigen-Based Cross-diffusion
and Heat Tracing for Brain State Profiling 142
   Mustafa Sağlam and Islem Rekik

Graph Domain Adaptation for Alignment-Invariant Brain
Surface Segmentation 152
   Karthik Gopinath, Christian Desrosiers, and Herve Lombaert

Min-Cut Max-Flow for Network Abnormality Detection: Application
to Preterm Birth 164
   Hassna Irzan, Lucas Fidon, Tom Vercauteren, Sebastien Ourselin,
   Neil Marlow, and Andrew Melbourne

Geometric Deep Learning for Post-Menstrual Age Prediction Based
on the Neonatal White Matter Cortical Surface 174
   Vitalis Vosylius, Andy Wang, Cemlyn Waters, Alexey Zakharov,
   Francis Ward, Loic Le Folgoc, John Cupitt, Antonios Makropoulos,
   Andreas Schuh, Daniel Rueckert, and Amir Alansary

The GraphNet Zoo: An All-in-One Graph Based Deep Semi-supervised
Framework for Medical Image Classification 187
   Marianne de Vriendt, Philip Sellars, and Angelica I. Aviles-Rivero

Intraoperative Liver Surface Completion with Graph Convolutional VAE. . . .   198
Simone Foti, Bongjin Koo, Thomas Dowrick, João Ramalhinho,
Moustafa Allam, Brian Davidson, Danail Stoyanov,
and Matthew J. Clarkson

HACT-Net: A Hierarchical Cell-to-Tissue Graph Neural Network
for Histopathological Image Classification   208
Pushpak Pati, Guillaume Jaume, Lauren Alisha Fernandes,
Antonio Foncubierta-Rodríguez, Florinda Feroce,
Anna Maria Anniciello, Giosue Scognamiglio, Nadia Brancati,
Daniel Riccio, Maurizio Di Bonito, Giuseppe De Pietro, Gerardo Botti,
Orcun Goksel, Jean-Philippe Thiran, Maria Frucci, and Maria Gabrani

Correction to: Graph Matching Based Connectomic Biomarker
with Learning for Brain Disorders. C1
Rui Sherry Shen, Jacob A. Alappatt, Drew Parker, Junghoon Kim,
Ragini Verma, and Yusuf Osmanlıoğlu

Author Index   221

UNSURE 2020

Image Registration via Stochastic Gradient Markov Chain Monte Carlo

Daniel Grzech$^{(\boxtimes)}$, Bernhard Kainz, Ben Glocker, and Loïc le Folgoc

Department of Computing, Imperial College London, London, UK
{d.grzech17,b.kainz,b.glocker,l.le-folgoc}@imperial.ac.uk

Abstract. We develop a fully Bayesian framework for non-rigid registration of three-dimensional medical images, with a focus on uncertainty quantification. Probabilistic registration of large images along with calibrated uncertainty estimates is difficult for both computational and modelling reasons. To address the computational issues, we explore connections between the *Markov chain Monte Carlo by backprop* and the *variational inference by backprop* frameworks in order to efficiently draw thousands of samples from the posterior distribution. Regarding the modelling issues, we carefully design a Bayesian model for registration to overcome the existing barriers when using a dense, high-dimensional, and diffeomorphic parameterisation of the transformation. This results in improved calibration of uncertainty estimates.

1 Introduction

Image registration is the problem of aligning images into a common coordinate system such that the discrete pixel locations carry the same semantic information. It is a common pre-processing step for many applications, *e.g.* the statistical analysis of imaging data and computer-aided diagnosis. Image registration methods based on deep learning tend to incorporate task-specific knowledge from large datasets [3], whereas traditional methods are more general purpose [11]. Many established models [9,11,14] are based on the iterative optimisation of an energy function consisting of task-specific similarity and regularisation terms, which leads to an estimated deformation field and has to be done independently for every pair of images to be registered.

VoxelMorph [2,3,6,7] changed this paradigm by learning a function that maps a pair of input images to a deformation field. This gave a speed-up of several orders of magnitude while maintaining an accuracy comparable to established methods. An overview of current learning-based methods for registration can be found in [16]. With a few notable exceptions [6,7], Bayesian methods are often shunned when designing novel medical image analysis algorithms because of their perceived conceptual challenges and computational overhead. Yet in order to fully explore the parameter space and to lessen the impact of ad-hoc hyperparameter choices, it is desirable to adopt a Bayesian point of view.

Markov chain Monte Carlo (MCMC) methods have been used for asymptotically exact sampling from the posterior distribution in rigid registration [13],

© Springer Nature Switzerland AG 2020
C. H. Sudre et al. (Eds.): UNSURE 2020/GRAIL 2020, LNCS 12443, pp. 3–12, 2020.
https://doi.org/10.1007/978-3-030-60365-6_1

and are popular for analysing non-rigid registration uncertainty in intra-subject studies [20]. Recent research shows that the computational burden of MCMC can be lessened by embedding it in a multilevel framework [21]. The problem of uncertainty quantification has also been addressed using variational Bayesian methods [22]. In [15] the authors compared the quality of uncertainty estimates from an efficient and approximate variational Bayesian model and a reversible jump MCMC model, which is asymptotically exact.

We use the stochastic gradient Markov chain Monte Carlo (SG-MCMC) algorithm to establish an efficient posterior sampling algorithm for non-rigid image registration. SG-MCMC is based on the idea of stochastic gradient descent interpreted as a stochastic process with a stationary distribution centred on the optimum and with a covariance structure that can be used to approximate the posterior distribution [5,18]. The following is the summary of our main contributions:

1. We propose an efficient SG-MCMC algorithm for three-dimensional diffeomorphic non-rigid image registration;
2. We propose a new regularisation loss, which allows to carry out inference of the regularisation strength in a setting with a very high number of degrees of freedom (d.f.);
3. We evaluate the performance of our model both qualitatively and quantitatively by analysing the output uncertainty estimates on inter-subject brain MRI data.

To our knowledge, this is the first time that SG-MCMC has been used for the task of image registration. The code is available in a public repository: https://github.com/dgrzech/ir-sgmcmc.

Related Work. Bayesian parameter estimation for established registration models was proposed in [27]. Bayesian frameworks have been used to characterize image intensities [10] and anatomic variability [26]. Kernel regression has also been used to tackle multi-modal image registration with uncertainty [12,28]. We believe that our work is the first that efficiently tackles Bayesian image registration and uncertainty estimation using a very high-dimensional parameterisation of the transformation.

2   Registration Model

We denote an image pair by $\mathcal{D} = (F, M)$, where $F : \Omega_F \to \mathbb{R}$ is a fixed image and $M : \Omega_M \to \mathbb{R}$ is a moving image. We assume that F can be generated from M if deformed by a transformation $\varphi : \Omega_F \to \Omega_M$ which is parameterised by w. The goal of registration is to align the underlying domains Ω_F and Ω_M using a mapping that roughly visually aligns the images F and $M(w) := M \circ \varphi^{-1}(w)$ and is physically plausible, *i.e.* find parameters w such that $F \simeq M(w)$. We parameterise the transformation using the stationary velocity field (SVF) formulation. The velocity field is integrated numerically through scaling-and-squaring which results in a diffeomorphic transformation [1].

Likelihood Model. The likelihood model $p(\mathcal{D} \mid w)$ specifies the relationship between the data and the transformation parameters through the choice of a similarity metric. Due to its robustness to linear intensity transformations we use a similarity metric based on local cross-correlation (LCC). However, because LCC is not meaningful in a probabilistic context, we opt for the sum of voxel-wise squared differences instead of the usual sum of the voxel-wise product of intensities. Thus we can also enhance the likelihood model with extra features.

Denote the fixed and the warped moving images, with intensities standardised to zero mean and unit variance inside a neighbourhood of 3 voxels, as $\overline{F}$ and $\overline{M(w)}$ respectively. Following the example in [15], in order to make the model more robust to high outlier values caused by acquisition artifacts and misalignment over the course of registration, we adopt a Gaussian mixture model (GMM) of intensity residuals. At voxel k, the corresponding intensity residual r_k is assigned to the l-th component of the mixture, $1 \leqslant l \leqslant L$, if the categorical variable $c_k \in \{1, \cdots, L\}$ is equal to l. It then follows a normal distribution $\mathcal{N}(0, \beta_l^{-1})$. The component assignment c_k follows a categorical distribution and takes value l with probability ρ_l. In all experiments we use $L = 4$ components.

We also use virtual decimation to account for the fact that voxel-wise residuals are not independent, preventing over-emphasis on the data term and allowing to better calibrate uncertainty estimates [23]. The full expression of the image similarity term is then given by:

$$\mathcal{E}_{\text{data}} = \alpha \times - \sum_{i=1}^{N} \log \sum_{l=1}^{L} \frac{\sqrt{\beta_l}}{\sqrt{2\pi}} \rho_l \exp\left(-\frac{\beta_l}{2} \|\overline{F} - \overline{M(w)}\|^2\right) \tag{1}$$

where α is the scalar virtual decimation factor.

Transformation Priors. In Bayesian models, the transformation parameters are typically regularised with use of a multivariate normal prior $p(w \mid \lambda) = |\lambda L^T L|^{\frac{1}{2}} (2\pi)^{-\frac{N}{2}} \exp^{-\frac{1}{2}\lambda(Lw)^T Lw}$ that ensures smoothness, where N is the number of voxels in the image, λ is a scalar parameter that controls the strength of regularisation, and L is the matrix of a differential operator, here chosen to penalise the magnitude of the first derivative of the velocity field. Note that $(Lw)^T Lw = \|Lw\|^2$.

The regularisation strength parameter λ can be either fixed [3] or learnt from the data. The latter has been done successfully only in the context of transformation parameterisations with a relatively low number of d.f., e.g. B-splines [23] or a sparse learnable parameterisation [15]. In case of an SVF, where the number of d.f. is orders of magnitude higher, the problem is even more difficult. The baseline method that we use for comparison with our proposed regularisation loss, which was described in [23], corresponds to an uninformative gamma prior.

In order to infer the regularisation strength we specify a prior on the scalar regularisation energy $\chi^2 := \|Lw\|^2$. We use a log-normal prior on χ^2 and derive a prior on the velocity field:

$$\log p(\chi^2) \propto \log \chi^2 + \log \sigma_{\chi^2} + \frac{(\log \chi^2 - \mu_{\chi^2})^2}{2\sigma_{\chi^2}^2} \qquad (2)$$

$$\log p(w) \propto \log p(\chi^2) + (\frac{\nu}{2} - 1) \cdot \log \chi^2 \qquad (3)$$

where $\nu = N \cdot 3$ is the number of d.f. Given semi-informative hyperpriors on μ_{χ^2} and $\sigma_{\chi^2}^2$, which we discuss in the next section, we can estimate the right regularisation strength from data. Overall, the regularisation term is given by $\mathcal{E}_{\text{reg}} = \log p(\chi^2) + \log p(w)$.

Hyperpriors. Parameters of the priors are treated as latent variables. We set the likelihood model hyperpriors similarly to [15], with the parameters β_l assigned independent log-normal priors Lognormal$(\beta_l \mid \mu_{\beta_0}, \sigma_{\beta_0}^2)$ and the mixture proportions $\rho = (\rho_1, \cdots, \rho_L)$ with an uninformative Dirichlet prior Dir$(\rho \mid \kappa)$, where $\kappa = (\kappa_1, \cdots, \kappa_L)$. The problem of inferring regularisation strength is difficult, so we use semi-informative priors for the transformation prior parameters. The exponential of the transformation prior parameter μ_{χ^2} follows a gamma distribution $\Gamma(\exp(\mu_{\chi^2}) \mid a_{\chi_0^2}, b_{\chi_0^2})$ and $\sigma_{\chi^2}^2$ has a log-normal prior Lognormal$(\sigma_{\chi^2}^2 \mid \mu_{\chi_0^2}, \sigma_{\chi_0^2}^2)$.

3 Variational Inference

To initialise the MCMC algorithm we use the result of variational inference (VI). We assume that the approximate posterior distribution of the transformation parameters $q_w \sim \mathcal{N}(\mu_w, \Sigma_w)$ is a multivariate normal distribution. Due to the dimensionality of the problem, computing the full covariance matrix is not possible, so we model it as a sum of diagonal and low-rank parts $\Sigma_w = \text{diag}(\sigma_w^2) + u_w u_w^T$, with σ_w^2 and u_w both of size $N \cdot 3 \times 1$. To carry out VI, we maximise the evidence lower bound (ELBO), which can be written as:

$$\mathcal{L}(q) = \mathbb{E}_q[\log p(\mathcal{D} \mid w)] - D_{\text{KL}}(q \parallel p) = -\langle \mathcal{E}_{\text{data}} + \mathcal{E}_{\text{reg}} \rangle_q + H(q) \qquad (4)$$

where $D_{\text{KL}}(q \parallel p)$ is the Kullback-Leibler divergence between the approximate posterior q and the prior p. This corresponds to the sum of similarity and regularisation terms, with an additional term equal to the entropy of the posterior distribution $H(q)$. We use the reparameterisation trick with two samples per update to backpropagate w.r.t. parameters of the approximate variational posterior q_w, i.e. μ_w, σ_w^2, and u_w.

In order to make optimisation less susceptible to undesired local minima we take advantage of Sobolev gradients [19]. Samples from q_w are convolved with a Sobolev kernel. To lower the computational cost, we approximate the 3D kernel by three separable 1D kernels [24].

4 Stochastic Gradient Markov Chain Monte Carlo

We use stochastic gradient Langevin dynamics (SGLD) [4,25] to sample the transformation parameters in an efficient way:

$$w_{k+1} \leftarrow w_k + \tau \sigma_w^2 \nabla \log q(w_k) + \sqrt{2\tau} \sigma_w \xi_k \qquad (5)$$

where τ is the step size, $\nabla \log q(w_k)$ is an estimate of the gradient of the posterior probability density function, and ξ_k is an independent draw from a multivariate normal distribution with zero mean and an identity covariance matrix.

Given a sufficient number of steps SGLD puts no restrictions on how the chain is initialised, but in order to lower the mixing time we set $w_0 \leftarrow \mu_w$. In the limit as $\tau \to 0$ and $k \to \infty$, it allows for asymptotically exact sampling from the posterior of the transformation parameters. The scheme suffers from similar issues as Gibbs sampling used in [15], *i.e.* high autocorrelation and slow mixing between modes. On the other hand, the term corresponding to the gradient of the posterior probability density function allows for more efficient landscape transversal. Moreover, simplicity of the formulation makes SGLD better suited to a high-dimensional problem like image registration.

The value of τ is important here and should be smaller than the width of the most constrained direction in the local energy landscape, which can be estimated using Σ_w. We discard the first 2,000 samples output by the algorithm to allow for the chain to reach the stationary distribution.

5   Experiments

The model was implemented in PyTorch. For all experiments we use three-dimensional brain MRI scans from the UK Biobank dataset. Input images were resampled to 96^3 voxels, with isotropic voxels of length $2.43\,\mathrm{mm}$, and registered with the affine component of *drop2* [8]. Note that the model is not constrained by memory, so it can be run on higher resolution images to produce output that is more clinically relevant, while maintaining a high speed of sampling.

We use the Adam optimiser with a learning rate of 5×10^{-3} for VI and the SGD optimiser with a learning rate of 1×10^{-1} for SG-MCMC. The hyperprior parameters are set to $\mu_{\beta_o} = 0$, $\sigma_{\beta_0}^2 = 2.3$, $\kappa = 0.5$, $a_{\chi_0^2} = 0.5 \cdot \nu$, $b_{\chi_0^2} = 0.5 \cdot \lambda_0$, $\mu_{\chi_0^2} = 2.8$, and $\sigma_{\chi_0^2}^2 = 5$, where λ_0 is the desired strength of equivalent $L2$ regularisation at initialisation. The model is particularly sensitive to the value of the transformation prior parameters. We start with an identity transformation, σ_w of half a voxel in each direction, and u_w set to zero, and VI is run until the loss value plateaus. We are unable to achieve convergence in the sense of the magnitude of updates to Σ_w.

Regularisation Strength. In the first experiment we show the benefits of the proposed regularisation loss. We compare the output of VI when using a fixed regularisation weight $\lambda \in \{0.01, 0.1\}$, the baseline method for learnable regularisation strength, and the novel regularisation loss. The result is shown in Fig. 1. The output transformation is highly sensitive to the regularisation weight and so is registration uncertainty, hence the need for a reliable method to infer regularisation strength from data.

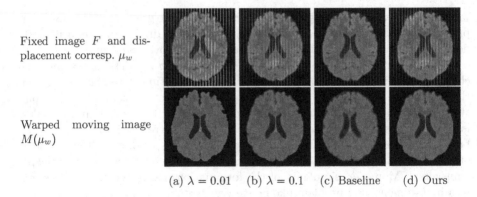

Fixed image F and displacement corresp. μ_w

Warped moving image $M(\mu_w)$

(a) $\lambda = 0.01$ (b) $\lambda = 0.1$ (c) Baseline   (d) Ours

Fig. 1. Output when using a fixed regularisation weight, the baseline method for learnable regularisation strength, and our regularisation loss. For the baseline, the regularisation strength is so high that it prevents alignment of the images, showing that the existing schemes for inferring regularisation strength from data are inadequate in cases with a very large number of d.f. Middle slice of 3D images in the axial plane.

In Fig. 2 we show the output of VI for two pairs of images which require different regularisation strengths. We choose a fixed image F, two moving images M_1 and M_2, and two regularisation weights $\lambda \in \{0.1, 0.4\}$. Use of our regularisation

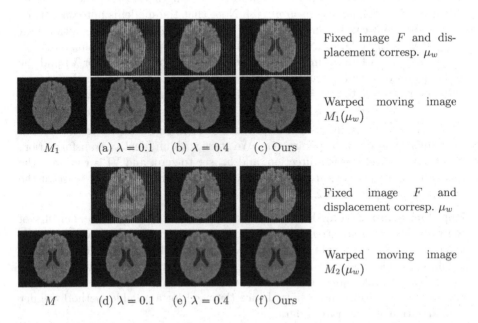

Fixed image F and displacement corresp. μ_w

Warped moving image $M_1(\mu_w)$

M_1 (a) $\lambda = 0.1$ (b) $\lambda = 0.4$ (c) Ours

Fixed image F and displacement corresp. μ_w

Warped moving image $M_2(\mu_w)$

M (d) $\lambda = 0.1$ (e) $\lambda = 0.4$ (f) Ours

Fig. 2. Output of VI for two pairs of images which require different regularisation strengths. At initialisation the strength of our loss corresponds to the fixed regularisation weight $\lambda = 0.4$. Middle slice of 3D images in the axial plane.

loss, which at initialisation corresponds to $\lambda = 0.4$, prevents oversmoothing. Due to its characteristics, it is preferable to initialise its strength to a higher value.

Uncertainty Quantification. To evaluate registration uncertainty we calculate the mean and the standard deviation of displacement using 50 samples selected at random from the output of SG-MCMC. Figure 3 shows the result for a pair of input images. In order to assess the results quantitatively, we use subcortical structure segmentations. We calculate Dice scores (DSC) and mean surface distances (MSD) between the fixed segmentation and the moving segmentation warped with the mean transformation, and compare them to those obtained using the 50 sample transformations. We report these metrics in Table 1 and Fig. 3.

The statistics prove that the posterior samples output by SG-MCMC are of high quality and varied. For a small number of structures (the left and right accumbens and thalamus, and the right caudate) the metrics are minimally worse for the mean transformation than before non-rigid registration. In case of the thalamus this can be attributed to a sub-optimal regularisation strength. The registration error for the accumbens and the caudate is likely caused by their tiny size. Thus the label distribution appears credible in the sense defined in [17]. The output is also consistent with previous findings on registration uncertainty, e.g. higher uncertainty in homogenous regions [23].

Table 1. DSC and MSD for a number of subcortical structures pre-registration and after applying the mean transformation calculated from the output of SG-MCMC.

Structure	DSC			MSD (mm)		
	Before	Mean	SD	Before	Mean	SD
Brain stem	0.815	0.879	0.002	1.85	1.17	0.03
L/R accumbens	0.593/0.653	0.637/0.592	0.036/0.022	1.20/1.13	1.03/1.18	0.13/0.10
L/R amygdala	0.335/0.644	0.700/0.700	0.019/0.015	2.18/1.44	1.12/1.12	0.08/0.08
L/R caudate	0.705/0.813	0.743/0.790	0.011/0.008	1.37/1.44	1.21/0.99	0.05/0.06
L/R hippocampus	0.708/0.665	0.783/0.781	0.009/0.009	1.45/1.60	1.00/1.03	0.05/0.05
L/R pallidum	0.673/0.794	0.702/0.798	0.014/0.014	1.56/1.12	1.29/0.98	0.07/0.08
L/R putamen	0.772/0.812	0.835/0.856	0.007/0.006	1.30/1.02	0.92/0.78	0.05/0.05
L/R thalamus	0.896/0.920	0.881/0.901	0.005/0.004	0.90/0.67	0.92/0.86	0.04/0.05

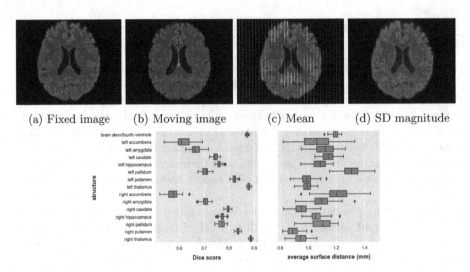

(a) Fixed image   (b) Moving image   (c) Mean   (d) SD magnitude

Fig. 3. Output of SG-MCMC for a pair of input images, calculated using 50 samples.

6   Discussion

Modelling Assumptions. The quality of uncertainty estimates is sensitive to the initialisation of regularisation loss hyperparameters and the validity of model assumptions. These include: 1. coinciding image intensities up to the expected spatial noise offsets, 2. ignoring spatial correlations between residuals, and 3. the spherical covariance structure of the approximate posterior in VI. The first assumption is valid in case of mono-modal registration but the model can be easily adapted to other settings by changing the data loss. In future work we plan to the use a frequency-domain model to deal with the last assumption.

Implementation and Computational Efficiency. The experiments were run on a system with an Intel i9-7900X CPU and a GeForce RTX 2080Ti GPU. VI took approx. 5 min per image pair and SG-MCMC produced 5 samples per second. Due to lack of data it is difficult to directly compare the runtime with that of other Bayesian image registration methods, but it is an order of magnitude better than in other recent work [15], while also being three- rather than two-dimensional.

7   Conclusion

In this paper we present an efficient Bayesian model for three-dimensional medical image registration. The newly proposed regularisation loss allows to tune the regularisation strength using a parameterisation of transformation that involves a very large number of d.f. Sampling from the posterior distribution via SG-MCMC makes it possible to quantify registration uncertainty for high-resolution images.

Acknowledgments. This research was conducted using the UK Biobank resources under application number 12579. DG is funded by the EPSRC CDT for Smart Medical Imaging EP/S022104/1 and LlF by EP/P023509/1.

References

1. Arsigny, V., Commowick, O., Pennec, X., Ayache, N.: A log-Euclidean framework for statistics on diffeomorphisms. In: Larsen, R., Nielsen, M., Sporring, J. (eds.) MICCAI 2006. LNCS, vol. 4190, pp. 924–931. Springer, Heidelberg (2006). https://doi.org/10.1007/11866565_113
2. Balakrishnan, G., Zhao, A., Sabuncu, M.R., Guttag, J., Dalca, A.V.: An unsupervised learning model for deformable medical image registration. In: CVPR (2018)
3. Balakrishnan, G., Zhao, A., Sabuncu, M.R., Guttag, J., Dalca, A.V.: VoxelMorph: a learning framework for deformable medical image registration. IEEE Trans. Med. Imaging **38**(8), 1788–1800 (2019)
4. Besag, J.: Comments on "representations of knowledge in complex systems" by U. Grenander and MI Miller. J. R. Stat. Soc. **56**, 591–592 (1993)
5. Chen, C., Carlson, D., Gan, Z., Li, C., Carin, L.: Bridging the gap between stochastic gradient MCMC and stochastic optimization. In: AISTATS (2016)
6. Dalca, A.V., Balakrishnan, G., Guttag, J., Sabuncu, M.R.: Unsupervised learning for fast probabilistic diffeomorphic registration. In: Frangi, A.F., Schnabel, J.A., Davatzikos, C., Alberola-López, C., Fichtinger, G. (eds.) MICCAI 2018. LNCS, vol. 11070, pp. 729–738. Springer, Cham (2018). https://doi.org/10.1007/978-3-030-00928-1_82
7. Dalca, A.V., Balakrishnan, G., Guttag, J., Sabuncu, M.R.: Unsupervised learning of probabilistic diffeomorphic registration for images and surfaces. MedIA Med. Image Anal. **57**, 226–236 (2019)
8. Glocker, B., Komodakis, N., Tziritas, G., Navab, N., Paragios, N.: Dense image registration through MRFs and efficient linear programming. Med. Image Anal. **12**(6), 731–741 (2008)
9. Glocker, B., Sotiras, A., Komodakis, N., Paragios, N.: Deformable medical image registration: setting the state of the art with discrete methods. Annu. Rev. Biomed. Eng. **13**, 219–244 (2011)
10. Hachama, M., Desolneux, A., Richard, F.J.: Bayesian technique for image classifying registration. IEEE Trans. Image Process. **21**(9), 4080–4091 (2012)
11. Heinrich, H.P., Jenkinson, M., Brady, M., Schnabel, J.A.: MRF-based deformable registration and ventilation estimation of lung CT. IEEE Trans. Med. Imaging **32**(7), 1239–1248 (2013)
12. Janoos, F., Risholm, P., Wells, W.: Bayesian characterization of uncertainty in multi-modal image registration. In: Dawant, B.M., Christensen, G.E., Fitzpatrick, J.M., Rueckert, D. (eds.) WBIR 2012. LNCS, vol. 7359, pp. 50–59. Springer, Heidelberg (2012). https://doi.org/10.1007/978-3-642-31340-0_6
13. Karabulut, N., Erdil, E., Çetin, M.: A Markov chain Monte Carlo based rigid image registration method. Technical report (2017)
14. Klein, S., Staring, M., Murphy, K., Viergever, M.A., Pluim, J.P.: Elastix: a toolbox for intensity-based medical image registration. IEEE Trans. Med. Imaging **29**(1), 196–205 (2009)
15. Le Folgoc, L., Delingette, H., Criminisi, A., Ayache, N.: Quantifying registration uncertainty with sparse Bayesian modelling. IEEE Trans. Med. Imaging **36**(2), 607–617 (2017)

16. Lee, M.C.H., Oktay, O., Schuh, A., Schaap, M., Glocker, B.: Image-and-spatial transformer networks for structure-guided image registration. In: Shen, D., et al. (eds.) MICCAI 2019. LNCS, vol. 11765, pp. 337–345. Springer, Cham (2019). https://doi.org/10.1007/978-3-030-32245-8_38

17. Luo, J., Sedghi, A., Popuri, K., Cobzas, D., Zhang, M., Preiswerk, F., Toews, M., Golby, A., Sugiyama, M., Wells, W.M., Frisken, S.: On the applicability of registration uncertainty. In: Shen, D., et al. (eds.) MICCAI 2019. LNCS, vol. 11765, pp. 410–419. Springer, Cham (2019). https://doi.org/10.1007/978-3-030-32245-8_46

18. Mandt, S., Hoffman, M.D., Blei, D.M.: Stochastic gradient descent as approximate Bayesian inference. J. Mach. Learn. Res. **18**, 1–35 (2017)

19. Neuberger, J.W., Dold, A., Takens, F.: Sobolev Gradients and Differential Equations. LNCS. Springer, Heidelberg (1997)

20. Risholm, P., Janoos, F., Norton, I., Golby, A.J., Wells, W.M.: Bayesian characterization of uncertainty in intra-subject non-rigid registration. Med. Image Anal. **17**, 538–555 (2013)

21. Schultz, S., Handels, H., Ehrhardt, J.: A multilevel Markov chain Monte Carlo approach for uncertainty quantification in deformable registration. In: SPIE Medical Imaging (2018)

22. Schultz, S., Krüger, J., Handels, H., Ehrhardt, J.: Bayesian inference for uncertainty quantification in point-based deformable image registration. In: SPIE Medical Imaging, p. 46, March 2019

23. Simpson, I.J., Schnabel, J.A., Groves, A.R., Andersson, J.L., Woolrich, M.W.: Probabilistic inference of regularisation in non-rigid registration. Neuroimage **59**(3), 2438–2451 (2012)

24. Slavcheva, M., Baust, M., Ilic, S.: SobolevFusion: 3D reconstruction of scenes undergoing free non-rigid motion. In: CVPR (2018)

25. Welling, M., Teh, Y.W.: Bayesian learning via stochastic gradient Langevin dynamics. In: ICML, pp. 681–688 (2011)

26. Zhang, M., Fletcher, P.T.: Bayesian principal geodesic analysis in diffeomorphic image registration. In: Golland, P., Hata, N., Barillot, C., Hornegger, J., Howe, R. (eds.) MICCAI 2014. LNCS, vol. 8675, pp. 121–128. Springer, Cham (2014). https://doi.org/10.1007/978-3-319-10443-0_16

27. Zhang, M., Singh, N., Fletcher, P.T.: Bayesian estimation of regularization and atlas building in diffeomorphic image registration. In: Gee, J.C., Joshi, S., Pohl, K.M., Wells, W.M., Zöllei, L. (eds.) IPMI 2013. LNCS, vol. 7917, pp. 37–48. Springer, Heidelberg (2013). https://doi.org/10.1007/978-3-642-38868-2_4

28. Zöllei, L., Jenkinson, M., Timoner, S., Wells, W.: A marginalized MAP approach and EM optimization for pair-wise registration. In: Karssemeijer, N., Lelieveldt, B. (eds.) IPMI 2007. LNCS, vol. 4584, pp. 662–674. Springer, Heidelberg (2007). https://doi.org/10.1007/978-3-540-73273-0_55

RevPHiSeg: A Memory-Efficient Neural Network for Uncertainty Quantification in Medical Image Segmentation

Marc Gantenbein, Ertunc Erdil[⊠], and Ender Konukoglu

Computer Vision Laboratory, ETH Zürich, Zürich, Switzerland
{ertunc.erdil,ender.konukoglu}@vision.ee.ethz.ch

Abstract. Quantifying segmentation uncertainty has become an important issue in medical image analysis due to the inherent ambiguity of anatomical structures and its pathologies. Recently, neural network-based uncertainty quantification methods have been successfully applied to various problems. One of the main limitations of the existing techniques is the high memory requirement during training; which limits their application to processing smaller field-of-views (FOVs) and/or using shallower architectures. In this paper, we investigate the effect of using reversible blocks for building memory-efficient neural network architectures for quantification of segmentation uncertainty. The reversible architecture achieves memory saving by exactly computing the activations from the outputs of the subsequent layers during backpropagation instead of storing the activations for each layer. We incorporate the reversible blocks into a recently proposed architecture called PHiSeg that is developed for uncertainty quantification in medical image segmentation. The reversible architecture, RevPHiSeg, allows training neural networks for quantifying segmentation uncertainty on GPUs with limited memory and processing larger FOVs. We perform experiments on the LIDC-IDRI dataset and an in-house prostate dataset, and present comparisons with PHiSeg. The results demonstrate that RevPHiSeg consumes ~30% less memory compared to PHiSeg while achieving very similar segmentation accuracy.

Keywords: Reversible neural network · UNet · Variational auto-encoder

1 Introduction

Segmentation has been a crucial problem in medical image analysis for clinical diagnosis and many downstream tasks. The majority of the segmentation algorithms in the literature aim to find a single segmentation as a solution which is a point estimate in the posterior distribution of a segmentation given an image [13]. However, having a point estimate does not provide a measure of the degree of confidence in that result, neither does it provide a picture of other probable

© Springer Nature Switzerland AG 2020
C. H. Sudre et al. (Eds.): UNSURE 2020/GRAIL 2020, LNCS 12443, pp. 13–22, 2020.
https://doi.org/10.1007/978-3-030-60365-6_2

solutions based on the data and the priors. Due to the inherent ambiguities and uncertainties in many medical images, characterization of the posterior distribution through its samples plays a crucial role in quantifying the uncertainty and revealing other plausible segmentations.

There have been some efforts in the literature for generating segmentation samples from the underlying posterior distribution. One group of methods aims at using Markov chain Monte Carlo (MCMC) techniques which ensure asymptotic convergence to the desired posterior [7–9]. However, these methods suffer from slow convergence and satisfying the necessary conditions of MCMC is nontrivial [8,9]. Another group of methods is based on variational inference which approximate the desired posterior density using a variational function. One of the pioneering variational inference-based methods that shows significant performance for segmentation uncertainty quantification is Probabilistic U-Net by Kohl et al. [12]. The method minimizes the Kullback-Leibler (KL) divergence between a posterior and a prior network during training. Then, the samples are generated from the learned latent distribution and appended to the penultimate layer of a U-Net [13] to generate segmentation samples. Recently, Baumgartner et al. [3] proposed a method called PHiSeg that samples from the learned distributions in every latent layer of a U-Net instead of the last latent level as in Probabilistic U-Net. PHiSeg achieves better performance compared to Probabilistic U-Net on various medical image segmentation datasets.

Although, both Probabilistic U-Net and PHiSeg achieve promising performance in terms of segmentation quality and uncertainty quantification, they suffer from a significant memory burden during training. This either limits their domain of applicability to processing images with small field-of-view which is not desired especially in medical domain or requires GPUs with large memories which are very expensive to obtain. To overcome this limitation, we investigate using reversible blocks for building a memory efficient architecture that generates segmentation samples for uncertainty quantification in medical image segmentation. To achieve this, we incorporate reversible blocks [10] into PHiSeg for a smaller memory consumption during training and built a new architecture called RevPHiSe.g. Reversible blocks have been previously used along with U-Net [13] for segmentation [4]. They allow us to recover the exact activation of each layer from the following layer during training and eliminate the need to store activations for each layer during backpropagation.

We perform experiments on two different datasets: LIDC-IDRI [1,2] and an in-house prostate data set. The results demonstrate that RevPHiSeg achieves ∼30% less memory consumption compared to PHiSeg by achieving very competitive results in terms of the quality of segmentation samples. The implementation of RevPHiSeg will be made available.[1]

---

[1] https://github.com/gigantenbein/UNet-Zoo.

2   Methods

In this section, we present RevPHiSeg after providing some background information on PHiSeg [3] and reversible blocks [10] for the sake of completeness.

2.1   PHiSeg

PHiSeg aims to approximate the posterior distribution $p(\mathbf{z}|\mathbf{s}, \mathbf{x})$ using a variational function as in [11], where $\mathbf{x}$ is the input image and $\mathbf{s}$ is the segmentation, and $\mathbf{z}$ is the latent representation. In PHiSeg, the latent variable $\mathbf{z} = \{\mathbf{z}_1, \dots, \mathbf{z}_L\}$ is modeled hierarchically as shown in the graphical model in Fig. 1.

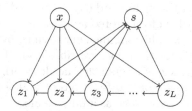

Fig. 1. Graphical model for hierarchical segmentation

Then, the posterior distribution of the segmentation $\mathbf{s}$ given an image $\mathbf{x}$ can be written for the general case of L latent levels as:

$$p(\mathbf{s}|\mathbf{x}) = \int_{\mathbf{z}_1, \dots, \mathbf{z}_L} p(\mathbf{s}|\mathbf{z}_1, \dots, \mathbf{z}_L)p(\mathbf{z}_1|\mathbf{z}_2, \mathbf{x}) \cdots p(\mathbf{z}_{L-1}|\mathbf{z}_L, \mathbf{x})p(\mathbf{z}_L|\mathbf{x})d\mathbf{z}_1 \dots d\mathbf{z}_L \tag{1}$$

The posterior distribution $p(\mathbf{z}|\mathbf{s}, \mathbf{x})$ can be approximated by a variational function $q(\mathbf{z}|\mathbf{s}, \mathbf{x})$ using variational inference. Minimizing the Kullback-Leibler (KL) divergence between $p(\mathbf{z}|\mathbf{s}, \mathbf{x})$ and $q(\mathbf{z}|\mathbf{s}, \mathbf{x})$ results in the following lower-bound estimate of $\log p(\mathbf{s}|\mathbf{x})$:

$$\log p(\mathbf{s}|\mathbf{x}) = \mathcal{L}(\mathbf{s}|\mathbf{x}) + \mathrm{KL}(q(\mathbf{z}|\mathbf{s}, \mathbf{x})||p(\mathbf{z}|\mathbf{s}, \mathbf{x})) \tag{2}$$

where, $\mathcal{L}$ is a lower-bound on $\log p(\mathbf{s}|\mathbf{x})$ with equality when the approximation q matches the posterior exactly. The lower bound $\mathcal{L}(\mathbf{s}|\mathbf{x})$ can be written as

$$\mathcal{L}(\mathbf{s}|\mathbf{x}) = \mathbb{E}_{q(\mathbf{z}_1, \dots, \mathbf{z}_L|\mathbf{x}, \mathbf{s})}[\log p(\mathbf{s}|\mathbf{z}_1, \dots, \mathbf{z}_L)] - \alpha_L \, \mathrm{KL}(q(\mathbf{z}_L|\mathbf{s}, \mathbf{x})||p(\mathbf{z}_L|\mathbf{x}))$$
$$- \sum_{l=1}^{L-1} \alpha_l \mathbb{E}_{q(\mathbf{z}_{l+1}|\mathbf{s}, \mathbf{x})}[\mathrm{KL}[q(\mathbf{z}_l|\mathbf{z}_{l+1}, \mathbf{s}, \mathbf{x})||p(\mathbf{z}_l|\mathbf{z}_{l+1}, \mathbf{x})]] \tag{3}$$

where, α_i is a weighting term which we set to 1 in our experiments.

In PHiSeg [3] the distributions $p(\mathbf{z}_l|\mathbf{z}_{L-1}, \mathbf{x})$ and $q(\mathbf{z}_l|\mathbf{z}_{L-1}, \mathbf{x}, \mathbf{s})$ are parametrized by axis-aligned normal distributions, which are defined as follows:

$$p(\mathbf{z}_l|\mathbf{z}_{l+1}, \mathbf{x}) = \mathcal{N}(\mathbf{z}|\phi_l^{(\mu)}(\mathbf{z}_{l+1}, \mathbf{x}), \phi_l^{(\sigma)}(\mathbf{z}_{l+1}, \mathbf{x})) \tag{4}$$

$$q(\mathbf{z}_l|\mathbf{z}_{l+1}, \mathbf{x}, \mathbf{s}) = \mathcal{N}(\mathbf{z}|\theta_l^{(\mu)}(\mathbf{z}_{l+1}, \mathbf{x}, \mathbf{s}), \theta_l^{(\sigma)}(\mathbf{z}_{l+1}, \mathbf{x}, \mathbf{s})) \tag{5}$$

where the functions ϕ and θ are parametrized by neural networks. The architecture is trained by minimizing Eq. 2.

2.2 Reversible Architectures

One of the major reasons for memory consumption in neural networks is due to storing the activations during the forward pass to be used in backpropagation. To alleviate the memory burden of the stored activations, Gomes et al. [10] propose reversible blocks that allow achieving memory savings by avoiding to store the activations in the forward pass by using reversible layers. Instead, the activations are computed from the previous layers when needed during backpropagation.

A reversible block consists of two functions $\mathcal{F}$ and $\mathcal{G}$ as shown in Fig. 2. $\mathcal{F}$ and $\mathcal{G}$ can be arbitrary functions such as a fully-connected layer, a convolutional layer or a nonlinearity. The functions are expected to have the same input and output dimensions since the performed operations have to be invertible.

Figure 2 shows the computations which take place during the forward (in Fig. 2a) and the backward (in Fig.2b) passes. Gomes et al. [10] partitions the input of the reversible block into two groups. The first group x_1 flows from the top batch while the second group uses the bottom one as shown in Fig. 2. The inputs x_1 and x_2 are recovered after the backward pass by inverting the operations in the forward pass with the gradients of $\mathcal{F}$ and $\mathcal{G}$ with respect to their parameters.

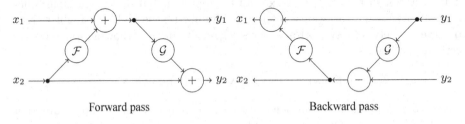

Forward pass   Backward pass

Fig. 2. Sketch of the computations of forward and backward passes in reversible blocks.

2.3 RevPHiSeg

To create a memory-efficient architecture for quantification of segmentation uncertainty, we incorporated reversible blocks into PHiSeg. When looking for an option to employ reversible blocks, the convolutional layer offer themselves due to the number of activations stored in them. To achieve memory savings, multiple reversible blocks have to be concatenated which then form a reversible sequence. Considering Fig. 2, the functions $\mathcal{F}$ and $\mathcal{G}$ would then correspond to a 3×3 convolutional layers with a nonlinearity. For our architecture RevPHiSeg, each sequence of convolutions in the original PHiSeg was replaced by a sequence of reversible blocks.

As stated in Sect. 2.2, replacing a function with a reversible block requires the function to have the same input and out dimensions. For convolutions, this implies that the convolution needs the same number of input and output channels. However, PHiSeg resembles a UNet architecture and thus contains convolutions with a different number of input and output channels. We thus decided to add a 1×1 convolution before every reversible sequence where the number of channels do change. The 1×1 convolution have different input and output dimensions and thus enable having the same input and output dimensions for the following 3×3 convolutions in the reversible blocks as can be seen in Fig. 3.

Applying the same process to each convolutional sequence in PHiSeg, we obtain the RevPHiSeg architecture shown in Fig. 4. As one can see, each convolutional sequence that features a dimension change is preceded by a 1×1 convolution.

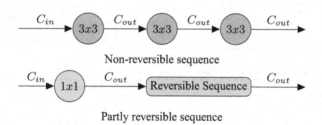

Fig. 3. Replacing a series of convolutions with a reversible sequence

3   Experimental Results

In this section, we present the experimental results of RevPHiSeg on two different data sets: LIDC-IDRI [1,2] and an in-house prostate dataset. We compare the results with PHiSeg in terms of both segmentation accuracy and memory consumption.

In our experiments, we chose the same number of latent and resolution levels as Baumgartner et al. to demonstrate the memory advantage of reversible blocks in PHiSeg architecture. Therefore, our configuration consisted of 5 latent layers, where a sampling step takes place, and 7 resolution layers with filters from 32 up to 192.

3.1   Evaluation Metrics

We obtain the quantitative results indicating the segmentation accuracy by comparing the ground truth segmentations of different experts with the segmentation samples generated by PHiSeg and RevPHiSeg. We exploit various evaluation metrics in our evaluations: Generalised Energy Distance (GED), Normalised Cross-Correlation (NCC) of the expected cross entropy between the mean segmentations and the mean of the generated samples, and the Dice score (DSC) [6] per label.

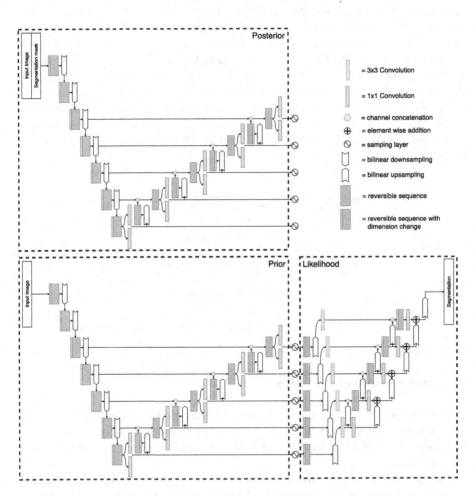

Fig. 4. Reversible PHiSeg with 5 latent levels and 7 resolution levels with corresponding Posterior, Prior and Likelihood network for training and inference

GED is defined as

$$D^2_{GED}(p_{gt}, p_s) = \frac{2}{nm} \sum_{i=1}^{n} \sum_{j=1}^{m} d(\mathbf{s}_i, \mathbf{y}_j) - \frac{1}{n^2} \sum_{i=1}^{n} \sum_{j=1}^{n} d(\mathbf{s}_i, \mathbf{s}_j) - \frac{1}{m^2} \sum_{i=1}^{m} \sum_{j=1}^{m} d(\mathbf{y}_i, \mathbf{y}_j)$$
(6)

where, $d(\cdot, \cdot) = 1 - \text{IoU}(\cdot, \cdot)$ with $\text{IoU}(\cdot, \cdot)$ as the intersection over union, m is the number of ground truth labels, n is the number of segmentation samples, y are the ground truth samples and s are the segmentation samples. The generalized energy distance is a measure of the distance between two probability distribution where we treat the generated segmentations as samples from the approximate distribution and the ground truth labels as samples from the ground truth distribution.

To quantify the pixel-wise differences between the samples and ground truths, we use the normalized cross-correlation(NCC) of the cross entropy between the mean of the ground truth labels ($\bar{\mathbf{y}}$) and the mean of the generated samples ($\bar{\mathbf{s}}$), which is defined as follows:

$$S_{NCC}(p_{gt}, p_s) = \mathbb{E}_{\mathbf{y} \sim p_{gt}}[\text{NCC}(\mathbb{E}_{\mathbf{s} \sim p_s}[\text{CE}(\bar{\mathbf{s}}, \mathbf{s})], \mathbb{E}_{\mathbf{s} \sim p_s}[\text{CE}(\bar{\mathbf{y}}, \mathbf{s})])$$
(7)

where p_{gt} is the ground truth distribution and p_s is the approximate distribution [3].

Furthermore, we use the Dice score (DSC) to measure the segmentation accuracy of each sample. DSC is a common metric that is used to quantify segmentation accuracy based on the overlap between the ground truth and the segmentation. When computing DSC we randomly choose a ground truth segmentation among different expert annotations, and calculate the DSC between the selected ground truth and the segmentation samples. We then average the DSC of these multiple draws.

We measure the memory consumption of the methods using the PyTorch function `max_memory_allocated()`. PHiSeg is originally implemented in Tensorflow. To have a fair comparison, we re-implemented PHiSeg in PyTorch.

3.2   Datasets

The LIDC-IDRI dataset contains 1018 lung CT scans each annotated by 4 radiologists. We use the same preprocessing as in [3,12] and crop a 128×128 squares centered around the lesions.

The prostate data set is an in-house data set that contains MR images from 68 patients. Each image in the data set has 6 annotations from 4 radiologists and 2 non-radiologists. We processed the data slice-by-slice (approx. 25 slices per volume), where we resampled each slice to a resolution of $0.6 \times 0.6 \, \text{mm}^2$ and took a central crop of size 192×192.

We divide both datasets into a training, testing and validation set using a random 60-20-20 split.

3.3 Experimental Setup

In our experiments, we use the network architecture shown in Fig. 4 for PHiSeg where we use 5 latent levels, $L = 5$, to generate samples as proposed for PHiSeg in [3]. The architecture we use for PHiSeg is similar to RevPHiSeg except for the reversible sequences and 1×1 convolutions.

We use the Adam optimizer with a learning rate of 10^{-3}. Furthermore, we used a weight decay of 10^{-5}. We use ReLU and batch normalization after each convolutional layer on non-output layer. We train both PHiSeg and RevPHiSeg for 48 h on an NVIDIA Titan X Pascal. While models are being trained, we calculate GED, NCC, and DSC on the validation sets. After 48h of training is done, we choose the model with the lowest GED score on the validation set. Finally, we evaluate the selected model on test sets to obtain the quantitative results. We conduct our experiments using an NVIDIA Titan Xp GPU with 12 GB of memory.

3.4 Experimental Results

We present the quantitative results on LIDC-IDRI dataset in Table 1. The quantitative results demonstrate that RevPHiSeg achieves almost 30% memory savings while being quite competitive with PHiSeg in terms of the segmentation quality.

Using the memory saving achieved by RevPHiSeg, we can process batch sizes of up to 56, where PHiSeg runs out of memory after batch size 48. Although, we do not observe any improvement in terms of the segmentation quality when using larger batch sizes, being able to process larger batches could lead to improvement depending on the application such as unsupervised contrastive learning [5].

Table 1. Quantitative results of RevPHiSeg and PHiSeg on LIDC-IDRI dataset.

	Batch size	LIDC-IDRI			
		D^2_{GED}	S_{NCC}	Dice	Memory (MB)
PHiSeg	12	0.2139	0.8533	0.4991	3251
RevPHiSeg	12	0.2365	0.7943	0.5220	**2194**
PHiSeg	24	0.2342	0.8296	0.5344	6076
RevPHiSeg	24	0.2396	0.7846	0.5525	**4070**
PHiSeg	36	0.2166	0.8387	0.5229	8905
RevPHiSeg	36	0.2677	0.7839	0.4995	**5903**
PHiSeg	48	0.2239	0.8409	0.5224	11374
RevPHiSeg	48	0.2436	0.8069	0.5459	**7948**
PHiSeg	56	–	–	-	–
RevPHiSeg	56	0.2478	0.7721	0.5361	**9238**

Table 2. Quantitative results of RevPHiSeg and PHiSeg on an in-house prostate dataset.

	Resolution	Prostate dataset			
		D^2_{GED}	S_{NCC}	Dice	Memory
PHiSeg	192	0.3578	**0.7801**	0.7480	6813
RevPHiSeg	192	0.3035	0.75	0.7871	**4621**
PHiSeg	256	–	–	–	–
RevPHiSeg	256	**0.2486**	0.6712	0.7094	7582

We present the quantitative results obtained on the in-house prostate dataset in Table 2. The reversible architecture achieves significant memory saving compared to the vanilla PHiSeg.

The memory saving achieved by RevPHiSeg allows us to process images with higher resolutions. We perform experiments with two different resolutions: 192×192 and 256×256. While RevPHiSeg can process both resolutions, PHiSeg cannot process resolutions higher than 192×192. Although processing higher resolutions lead to a better score in terms of GED, the NCC and DSC results get slightly worse. This may be caused due to the architecture used for 192×192 is not large enough to learn effectively from 256×256 images or that the training time of 48 h was not long enough for the resolution of 256×256.

4   Discussion and Conclusion

We investigate using reversible blocks for building a memory-efficient neural network architecture for generating segmentation samples to quantify segmentation uncertainty in medical images. To this end, we modified a state-of-the-art method, PHiSeg, by adding reversible blocks to make it memory efficient. We present quantitative results on two different medical datasets. The results demonstrate that RevPHiSeg consumes significantly less memory compared to the non-reversible architecture PHiSe.g. The memory saving enables training RevPHiSeg on GPUs with limited memory, processing larger resolutions and using larger batches. Besides the memory saving, RevPHiSeg is quite competitive with PHiSeg in terms of segmentation quality.

References

1. Armato III, S.G., et al.: Data from LIDC-IDRI (2015). http://doi.org/10.7937/K9/TCIA.2015.LO9QL9SX
2. Armato III, S.G., et al.: The lung image database consortium (LIDC) and image database resource initiative (IDRI): a completed reference database of lung nodules on CT scans. Med. Phys. **38**, 915–931 (2011). https://doi.org/10.1118/1.3528204
3. Baumgartner, C.F., et al.: PHiSeg: capturing uncertainty in medical image segmentation. In: Shen, D., et al. (eds.) MICCAI 2019, Part II. LNCS, vol. 11765, pp. 119–127. Springer, Cham (2019). https://doi.org/10.1007/978-3-030-32245-8_14

4. Brügger, R., Baumgartner, C.F., Konukoglu, E.: A partially reversible U-Net for memory-efficient volumetric image segmentation. In: Shen, D., et al. (eds.) MIC-CAI 2019, Part III. LNCS, vol. 11766, pp. 429–437. Springer, Cham (2019). https://doi.org/10.1007/978-3-030-32248-9_48
5. Chen, T., Kornblith, S., Norouzi, M., Hinton, G.: A simple framework for contrastive learning of visual representations. arXiv preprint arXiv:2002.05709 (2020)
6. Dice, L.R.: Measures of the amount of ecologic association between species. Ecology **26**(3), 297–302 (1945)
7. Erdil, E., Yildirim, S., Tasdizen, T., Cetin, M.: Pseudo-marginal MCMC sampling for image segmentation using nonparametric shape priors. IEEE Trans. Image Process. **28**, 5702–5715 (2019). https://doi.org/10.1109/TIP.2019.2922071
8. Erdil, E., Yildirim, S., Cetin, M., Tasdizen, T.: MCMC shape sampling for image segmentation with nonparametric shape priors. In: The IEEE Conference on Computer Vision and Pattern Recognition (CVPR), June 2016
9. Fan, A.C., Fisher, J.W., Wells, W.M., Levitt, J.J., Willsky, A.S.: MCMC curve sampling for image segmentation. In: Ayache, N., Ourselin, S., Maeder, A. (eds.) MICCAI 2007. LNCS, vol. 4792, pp. 477–485. Springer, Heidelberg (2007). https://doi.org/10.1007/978-3-540-75759-7_58
10. Gomez, A.N., Ren, M., Urtasun, R., Grosse, R.B.: The reversible residual network: backpropagation without storing activations. In: Guyon, I., et al. (eds.) Advances in Neural Information Processing Systems 30, pp. 2214–2224. Curran Associates, Inc. (2017). http://papers.nips.cc/paper/6816-the-reversible-residual-network-backpropagation-without-storing-activations.pdf
11. Kingma, D.P., Mohamed, S., Rezende, D.J., Welling, M.: Semi-supervised learning with deep generative models. In: Advances in Neural Information Processing Systems 27: Annual Conference on Neural Information Processing Systems 2014, Montreal, Quebec, Canada, 8–13 December 2014, pp. 3581–3589 (2014). http://papers.nips.cc/paper/5352-semi-supervised-learning-with-deep-generative-models
12. Kohl, S., et al.: A probabilistic U-Net for segmentation of ambiguous images. In: Advances in Neural Information Processing Systems 31: Annual Conference on Neural Information Processing Systems 2018, NeurIPS 2018, Montréal, Canada, 3–8 December 2018, pp. 6965–6975 (2018). http://papers.nips.cc/paper/7928-a-probabilistic-u-net-for-segmentation-of-ambiguous-images
13. Ronneberger, O., Fischer, P., Brox, T.: U-Net: convolutional networks for biomedical image segmentation. In: Navab, N., Hornegger, J., Wells, W.M., Frangi, A.F. (eds.) MICCAI 2015, Part III. LNCS, vol. 9351, pp. 234–241. Springer, Cham (2015). https://doi.org/10.1007/978-3-319-24574-4_28

Hierarchical Brain Parcellation
with Uncertainty

Mark S. Graham[1]([✉]), Carole H. Sudre[1], Thomas Varsavsky[1],
Petru-Daniel Tudosiu[1], Parashkev Nachev[2], Sebastien Ourselin[1],
and M. Jorge Cardoso[1]

[1] Biomedical Engineering and Imaging Sciences, King's College London, London, UK
mark.graham@kcl.ac.uk
[2] Institute of Neurology, University College London, London, UK

Abstract. Many atlases used for brain parcellation are hierarchically organised, progressively dividing the brain into smaller sub-regions. However, state-of-the-art parcellation methods tend to ignore this structure and treat labels as if they are 'flat'. We introduce a hierarchically-aware brain parcellation method that works by predicting the decisions at each branch in the label tree. We further show how this method can be used to model uncertainty separately for every branch in this label tree. Our method exceeds the performance of flat uncertainty methods, whilst also providing decomposed uncertainty estimates that enable us to obtain self-consistent parcellations and uncertainty maps at any level of the label hierarchy. We demonstrate a simple way these decision-specific uncertainty maps may be used to provided uncertainty-thresholded tissue maps at any level of the label tree.

1 Introduction

Brain parcellation seeks to partition the brain into spatially homogeneous structural and functional regions, a task fundamental for allowing us to study the brain in both function and dysfunction. The brain is hierarchically organised, with smaller subregions performing increasingly specialised functions, and the atlases classically used for parcellation typically reflect this by defining labels in a hierarchical tree structure. Manual parcellation is also typically performed hierarchically; typically semi-automated methods are used to help delineate larger structures with sufficient tissue contrast, and these are then manually sub-parcellated using anatomical or functional landmarks [1].

The state-of-the-art for brain parcellation has come to be dominated by convolutional neural networks (CNNs). These methods tend to ignore the label hierarchy, instead adopting a 'flat' label structure. However, methods that are

---

Electronic supplementary material The online version of this chapter (https://doi.org/10.1007/978-3-030-60365-6_3) contains supplementary material, which is available to authorized users.

C. H. Sudre et al. (Eds.): UNSURE 2020/GRAIL 2020, LNCS 12443, pp. 23–31, 2020.
https://doi.org/10.1007/978-3-030-60365-6_3

aware of the label hierarchy are desirable for many reasons. Such methods could degrade their predictions gracefully, for example labelling a noisy region with the coarser label 'cortex' rather then trying to assign a particular cortical division. They also offer the opportunity to train on multiple datasets with differing degrees of label granularity, assuming those labels can be mapped onto a single hierarchy.

Hierarchical methods also enable uncertainty to be modelled at different levels of the label tree. There has been recent interest in using uncertainty estimates provided by CNNs [8,9] to obtain confidence intervals for downstream biomarkers such as regional volumes [4,15], which is key if these biomarkers are to be integrated into clinical pipelines. Flat methods provide only a single uncertainty measure per voxel, which prevents attribution of the uncertainty to a specific decision. Hierarchical methods can provide uncertainty for each decision along the label hierarchy, for example enabling the network to distinguish between relatively easy decisions (e.g. cortex vs non-cortex) and more challenging decisions, such as delineating cortical sub-regions that are ill-defined on MRI. This could facilitate more specific and informative confidence bounds for derived biomarkers used in clinical decision making.

Whilst hierarchical methods have been applied to classification, [3,6,14,16], there are very few CNN-based methods that attempt hierarchical segmentation. A method proposed by Liang et al. [12] has been applied to perform hierarchical parcellation of the cerebellum [5]. A drawback of this approach is that the tree structure is directly built into the model architecture, requiring a tailored model to be built for each new label tree.

In this work we make two contributions. Firstly, we extend a method previously proposed for hierarchical classification [14] to hierarchically-aware segmentation. The method works by predicting decisions at each branch in the label tree, and has the advantage that it requires no alteration to the network architecture. Secondly, we show it is possible to use such a model to estimate uncertainty at each branch in the label tree. Our model with uncertainty matches the performance of 'flat' uncertainty methods, whilst providing us with decomposed uncertainty estimates that enable us to obtain consistent parcellations with corresponding uncertainty at any level of the label tree. We demonstrate how these decision-specific uncertainty maps can be used to provide uncertainty-thresholded tissue segmentations at any level of the label tree.

2   Methods

We first review existing flat segmentation models with uncertainty, before describing how we apply an existing classification model to perform hierarchical parcellation. We then show how such a model can be used to provide hierarchical uncertainty estimates. We focus on modelling intrinsic uncertainty in this work, although the methods presented can be straightforwardly extended to estimating model uncertainty, too.

2.1   Flat Parcellation

In a flat segmentation scenario, we consider the task as per-voxel classification, where the likelihood for a voxel is given by $p(\mathbf{y}|\mathbf{W}, \mathbf{x}) = \text{Softmax}\left(\mathbf{f}^{\mathbf{W}}(\mathbf{x})\right)$ where $\mathbf{f}^{\mathbf{W}}(\mathbf{x})$ is the output of a neural network with weights $\mathbf{W}$, input $\mathbf{x}$ is a 3D image volume, and $\mathbf{y}$ encodes the C segmentation classes. We seek the weights $\mathbf{W}$ that minimise the negative log-likelihood, yielding the standard cross-entropy loss function, $\text{CE}\left(y = c, \mathbf{f}^{\mathbf{W}}(\mathbf{x})\right) = -\log\text{Softmax}\left(f_c^{\mathbf{W}}(\mathbf{x})\right)$. As in Kendall et al. [8], heteroscedastic intrinsic uncertainty can be modelled by considering scaling the logits by a second network output, $\sigma^{\mathbf{W}}(\mathbf{x})$, giving a likelihood of $p(\mathbf{y}|\mathbf{W}, \mathbf{x}, \sigma) = \text{Softmax}\left(\frac{1}{\sigma^2(\mathbf{x})}\mathbf{f}^{\mathbf{W}}(\mathbf{x})\right)$. $\sigma^{\mathbf{W}}(\mathbf{x})$ is a per-voxel estimate, so it has the same dimension as $\mathbf{x}$. Employing the approximation $\frac{1}{\sigma^{\mathbf{W}}(\mathbf{x})^2}\sum_c \exp\left(\frac{1}{\sigma^{\mathbf{W}}(\mathbf{x})^2}f_c^{\mathbf{W}}(\mathbf{x})\right) \approx \left(\sum_c \exp\left(f_c^{\mathbf{W}}(\mathbf{x})\right)\right)^{\sigma^{\mathbf{W}}(\mathbf{x})^{-2}}$ used in [9] allows us to write the negative log-likelihood as

$$\mathcal{L}(y = c, \mathbf{x}; \mathbf{W}) = \frac{\text{CE}\left(y = c, \mathbf{f}^{\mathbf{W}}(\mathbf{x})\right)}{\sigma^{\mathbf{W}}(\mathbf{x})^2} + \log\sigma^{\mathbf{W}}(\mathbf{x})$$

2.2   Hierarchical Parcellation

Here we describe the hierarchical classification/detection model proposed by Redmon et al. [14], and discuss how it can be adapted for segmentation tasks. The methods described here are general to all label taxonomy trees, but in this work we specifically consider the tree shown in Fig. 1, described in more detail in Sect. 3.1. The probabilities at each node obey simple rules: the probabilities of all a node's children sum to the probability of the node itself, and so if we take $p(\text{root}) = 1$ the probabilities of all leaf nodes sum to 1. Leaf node probabilities can be expressed as the product of conditional probabilities down the tree; for example using the hierarchy in Fig. 1 we can express $p(\text{Right cingulate WM})$ as

$$p(\text{Right cingulate WM}) = p(\text{Right cingulate}|\text{Right WM})p(\text{Right WM}|\text{WM})\dots$$
$$p(\text{WM}|\text{Supra tentorial})p(\text{Supra tentorial}|\text{Cranium})\dots$$
$$p(\text{Cranium})$$

where $p(\text{Cranium}) = 1$. Our model predicts the conditional probabilities for each node, and is optimised using a cross-entropy loss at every level of the tree.

More formally, we label each node i at level l as $N_{i,l}$, where $l = 0$ denotes the root and $l = L$ the deepest level, giving a maximum height of $L + 1$. Our model $\mathbf{f}^{\mathbf{W}}(\mathbf{x})$ produces a score for each node in the tree, $f^{\mathbf{W}}(\mathbf{x})_{i,l}$. We define a hierarchical softmax - essentially a softmax over the siblings for a given node - to produce the conditional probabilities at each node,

$$p_{i,l} = \frac{\exp\left(f^{\mathbf{W}}(\mathbf{x})_{i,l}\right)}{\sum_{N_{j,l}=S[N_{i,l}]} \exp\left(f^{\mathbf{W}}(\mathbf{x})_{j,l}\right)}$$

where $S[N_{i,l}]$ denotes all the sibling nodes of $N_{i,l}$, including itself.

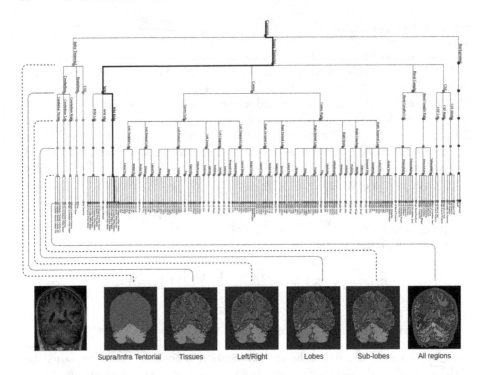

Fig. 1. The neuro-anatomical label hierarchy considered in this paper, with the path from the root to the right cingulate highlighted. A larger version of this tree is included in the supplementary materials.

In the flat case we had a single label per voxel, y_c. In the hierarchical case y_c denotes a leaf node of the tree, and we consider the label superset $A[y_c] = \{N_{i,l}\}$ comprising all the nodes traversed from the root to the label's leaf node, excluding the root node but including itself. The total loss is the summation of a CE loss calculated at each level of the tree,

$$\mathcal{L}\left(y = c, \mathbf{x}; \mathbf{W}\right) = -\sum_{N_{i,l} \in A[y_c]} \log p_{i,l}$$

For parcellation the network makes a prediction per voxel, that is $\mathbf{f}^{\mathbf{W}}(\mathbf{x}) \in \mathbb{R}^{x \times y \times z \times H}$ where H is the total number of nodes, making the considerably more computationally expensive than in classification tasks. The denominator of the hierarchical softmax can be efficiently calculated as a matrix multiplication, allowing $p_{i,l}$ to be calculated from the elementwise division of two matrices.

2.3 Hierarchical Uncertainty

We extend the model by modelling an uncertainty for every decision made along the tree. The network output $\sigma^{\mathbf{W}}(\mathbf{x})$ is now vector-valued, and exists for every non-leaf node, $\sigma^{\mathbf{W}}(\mathbf{x})_{i,l}$. The loss becomes:

$$\mathcal{L}\left(y=c,\mathbf{x};\mathbf{W}\right) = - \sum_{N_{i,l}\in A[y_c]} \frac{\log p_{i,l}}{\sigma^{\mathbf{W}}(\mathbf{x})_{i,l-1}^2} + \log\sigma^{\mathbf{W}}(\mathbf{x})_{i,l-1}$$

In this formulation the uncertainty values in a given voxel are unconstrained if they do not fall along the decision path for that voxel; for example values of σ relating to cortical parcellation do not enter into the loss in white matter voxels. We add a penalty term to encourage shrinking every value of $\sigma_{i,l}$ that does not fall along the path from the true leaf node to the root node, giving a final loss of

$$\mathcal{L}\left(\mathbf{y}=c,\mathbf{x};\mathbf{W}\right) = - \sum_{N_{i,l}\in A[y_c]} \left(\frac{\log p_{i,l}}{\sigma^{\mathbf{W}}(\mathbf{x})_{i,l-1}^2} + \log\sigma^{\mathbf{W}}(\mathbf{x})_{i,l-1} \right) \\ + \lambda \sum_{N_{i,l}\notin A[y_c]} \log\sigma^{\mathbf{W}}(\mathbf{x})_{i,l-1} \tag{1}$$

where λ controls the strength of this penalty.

2.4   Architecture and Implementation Details

The network is a 3D UNet based on the implementation described in the nnUNet paper [7] and implemented in PyTorch. Our implementation contains three pooling layers and separate, identical decoder branches for the segmentation and uncertainty outputs. The parcellation branch predicts an output for each leaf node in the tree for the flat case - 151 for the tree considered in this work - and in the hierarchical case predicts an output for each node in the tree. As the hierarchical network does not make any predictions for nodes with no siblings, as $p(\text{node}|\text{parent}) = 1$ always for such nodes, the hierarchical model predicts 213 outputs per voxel for the same tree. The uncertainty branch predicts a single channel for flat models, and a number of channels equal to the number of branches in the label tree for hierarchical models - 61 for the tree in this work. In practice, $\log(\sigma^2)$ is predicted for numerical stability. We set the penalty term in the hierarchical loss $\lambda = 0.1$. Networks were trained on 110^3 patches randomly sampled from the training volume. Group normalisation was used, enabling a batch size of 1 to be coupled with gradient accumulation to produce an effective batch size of 3. Models were trained with the Adam optimiser [10] using a learning rate of $4e^{-3}$. Each model was trained for a maximum of 300 epochs with early stopping if the minimum validation loss did not improve for 15 epochs.

3   Experiments and Results

3.1   Data

We use the hierarchical label tree from the GIF label-fusion framework [2], which is based on the labelling from the MICCAI 2012 Grand Challenge on label fusion [11]. In total, there are 151 leaf classes and a hierarchical depth of 6, see Fig. 1.

We use 593 T1-weighted MRI scans from the ADNI2 dataset [13], with an average voxel size of $1.18 \times 1.05 \times 1.05 \, \text{mm}^3$ and dimension $182 \times 244 \times 246$. Images were bias-field corrected, oriented to a standard RAS orientation and cropped using a tight mask. Silver-standard labels were produced using GIF on multimodal input data, followed by manual quality control and editing where necessary. 543 scans were used for training and validation, and 50 were reserved for testing.

Table 1. Dice scores averaged over all classes on the test set for the flat (F) and the proposed hierarchical (H) model. Uncertainty-aware models are denoted with an unc subscript. Values are Median (IQR) across the 50 subjects in the test set. Bold indicates significantly better performance between model pairs (F vs H, F_{unc} vs H_{unc}), at $p < 0.05$, using p-values obtained from a Wilcoxon paired test.

Tree level	F	H (ours)	P	F_{unc}	H_{unc} (ours)	P
Supra/Infra	**0.986 (0.003)**	0.985 (0.002)	<0.00005	**0.984 (0.003)**	0.984 (0.002)	0.009
Tissue	**0.942 (0.007)**	0.941 (0.008)	<0.00005	0.934 (0.007)	0.934 (0.007)	0.95
Left/Right	**0.942 (0.006)**	0.938 (0.008)	<0.00005	0.932 (0.005)	**0.933 (0.006)**	0.006
Lobes	**0.924 (0.008)**	0.922 (0.009)	0.00001	0.913 (0.008)	**0.917 (0.008)**	<0.00005
Sub-lobes	**0.891 (0.011)**	0.884 (0.013)	<0.00005	0.870 (0.013)	**0.880 (0.012)**	<0.00005
All regions	**0.861 (0.011)**	0.848 (0.015)	<0.00005	0.831 (0.018)	**0.845 (0.013)**	<0.00005

3.2 Experiments

We consider the following four models: 1) a baseline network trained on flat labels with weighted cross-entropy (F) 2) the same as (F) but with uncertainty estimates (F_{unc}), 3) a network trained on hierarchical labels (H), 4) a hierarchically-trained network with hierarchical uncertainty estimates (H_{unc}). The following experiments were performed:

- Performance comparison using dice overlap on the withheld test data at all six levels of the tree.
- Qualitative assessment of the uncertainty maps provided by H_{unc} and F_{unc}.
- Comparison of uncertainty-thresholded segmentations from H_{unc} and F_{unc}.

3.3 Results and Discussion

Dice scores for all the models are reported in Table 1. Despite predicting a tree-structure with >41% more predictions per voxel than the flat model, performance for H only drops marginally when compared to F, consistent with existing performance comparisons between flat and hierarchical models in classification and object detection settings [14]. H_{unc} outperforms F_{unc} for the four more fine-grained levels of the label tree. This is likely due to the empirically observed difficult in stably training F_{unc}; we found no such problems with H_{unc}, which was easy to optimise.

Figure 2 compares the uncertainty map from F_{unc} with the total uncertainty map from H_{unc}, obtained by summing all uncertainty components at each voxel. They look visually similar, and the joint histograms demonstrate expected trade-offs between uncertainty and error rate. Ideally, we would see low counts in the top-left of the joint histograms, indicating the models do not make confidently wrong predictions with low uncertainty. We see this desired behavior for H_{unc} more strongly than F_{unc}.

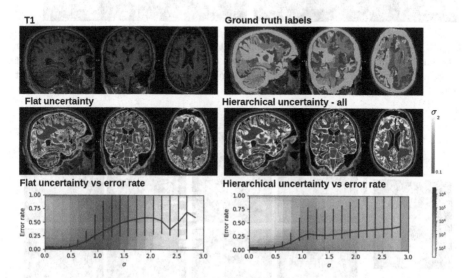

Fig. 2. Evaluation of the uncertainty from F_{unc} and the total uncertainty for H_{unc} obtained by summing all uncertainty components. Joint histograms show voxel counts for σ against (1-predicted probability for true class), averaged across all test subjects. Blue lines represent the mean error rate and error bars are 25–75 percentiles.

Figure 3 shows uncertainty maps predicted by H_{unc} for different branches of the label tree. The model provides sensibly decomposed uncertainty maps for each decision along the label tree, with uncertainty strongly localised along decision boundaries. The maps reflect the uncertainty we expect for different decisions: for example there is highly localised uncertainty along the well contrasted WM-CSF boundary, but uncertainty is more spread out on boundaries between cortical regions which are poorly defined, and subject to high inter-rater variability.

Figure 4 demonstrates a simple uncertainty-based thresholding method to obtain upper- and lower-bound cortical maps. They show that the cortical-specific uncertainty component from H_{unc} can be used to sensibly threshold predictions for non-leaf classes, in a way that is not possible for the uncertainty map from F_{unc} which lacks specificity to non-leaf nodes.

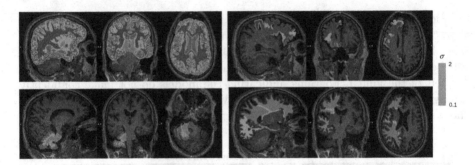

Fig. 3. Demonstration of different uncertainty components for model H_{unc} at four different branches of the label hierarchy, shown alongside the tissue class options at that branch. Colours have been selected to maximise distinguishability between adjacent classes.

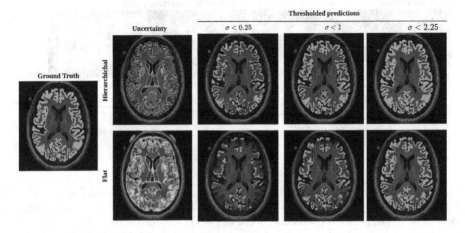

Fig. 4. Demonstration of thresholding predictions according to uncertainty. Ground truth cortical segmentation is shown on left. Using H_{unc} a cortex-specific uncertainty map can be produced, that can be sensibly thresholded to create cortical predictions at different uncertainty levels. The lack of decision specificity in the single uncertainty map provided by F_{unc} means we cannot perform cortex-specific thresholding - see in particular the map thresholded at $\sigma < 0.25$.

4   Conclusions

We have proposed a hierarchically-aware parcellation model, and demonstrated how it may be used to produce per-decision measures of uncertainty on the label tree. Our method outperforms the flat uncertainty model in terms of dice score, and was less likely than the flat model to make wrong predictions with both high confidence and low uncertainty. Furthermore we demonstrate the decomposed uncertainty enables us to produce consistent parcellations along with uncertainty maps for classes higher up the label tree, which is not possible with flat uncertainty models.

References

1. Whole-brain segmentation protocol. http://neuromorphometrics.com/Seg/
2. Cardoso, M.J., Modat, M., Wolz, R., Melbourne, A., Cash, D., Rueckert, D., Ourselin, S.: Geodesic information flows: spatially-variant graphs and their application to segmentation and fusion. IEEE Trans. Med. Imaging **34**(9), 1976–1988 (2015)
3. Demyanov, S., et al.: Tree-loss function for training neural networks on weakly-labelled datasets. In: 2017 IEEE 14th International Symposium on Biomedical Imaging (ISBI 2017), pp. 287–291. IEEE (2017)
4. Eaton-Rosen, Z., Bragman, F., Bisdas, S., Ourselin, S., Cardoso, M.J.: Towards safe deep learning: accurately quantifying biomarker uncertainty in neural network predictions. In: Frangi, A.F., Schnabel, J.A., Davatzikos, C., Alberola-López, C., Fichtinger, G. (eds.) MICCAI 2018. LNCS, vol. 11070, pp. 691–699. Springer, Cham (2018). https://doi.org/10.1007/978-3-030-00928-1_78
5. Han, S., Carass, A., Prince, J.L.: Hierarchical parcellation of the cerebellum. In: Shen, D., et al. (eds.) MICCAI 2019. LNCS, vol. 11766, pp. 484–491. Springer, Cham (2019). https://doi.org/10.1007/978-3-030-32248-9_54
6. Hu, H., Zhou, G.T., Deng, Z., Liao, Z., Mori, G.: Learning structured inference neural networks with label relations. In: Proceedings of the IEEE Conference on Computer Vision and Pattern Recognition, pp. 2960–2968 (2016)
7. Isensee, F., Petersen, J., Kohl, S.A.A., Jäger, P.F., Maier-Hein, K.H.: nnU-net: breaking the spell on successful medical image segmentation (2019)
8. Kendall, A., Gal, Y.: What uncertainties do we need in Bayesian deep learning for computer vision? In: Advances in Neural Information Processing Systems, pp. 5574–5584 (2017)
9. Kendall, A., Gal, Y., Cipolla, R.: Multi-task learning using uncertainty to weigh losses for scene geometry and semantics. In: Proceedings of the IEEE Conference on Computer Vision and Pattern Recognition, pp. 7482–7491 (2018)
10. Kingma, D.P., Ba, J.: Adam: a method for stochastic optimization. arXiv preprint arXiv:1412.6980 (2014)
11. Landman, B., Warfield, S.: MICCAI 2012 workshop on multi-atlas labeling. In: Medical Image Computing and Computer Assisted Intervention Conference (2012)
12. Liang, X., Zhou, H., Xing, E.: Dynamic-structured semantic propagation network. In: Proceedings of the IEEE Conference on Computer Vision and Pattern Recognition, pp. 752–761 (2018)
13. Petersen, R.C., et al.: Alzheimer's disease neuroimaging initiative (ADNI): clinical characterization. Neurology **74**(3), 201–209 (2010)
14. Redmon, J., Farhadi, A.: Yolo9000: better, faster, stronger. In: Proceedings of the IEEE Conference on Computer Vision and Pattern Recognition, pp. 7263–7271 (2017)
15. Wang, G., Li, W., Vercauteren, T., Ourselin, S.: Automatic brain tumor segmentation based on cascaded convolutional neural networks with uncertainty estimation. Front. Comput. Neurosci. **13**, 56 (2019)
16. Wu, C., Tygert, M., LeCun, Y.: A hierarchical loss and its problems when classifying non-hierarchically. PLoS ONE **14**(12), e0226222 (2019)

Quantitative Comparison of Monte-Carlo Dropout Uncertainty Measures for Multi-class Segmentation

Robin Camarasa[1,2(✉)], Daniel Bos[2,3(✉)], Jeroen Hendrikse[4(✉)],
Paul Nederkoorn[5(✉)], Eline Kooi[6(✉)], Aad van der Lugt[2(✉)],
and Marleen de Bruijne[1,2,7(✉)]

[1] Biomedical Imaging Group Rotterdam, Erasmus MC, Rotterdam, The Netherlands
{r.camarasa,marleen.debruijne}@erasmusmc.nl
[2] Department of Radiology and Nuclear Medicine, Erasmus MC,
Rotterdam, The Netherlands
{d.bos,a.vanderlugt}@erasmusmc.nl
[3] Department of Epidemiology, Erasmus MC, Rotterdam, The Netherlands
[4] Department of Radiology, University Medical Center Utrecht,
Utrecht, The Netherlands
j.hendrikse@umcutrecht.nl
[5] Department of Neurology, Academic Medical Center University of Amsterdam,
Amsterdam, The Netherlands
p.j.nederkoorn@amsterdamumc.nl
[6] Department of Radiology, Cardiovascular Research Institute Maastricht (CARIM),
Maastricht University Medical Center, Maastricht, The Netherlands
eline.kooi@mumc.nl
[7] Department of Computer Science, University of Copenhagen,
Copenhagen, Denmark

Abstract. Over the past decade, deep learning has become the gold standard for automatic medical image segmentation. Every segmentation task has an underlying uncertainty due to image resolution, annotation protocol, etc. Therefore, a number of methods and metrics have been proposed to quantify the uncertainty of neural networks mostly based on Bayesian deep learning, ensemble learning methods or output probability calibration. The aim of our research is to assess how reliable the different uncertainty metrics found in the literature are. We propose a quantitative and statistical comparison of uncertainty measures based on the relevance of the uncertainty map to predict misclassification. Four uncertainty metrics were compared over a set of 144 models. The application studied is the segmentation of the lumen and vessel wall of carotid arteries based on multiple sequences of magnetic resonance (MR) images in multi-center data.

© Springer Nature Switzerland AG 2020
C. H. Sudre et al. (Eds.): UNSURE 2020/GRAIL 2020, LNCS 12443, pp. 32–41, 2020.
https://doi.org/10.1007/978-3-030-60365-6_4

1   Introduction

Bayesian methods for neural networks [2,6,14] offer a mathematically grounded framework to analyse uncertainties. Nonetheless, the early Bayesian networks were computationally expensive to train, hard to implement and required more storage than conventional ones. The work of Gal et al. [3] renewed the interest in the field demonstrating the Bayesian properties of networks using dropout. The fast uptake of this technique in the field can be mainly attributed to the light alteration of the original model required.

The uncertainty estimation provided by Bayesian deep learning methods can be considered in every downstream tasks such as biomarkers extraction, surgery planning etc. Therefore, Bayesian techniques have known a rising interest in medical imaging for classification [12], segmentation [15,22] and registration [18].

Little research focuses on comparing the quality of different uncertainties metrics. A straightforward approach is to investigate the relationship between different uncertainty metrics and inter-observer variability [1,4]. Alternatively, in a classification problem, Van Molle et al. [22] introduces an uncertainty metric based on distribution similarity of the two most probable classes. Authors recommend the use of this uncertainty metric compared to variance based ones since it is more interpretable. In another work, Mehrtash et al. [9] compares calibrated and uncalibrated segmentation with negative log likelihood and Brier score. Finally, Nair et al. [13] compared the gain in segmentation performance when filtering out the most uncertain voxels for different uncertainty metrics. However, none of these approaches compare uncertainty metrics for multi-class segmentation which provide a larger spectrum of uncertainty measures.

To the best of our knowledge, this is the first work, in medical imaging, that compares quantitatively and statistically the ability of different uncertainty measures to predict misclassification in a multi-class segmentation context over a large set of models with widely varying performance, including different variations of Monte-Carlo dropout (MC dropout) techniques.

2   Methods

2.1   MC Dropout

In the following, $\theta \in \Omega$ represents the parameters of the model, f_θ the network with parameters θ, $(n_x, n_y, n_z) \in \mathbb{N}^3$ the dimensions of the input images, M the number of input modalities, C the number of output classes, $(x, t) \in \mathbb{R}^{n_x \times n_y \times n_z \times M} \times \mathbb{R}^{n_x \times n_y \times n_z \times C}$ a pair input image x with ground truth label image t, and $j \in J = \{0, ..., n_x - 1\} \times \{0, ..., n_y - 1\} \times \{0, ..., n_z - 1\}$ a 3D coordinate.

The different models used for carotid artery segmentation are based on the MC dropout method [3]. To obtain several estimates of the multi-class segmentation at test time, we sample T sets of parameters $(\theta_1, ..., \theta_T)$. From those parameters, we can evaluate T outputs $(f^{\theta_1}(x), ..., f^{\theta_T}(x))$ which represent a sample of the output distribution $q(y|x)$. From this sample, one can derive the mean and the covariance of output probabilities at a voxel level in Eq. 1.

$$\begin{cases} \mathbb{E}(q(y_j|x)) \approx \frac{1}{T}\sum_{t=1}^{T} f_j^{\theta_t}(x) \\ \mathrm{Var}(q(y_j|x)) \approx \frac{1}{T}\sum_{t=1}^{T} f_j^{\theta_t}(x)^T f_j^{\theta_t}(x) - \mathbb{E}(q(y_j|x))^T\mathbb{E}(q(y_j|x)) \end{cases} \tag{1}$$

An alternative to the original (Bernoulli) dropout that applies binary multiplicative noise is to use Gaussian multiplicative noise [20]. To make the two dropout methods comparable, one has to match the expected mean and the variance of the dropout distributions as shown in the following Eq. 2.

$$\begin{cases} B = \lambda A \\ \lambda_{Bernoulli} \sim \frac{1}{1-p}\mathcal{B}(1-p) \\ \lambda_{Gaussian} \sim \mathcal{N}(1, \frac{p}{1-p}) \end{cases} \tag{2}$$

where A is part of the feature maps of a dropout layer input, B is the corresponding feature map of that dropout layer output, $\lambda \in \mathbb{R}$ is randomly sampled from the dropout distribution, p is the dropout rate, $\mathcal{B}$ is a Bernoulli distribution and $\mathcal{N}$ is a Gaussian distribution.

2.2 Uncertainty Metrics

Distribution Description. A conventional approach to estimate uncertainty in a multi-class segmentation is to average the variance over classes [5,19]. In practice, this is obtained, at a voxel level, averaging the diagonal elements of the covariance matrix, Eq. 3.

$$u^v(q(y_j|x)) = \frac{1}{C}\mathrm{Tr}[\mathrm{Var}(q(y_j|x))] \tag{3}$$

where u^v is the averaged variance uncertainty metric and Tr is the trace of the matrix.

Another widely used uncertainty metric for segmentation is the entropy [23]. In contrast with the variance metric which can be directly computed from data sampled with MC dropout from the distribution $q(y_j|x)$, it requires the estimation of an integral defined in Eq. 4.

$$u^h(q(y_j|x)) = \frac{1}{C}\sum_{i=0}^{C-1}\int_0^1 -q_c(y_j = t|x)\log[q_c(y_j = t|x)]dt \tag{4}$$

where u^h is the averaged entropy uncertainty metric, $q_c(y_j|x)$ is the output distribution of the class c of the voxel j.

Distribution Similarity. Another option to define (voxelwise) classification uncertainty, is to consider the overlap of the distributions of the two most probable classes for a given voxel. Van der Molle et al. [22] considered the Bhattacharya coefficient, since it is interpretable (0: certain, 1: uncertain), Eq. 5.

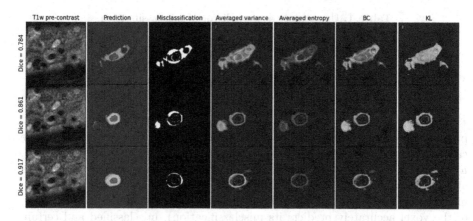

Fig. 1. Example of the different uncertainty metrics. From left to right columns represent, the T1w pre-contrast MR image, the multi-class prediction (blue = background, green = vessel wall, red = lumen, the level of brightness corresponds to the probability of the predicted class), the misclassification map and the different uncertainty maps (averaged variance, averaged entropy, BC, and KL). The rows correspond to predictions with different networks and level of performances. The indicated Dice is the averaged Dice over classes (Color figure online)

$$u^b(q(y_j|x)) = \int_0^1 \sqrt{q_{c_1}(y_j = t|x)q_{c_2}(y_j = t|x)}dt \tag{5}$$

where u^b is the Bhattacharya coefficient based uncertainty metric (BC), c_1 and c_2 are the two top classes for voxel j.

Alternatively, Kullback-Leibler divergence provides another measure of distribution similarity. However, unlike the previous presented uncertainty measures, a high value represents a small overlap among distributions. Therefore, the negative of the metric is considered. In addition, the Kullback-Leibler is made symmetric with respect to the classes c_1 and c_2, resulting in Eq. 6.

$$u^{kl}(q(y_j|x)) = -D_{KL}[q_{c_1}(y_j|x)||q_{c_2}(y_j|x)] - D_{KL}[q_{c_2}(y_j|x)||q_{c_1}(y_j|x)] \tag{6}$$

where u^{kl} is the Kullback-Leibler based uncertainty metric (KL) and D_{KL} is the Kullback-Leibler divergence.

The distribution $q(y_j|x)$ and $q_c(y_j|x)$ of Eqs. 3, 4, 5 and 6 are approximated by the distribution of the T outputs $(f^{\theta_1}(x), ..., f^{\theta_T}(x))$. The integrals of Eqs. 4, 5 and 6 are estimated with a left Riemann sum with a discretisation of the interval in n_{bins}.

2.3   Evaluation

Uncertainty Map Quality. To assess the quality of the uncertainty metrics, we applied the framework developed by Mobiny et al. [11] to the different type of uncertainty maps. The main idea is to consider uncertainty as a score that

Table 1. Uncertainty as a predictor of misclassification

	Uncertain $(u(q(y_j|x)) \geq th)$	Certain $(u(q(y_j|x)) < th)$
Misclassified	$TP(th)$	$FN(th)$
Correctly classified	$FP(th)$	$TN(th)$

predicts misclassification. From the MC estimates and the ground-truth, one can obtain a misclassification map m and an uncertainty map u (either u^v, u^h, u^b, u^{KL}) as described in Fig. 2. Once an uncertainty map is thresholded at a value th, one can define four types of voxels as summarized in Table 1: misclassified and uncertain (True Positive (TP) in a sense that the uncertainty of the voxel accurately predicts its misclassification), misclassified and certain (False Negative (FN)), correctly classified and uncertain (False Positive (FP)) and correctly classified and certain (True Negative (TN)).

For a given value of the uncertainty threshold th, it is possible to compute the precision and the recall of uncertainty as a misclassification predictor following: $\text{Pr}(th) = \frac{TP(th)}{TP(th)+FP(th)}$ and $\text{Rc}(th) = \frac{TP(th)}{TP(th)+FN(th)}$. By varying the threshold over the range of the values of u, one can derive the area under the precision recall curve (AUC-PR), Eq. 7.

$$\text{AUC-PR} = \sum_{i=1}^{|J|} Pr(u_i).[Rc(u_i) - Rc(u_{i+1})] \tag{7}$$

where $u_1 = u(q(y_{\phi^{-1}\circ\sigma(1)}|x)) \leq u_2 = u(q(y_{\phi^{-1}\circ\sigma(2)}|x)) \leq ... \leq u_{|J|} = u(q(y_{\phi^{-1}\circ\sigma(|J|)}|x))$ with $\phi : i, j, k \to 1 + k + i.n_x + j.n_x.n_y$ transforms 3D coordinates into indices and $\sigma \in \mathfrak{S}_{|J|}$ is a permutation.

The main advantage of this metric is its independence from uncertainty map scaling and distribution, as only the order of the voxels in the uncertainty map matters. For this reason, AUC-PR provides a quantitative evaluation of the uncertainty map quality that can reliably compare different uncertainty metrics.

Statistical Significance. To assess the statistical significance of our findings a Bayesian point of view is adopted. One can estimate the posterior distribution $p_{A,B}$ of the proportion of experiments where the uncertainty metric A has a higher average of AUC-PR (Eq. 7) over the test set than uncertainty metric B (with metric A and metric B different). In a Bayesian fashion, we choose a non-informative prior distribution of $p_{A,B} \sim \text{Beta}(1, 1)$ which corresponds to a uniform distribution. Over the N experiments, we observe $k_{A,B}$ experiments where metric A gives a better estimate of misclassification than metric B. Then, using Bayes rules, the posterior distribution is the following beta distribution, $p_{A,B} \sim \text{Beta}(1+k_{A,B}, 1+N-k_{A,B})$. From this Bayesian analysis, one can derive $I_{95\%}$, the 95% equally tailed credible interval of the parameter $p_{A,B}$, [7,8].

3   Experiments

Dataset. We used carotid artery MR images acquired within the multi-center, multi-scanner PARISK study [21], a large prospective study to improve risk stratification in patient with mild to moderate carotid artery stenosis (<70%). The standardized MR images acquisition protocol is described in Table 2. We used the images of all enrolled subjects (n = 145) at three of the four study centers as these centers have used the same protocol resulting in a homogeneous set of data: Amsterdam Medical Center (AMC), the Maastricht University Medical Center (MUMC) and the University Medical Center of Utrecht (UMCU). The dataset was split as followed 69 patients in the training set (all from MUMC), 24 patients in the validation set (all from MUMC) and 52 patients in the test set (15 from MUMC, 24 from UMCU and 13 from AMC).

Table 2. MR images scan parameters (QIR = quadruple inversion recovery, TSE = turbo spin echo, IR = inversion recovery, FFE = fast field echo and, TFE = turbo field echo, FA = flip angle, AVS = acquired voxel size, RVS = reconstructed voxel size)

Pulse	T1wQIR TSE		TOF FFE	IR-TFE	T2w TSE
sequence	Pre-contrast	Post-contrast			
Repetion time (ms)	800	800	20	3.3	4800
Echo time (ms)	10	10	5	2.1	49
Inversion time (ms)	282,61	282,61		304	
FA (degrees)	90	90	20	15	90
AVS (mm^2)	0.62×0.67	0.62×0.67	0.62×0.62	0.62×0.63	0.62×0.63
RVS (mm^2)	0.30×0.30	0.30×0.30	0.30×0.30	0.30×0.24	0.30×0.30
Slice thickness (mm)	2	2	2	2	2

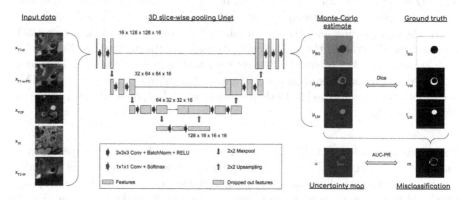

Fig. 2. Description of the network architecture and of the uncertainty map testing framework. The dimensions corresponds to the number of feature maps and the size of the feature maps

MR sequences were semi-automatically affinely and elastically registered to the T1w precontrast sequence. The vessel lumen and outer wall were annotated manually slice-wise, by trained observers with 3 years of experience, in the T1w precontrast sequence. Registration and annotation were achieved with Vessel-Mass software[1]. The intensity histogram was linearly scaled per image such that the 5th % was set to 0 and the 95th % was set to 1. The networks were trained and tested on a region of interest of $128 \times 128 \times 16$ voxels covering one of the common and internal carotid arteries per scan (either left or right).

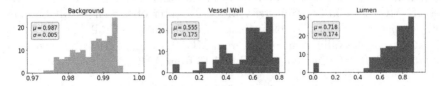

Fig. 3. Distribution over the experiments of the average Dice coefficient, for each of the three classes.

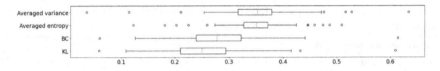

Fig. 4. Distribution over the experiments of the average AUC-PR computed on the test set. The whiskers represent the 5% and 95% interval.

Network Implementation. The networks used for our experiments are based on a 3D U-net architecture [17] as shown in Fig. 2. Because of the low resolution of our problem in the z-axis compared to the resolution on the x-and y-axis, we apply 2D max-pooling and 2D up-sampling slice-wise instead of their usual 3D alternatives. We trained the model using Adadelta optimizer [24] for 600 epochs with training batches of size 1. The network was optimized with the Dice loss [10]. As data augmentation, on the fly random flips along x axis were used. The networks were implemented in Python using Pytorch [16], on a NVIDIA GeForce 2080 RTX GPU.

Parameters Under Study. We varied three parameters in our experiments: the number of images in the training sample to analyse the robustness of the metrics to networks with different level of segmentation performances, the dropout rate, and the dropout type to test different variations of MC dropout. Eight values of number of images in the training set were used: 3, 5, 9, 15, 25, 30, 40 and 69 images. Also, nine dropout rates were used: 0.1, 0.2, 0.3, 0.4, 0.5, 0.6, 0.7, 0.8 and 0.9. Finally the two types of dropout (Bernoulli and Gaussian

---

[1] https://medisimaging.com/apps/vesselmass-re/.

dropout) described in Sect. 2 were considered. For every combination of those three parameters, we trained a network following the procedure detailed in previous paragraph. At evaluation time, we discretized the integrals of Eqs. 5, 4 and 6 in $n_{bins} = 100$ bins and we sampled $T = 50$ times using MC dropout method.

Results. A visualization of the different uncertainty measures for different level of performances can be found in Fig. 1. One can find the distribution of the average Dice per class in Fig. 3. The experiment with the highest averaged Dice over classes was observed with a model trained with Gaussian dropout and a dropout rate of 0.3 on the whole training set (69 samples). This method achieved Dice scores of 0.994 on the background, 0.764 on the vessel wall and 0.885 on the lumen. Figure 4 shows the distribution over experiments of the AUC-PR averaged over the test set for the four uncertainty metrics presented in this article.

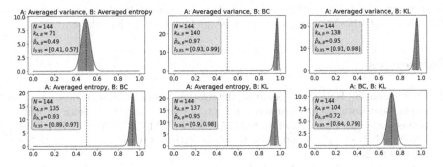

Fig. 5. Posterior distribution of $p_{A,B}$ for different metric pairs A and B, the red dashed line represents the expected value if compared metrics perform equally and the blue area under the curve represents the 95% credible interval

In our pairwise comparison of the four metrics, ten of the twelve combinations of metrics under study showed statistically significant differences over the 144 experiments ($I_{0.95}$ does not contain 0.5). Due to the nature of the beta distributions, the distribution of $p_{a,b}$ and $p_{b,a}$ are symmetric with respect to $y = 0.5$ axis. Therefore, to avoid redundancy only half of the combinations of metric analysis are reported in Fig. 5.

4   Discussion and Conclusion

We presented a quantitative analysis of four uncertainty metrics as predictors of misclassification over a large set of MC dropout variations applied to multiclass segmentation of carotid artery on MR images. This analysis which ranks voxels based on their uncertainty does not take into account the calibration of the different metrics. However, calibration can be performed easily for all metrics based on the validation set, without altering the rank of uncertainty values for individual voxels [12].

Our results showed that metrics considering the statistical description of a distribution averaged over classes performed significantly better than metrics based on distribution similarity of the top two classes when it comes to predict misclassification. Furthermore, BC performed better than KL. Those observations could be attributed to the over-confidence of the softmax output that tends to polarize the distributions to their extreme values (0 or 1) and how sensitive are the different metrics to this polarization. Therefore, in vessel segmentation, taking computation time and metrics performances into account, we advise the use of the averaged variance which does not require the discretisation of an integral voxel-wise. Finally, the good performances of the averaged variance and averaged entropy are consistent with their extensive use in the literature [5,19,23].

Acknowledgments. This work was funded by Netherlands Organisation for Scientific Research (NWO) VICI project VI.C.182.042. The PARISK study was funded within the framework of CTMM, the Center for Translational Molecular Medicine, project PARISK (grant 01C-202), and supported by the Dutch Heart Foundation.

References

1. Chotzoglou, E., Kainz, B.: Exploring the relationship between segmentation uncertainty, segmentation performance and inter-observer variability with probabilistic networks. In: Zhou, L., et al. (eds.) LABELS/HAL-MICCAI/CuRIOUS -2019. LNCS, vol. 11851, pp. 51–60. Springer, Cham (2019). https://doi.org/10.1007/978-3-030-33642-4_6

2. Denker, J.S., LeCun, Y.: Transforming neural-net output levels to probability distributions. In: Advances in Neural Information Processing Systems, pp. 853–859 (1991)

3. Gal, Y., Ghahramani, Z.: Dropout as a Bayesian approximation: representing model uncertainty in deep learning. In: International Conference on Machine Learning, pp. 1050–1059 (2016)

4. Jungo, A., et al.: On the effect of inter-observer variability for a reliable estimation of uncertainty of medical image segmentation. In: Frangi, A.F., Schnabel, J.A., Davatzikos, C., Alberola-López, C., Fichtinger, G. (eds.) MICCAI 2018. LNCS, vol. 11070, pp. 682–690. Springer, Cham (2018). https://doi.org/10.1007/978-3-030-00928-1_77

5. Kendall, A., Badrinarayanan, V., Cipolla, R.: Bayesian SegNet: model uncertainty in deep convolutional encoder-decoder architectures for scene understanding. arXiv preprint arXiv:1511.02680 (2015)

6. MacKay, D.J.: A practical Bayesian framework for backpropagation networks. Neural Comput. **4**(3), 448–472 (1992)

7. Makowski, D., Ben-Shachar, M., Lüdecke, D.: bayestestR: describing effects and their uncertainty, existence and significance within the Bayesian framework. J. Open Source Softw. **4**(40), 1541 (2019)

8. McElreath, R.: Statistical Rethinking: A Bayesian Course with Examples in R and Stan. CRC Press, Boca Raton (2020)

9. Mehrtash, A., Wells III, W.M., Tempany, C.M., Abolmaesumi, P., Kapur, T.: Confidence calibration and predictive uncertainty estimation for deep medical image segmentation. arXiv preprint arXiv:1911.13273 (2019)
10. Milletari, F., Navab, N., Ahmadi, S.A.: V-Net: fully convolutional neural networks for volumetric medical image segmentation. In: 2016 Fourth International Conference on 3D Vision (3DV), pp. 565–571. IEEE (2016)
11. Mobiny, A., Nguyen, H.V., Moulik, S., Garg, N., Wu, C.C.: DropConnect is effective in modeling uncertainty of Bayesian deep networks. arXiv preprint arXiv:1906.04569 (2019)
12. Mobiny, A., Singh, A., Van Nguyen, H.: Risk-aware machine learning classifier for skin lesion diagnosis. J. Clin. Med. 8(8), 1241 (2019)
13. Nair, T., Precup, D., Arnold, D.L., Arbel, T.: Exploring uncertainty measures in deep networks for multiple sclerosis lesion detection and segmentation. Med. Image Anal. 59, 101557 (2020)
14. Neal, R.M.: Bayesian learning via stochastic dynamics. In: Advances in Neural Information Processing Systems, pp. 475–482 (1993)
15. Orlando, J.I., et al.: U2-Net: a Bayesian U-Net model with epistemic uncertainty feedback for photoreceptor layer segmentation in pathological oct scans. In: 2019 IEEE 16th International Symposium on Biomedical Imaging (ISBI 2019), pp. 1441–1445. IEEE (2019)
16. Paszke, A., et al.: PyTorch: an imperative style, high-performance deep learning library. In: Advances in Neural Information Processing Systems, pp. 8024–8035 (2019)
17. Ronneberger, O., Fischer, P., Brox, T.: U-Net: convolutional networks for biomedical image segmentation. In: Navab, N., Hornegger, J., Wells, W.M., Frangi, A.F. (eds.) MICCAI 2015. LNCS, vol. 9351, pp. 234–241. Springer, Cham (2015). https://doi.org/10.1007/978-3-319-24574-4_28
18. Sedghi, A., Kapur, T., Luo, J., Mousavi, P., Wells, W.M.: Probabilistic image registration via deep multi-class classification: characterizing uncertainty. In: Greenspan, H., et al. (eds.) CLIP/UNSURE -2019. LNCS, vol. 11840, pp. 12–22. Springer, Cham (2019). https://doi.org/10.1007/978-3-030-32689-0_2
19. Seeböck, P., et al.: Exploiting epistemic uncertainty of anatomy segmentation for anomaly detection in retinal OCT. IEEE Trans. Med. Imaging 39(1), 87–98 (2019)
20. Srivastava, N., Hinton, G., Krizhevsky, A., Sutskever, I., Salakhutdinov, R.: Dropout: a simple way to prevent neural networks from overfitting. J. Mach. Learn. Res. 15(1), 1929–1958 (2014)
21. Truijman, M., et al.: Plaque At RISK (PARISK): prospective multicenter study to improve diagnosis of high-risk carotid plaques. Int. J. Stroke 9(6), 747–754 (2014)
22. Van Molle, P., et al.: Quantifying uncertainty of deep neural networks in skin lesion classification. In: Greenspan, H., et al. (eds.) CLIP/UNSURE -2019. LNCS, vol. 11840, pp. 52–61. Springer, Cham (2019). https://doi.org/10.1007/978-3-030-32689-0_6
23. Wang, G., Li, W., Aertsen, M., Deprest, J., Ourselin, S., Vercauteren, T.: Aleatoric uncertainty estimation with test-time augmentation for medical image segmentation with convolutional neural networks. Neurocomputing 338, 34–45 (2019)
24. Zeiler, M.D.: ADADELTA: an adaptive learning rate method. arXiv preprint arXiv:1212.5701 (2012)

Uncertainty Estimation in Landmark Localization Based on Gaussian Heatmaps

Christian Payer[1]([⊠]) [iD], Martin Urschler[2] [iD], Horst Bischof[1] [iD], and Darko Štern[3] [iD]

[1] Institute of Computer Graphics and Vision, Graz University of Technology, Graz, Austria
christian.payer@icg.tugraz.at
[2] School of Computer Science, The University of Auckland, Auckland, New Zealand
[3] Gottfried Schatz Research Center: Biophysics, Medical University of Graz, Graz, Austria

Abstract. In landmark localization, due to ambiguities in defining their exact position, landmark annotations may suffer from both large inter- and intra-observer variabilites, which result in uncertain annotations. Therefore, predicting a single coordinate for a landmark is not sufficient for modeling the distribution of possible landmark locations. We propose to learn the Gaussian covariances of target heatmaps, such that covariances for pointed heatmaps correspond to more certain landmarks and covariances for flat heatmaps to more uncertain or ambiguous landmarks. By fitting Gaussian functions to the predicted heatmaps, our method is able to obtain landmark location distributions, which model location uncertainties. We show on a dataset of left hand radiographs and on a dataset of lateral cephalograms that the predicted uncertainties correlate with the landmark error, as well as inter-observer variabilities.

Keywords: Landmark localization · Uncertainty estimation

1 Introduction

Anatomical landmark localization is an important topic in medical image analysis, e.g., as a preprocessing step for segmentation [1,9], registration [11,19], as well as for deriving surgical or diagnostic measures like the location of bones in the hip [2], the curvature of the spine [20], and the misalignment of teeth or the jaw [21]. Unfortunately, anatomical landmarks can be difficult to define unambiguously, especially for landmarks that do not lie on distinct anatomical structures like the tip of the incisor, but on smooth edges like the tip of the chin. Such ambiguous landmarks are specifically difficult to annotate, which

Electronic supplementary material The online version of this chapter (https://doi.org/10.1007/978-3-030-60365-6_5) contains supplementary material, which is available to authorized users.

C. H. Sudre et al. (Eds.): UNSURE 2020/GRAIL 2020, LNCS 12443, pp. 42–51, 2020.
https://doi.org/10.1007/978-3-030-60365-6_5

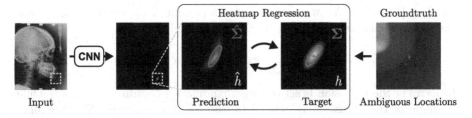

Fig. 1. Schematic representation of our proposed method to model annotation ambiguities. Although ambiguities are not observable from a single groundtruth annotation (green cross), they are present in the entirety of the annotated images (red dots). We model landmark ambiguities with a Gaussian function with covariance Σ that is learned during training and represents a *dataset-based uncertainty*. The predicted heatmap $\hat{h}$ is fitted with covariance $\hat{\Sigma}$ to represent the predicted landmark locations as a distribution, modeling an *image-based uncertainty*. (Color figure online)

may lead not only to a large inter-observer variability between different annotators, but also to a large intra-observer variability that is dependent on the daily constitution of a single annotator. Due to this uncertainty, a machine learning predictor that has been trained on potentially ambiguous annotations should model landmarks not only as single locations, but rather as distributions over possible locations. Predicting such uncertainty measures helps interpreting the output of machine learning programs [6], which is especially useful in the medical imaging domain [14,22,23] where explainability is crucial [8].

Methods in anatomical landmark localization predominantly use machine learning. While random forests have been successfully applied [5,13,18], recently, convolutional neural networks (CNNs) outperformed other techniques, especially when doing heatmap regression [2,15–17,24]. In these works, heatmaps have only been used for predicting single locations, e.g., as the maximum response, and not for obtaining distributions of possible landmark locations.

We hypothesize that the heatmap regression framework may be used to model landmark uncertainties (see Fig. 1). We adapt the framework to learn the optimal shape of target heatmaps, which models an uncertainty based on annotation ambiguities in the training dataset. Furthermore, by fitting a Gaussian function to the predicted heatmap during inference, we do not only predict the most probable landmark location but its distribution, which models a prediction uncertainty. Evaluation on datasets of left hand radiographs and lateral cephalograms shows that the uncertainties correlate with the magnitude and direction of the average localization error, as well as the inter-observer variabilities.

2 Heatmap Regression for Dataset-Based Uncertainty

We perform anatomical landmark localization with CNNs using heatmap regression [2,15–17,24]. For N target landmarks, the CNN with parameters w predicts N heatmaps $\hat{h}_i(x; w)$, while each heatmap corresponds to a single landmark L_i

with $i = \{1, ..., N\}$. A target heatmap is represented as an image of a two-dimensional Gaussian function $h_i(\boldsymbol{x}; \boldsymbol{\Sigma}_i) : \mathbb{R}^2 \to \mathbb{R}$, i.e.,

$$h_i(\boldsymbol{x}; \boldsymbol{\Sigma}_i) = \frac{\gamma}{\sqrt{(2\pi)^2 \det \boldsymbol{\Sigma}_i}} \exp\left(-\frac{1}{2}(\boldsymbol{x} - \boldsymbol{x}_i)^T \boldsymbol{\Sigma}_i^{-1}(\boldsymbol{x} - \boldsymbol{x}_i)\right). \qquad (1)$$

The mean of the Gaussian is set to target landmark's coordinate $\boldsymbol{x}_i \in \mathbb{R}^2$, while the shape of the Gaussian is defined by the covariance matrix $\boldsymbol{\Sigma}_i$. A scaling factor γ is used to avoid numerical instabilities during training.

Differently to other heatmap regression methods, which represent the covariance of the Gaussian with only a single parameter σ_i, we allow anisotropic Gaussian functions with a general covariance matrix $\boldsymbol{\Sigma}_i$. This way, we do not model isotropic, axis-aligned Gaussian functions with varying extents but anisotropic Gaussian functions that have different extents in different directions. The covariance matrix $\boldsymbol{\Sigma}_i$ may be decomposed into

$$\boldsymbol{\Sigma}_i = \mathbf{R}_i \boldsymbol{\Sigma}_i^* \mathbf{R}_i^T, \text{ with } \mathbf{R}_i = \begin{bmatrix} \cos\theta_i & -\sin\theta_i \\ \sin\theta_i & \cos\theta_i \end{bmatrix} \text{ and } \boldsymbol{\Sigma}_i^* = \begin{bmatrix} \sigma_i^{\text{maj}} & 0 \\ 0 & \sigma_i^{\text{min}} \end{bmatrix}, \qquad (2)$$

where θ_i represents the rotation of the Gaussian function's major axis, and σ_i^{maj} and σ_i^{min} represent its extent in major and minor axis, respectively.

The loss function for simultaneously regressing N heatmaps is defined as

$$\min_{\boldsymbol{w}, \boldsymbol{\Sigma}_1, ..., \boldsymbol{\Sigma}_N} \sum_{i=1}^{N} \sum_{\boldsymbol{x}} \|\hat{h}_i(\boldsymbol{x}; \boldsymbol{w}) - h_i(\boldsymbol{x}; \boldsymbol{\Sigma}_i)\|_2^2 + \alpha \sum_{i=1}^{N} \sigma_i^{\text{maj}} \sigma_i^{\text{min}}. \qquad (3)$$

The first term in (3) minimizes the differences between the predicted heatmaps $\hat{h}_i$ and the target heatmaps h_i for all landmarks L_i. Since we also treat the covariance parameters of the Gaussian function (θ_i, σ_i^{maj}, and σ_i^{min}) as unknowns, we enable learning them in addition to the network parameters $\boldsymbol{w}$. Unfortunately, minimizing the difference between $\hat{h}_i$ and h_i could lead to the trivial solution $\sigma_i^{\text{maj}} \sigma_i^{\text{min}} \to \infty$ with $h_i \approx 0$. To avoid that $\sigma_i^{\text{maj}} \sigma_i^{\text{min}} \to \infty$, the second term in (3) penalizes $\sigma_i^{\text{maj}} \sigma_i^{\text{min}}$ with factor α.

Analyzing (3) in more detail, not only the predicted heatmaps $\hat{h}_i$ aim to be close to the target heatmaps h_i but also the target heatmaps h_i aim to be close to the predicted heatmaps $\hat{h}_i$. For each landmark L_i, $\hat{h}_i$ and h_i receive feedback from each other during training (see Fig. 1). While the network parameters $\boldsymbol{w}$ are updated to better model the shape of the target heatmap $\hat{h}_i$, at the same time, the covariance $\boldsymbol{\Sigma}_i$ parameters of each target heatmap h_i (θ_i, σ_i^{maj}, and σ_i^{min}) are updated to better model the shape of the predicted heatmap $\hat{h}_i$. Note that $\boldsymbol{\Sigma}_i$ is learned only from single annotations per image, but from all annotated training images, thus, modeling the ambiguities of landmark annotations for the whole training dataset and representing a *dataset-based uncertainty*.

3   Heatmap Fitting for Image-Based Uncertainty

As the output of heatmap regression networks are N heatmaps that correspond to the N landmarks L_i, the landmark's coordinate $\hat{\boldsymbol{x}}_i$ needs to be obtained from the predicted heatmaps $\hat{h}_i$. Previous work often uses the coordinate of the maximum response or the center of mass of the predicted heatmaps as the landmark's coordinate. However, this represents only the most probable landmark location, but not the whole distribution of possible landmark locations.

As the target heatmaps are modeled as Gaussian functions (see (1)), we expect also the predicted heatmaps to be a Gaussian function. Hence, we capture the distribution of possible landmark locations by fitting Gaussian functions to the predicted heatmaps $\hat{h}$. We use a robust least squares curve fitting method [3] to fit the Gaussian function (see (1)) around the maximum of the predicted heatmaps $\hat{h}_i$ and obtain the fitted Gaussian parameters $\hat{x}_i$ and $\hat{\Sigma}_i$ with $i = \{1, ..., N\}$. As the fitted Gaussian function models the distribution of possible locations, the parameters represent a directional *image-based uncertainty* of the landmark location during inference.

4   Experimental Setup

Networks: Our proposed method to learn anisotropic Gaussian heatmaps can be combined with any image-to-image based network architecture. In this work, we use the SpatialConfiguration-Net (SCN [16]), due to its state-of-the-art performance and publicly available code. We implement learning of Gaussian functions with arbitrary covariance matrices. We use the SCN with the default parameters trained for 40,000 iterations. We use training data augmentation, i.e., random intensity shift and scale, translation, scaling, rotation, and elastic deformation. We use L_2 weight regularization with a factor of $\lambda = 0.001$. In (1) we set $\gamma = 100$; in (3), we initialize $\sigma_i^{\mathrm{maj}} = \sigma_i^{\mathrm{min}} = 3$, $\theta_i = 0$, and set $\alpha = 5$.

We perform an ablation study on different strategies of using Gaussians. First, we distinguish whether the target Gaussian heatmaps in (2) are isotropic, i.e., $\sigma^{\mathrm{maj}} = \sigma^{\mathrm{min}}$, or anisotropic during training. Second, we distinguish how the location is obtained from the predicted heatmaps during inference. This can be done by either taking the maximum [15–17,24], or, as we are proposing, by fitting Gaussians. We compare networks using isotropic Gaussians as target and taking the maximum (σ-target, max), fitting isotropic (σ-target, $\hat{\sigma}$-fit) and anisotropic Gaussians (σ-target, $\hat{\Sigma}$-fit), as well as networks using anisotropic Gaussians for target only (Σ-target, $\hat{\sigma}$-fit), and for both target and fitting (Σ-target, $\hat{\Sigma}$-fit).

Datasets: We evaluate our proposed method on two publicly available datasets for anatomical landmark localization. The first dataset consists of 895 radiographs of left hands of the Digital Hand Atlas Database System [7,25] with 37 annotated landmarks per image. Each image has been annotated by one of three experts. The second dataset consists of 400 lateral cephalograms with 19 annotated landmarks per image. This dataset has been used for the ISBI 2015 Cephalometric X-ray Image Analysis Challenge [21], in which each image has been annotated by both a senior and a junior radiologist. As every image has been annotated by two radiologists, we are able to measure the inter-observer variability in this dataset and can compare it with the predicted uncertainty.

Metrics: For evaluating the landmark localization performance, we use the point-to-point error PE, i.e., the Euclidean distance between groundtruth x and prediction $\hat{x}$. We also calculate the number of outliers $\#O_r$ for radius r, which is defined as the number of landmarks with a larger PE of r mm. The outlier ratio OR_r is the percentage of outliers to all predicted landmarks; the success detection rate is defined as $SDR_r = 100 - OR_r$.

Table 1. Quantitative localization results. Top: Results for the cross-validation (CV) on the hand radiographs. Bottom: Results on the test sets (using the mean annotation of junior and senior), as well as the CV (using the junior's annotation) for the lateral cephalograms. Best values are marked in bold.

hand	Method	PE (in mm)		$\#O_r$ (OR_r in %)		
		median	mean $\pm$ SD	$r = 2$ mm	$r = 4$ mm	$r = 10$ mm
CV	Lindner et al. [12]	0.64	0.85 $\pm$ 1.01	2094 (6.32%)	347 (1.05%)	20 (0.06%)
	Urschler et al. [18]	0.51	0.80 $\pm$ 0.93	2586 (7.81%)	510 (1.54%)	18 (0.05%)
	Payer et al. [16]	0.43	0.66 $\pm$ 0.74	1659 (5.01%)	241 (0.73%)	**3 (0.01%)**
	(σ-target, max)	0.40	0.62 $\pm$ 0.72	1507 (4.55%)	263 (0.79%)	4 (0.01%)
	(σ-target, $\hat{\sigma}$-fit)	0.40	**0.61 $\pm$ 0.67**	1381 (4.17%)	185 (0.56%)	**3 (0.01%)**
	(σ-target, $\hat{\Sigma}$-fit)	0.40	**0.61 $\pm$ 0.66**	1354 (4.09%)	161 (0.49%)	**3 (0.01%)**
	(Σ-target, $\hat{\sigma}$-fit)	**0.39**	**0.61 $\pm$ 0.68**	1404 (4.24%)	169 (0.51%)	5 (0.02%)
	(Σ-target, $\hat{\Sigma}$-fit)	**0.39**	**0.61 $\pm$ 0.67**	**1349 (4.07%)**	**151 (0.46%)**	4 (0.01%)
ceph.	Method	PE (in mm)	SDR$_r$ in %			
		mean $\pm$ SD	$r = 2$ mm	$r = 2.5$ mm	$r = 3$ mm	$r = 4$ mm
Test1	Ibragimov et al. [10]	1.67 $\pm$ n/a	71.72%	77.40%	81.93%	88.04%
	Lindner et al. [12]	1.84 $\pm$ n/a	73.68%	80.21%	85.19%	91.47%
	Zhong et al. [26]	1.12 $\pm$ 0.88	86.91%	91.82%	94.88%	97.90%
	Chen et al. [4]	1.17 $\pm$ n/a	86.67%	**92.67%**	**95.54%**	**98.53%**
	(Σ-target, $\hat{\Sigma}$-fit)	**1.07 $\pm$ 1.02**	**87.37%**	91.86%	94.81%	97.79%
Test2	Ibragimov et al. [10]	1.92 $\pm$ n/a	62.74%	70.47%	76.53%	85.11%
	Lindner et al. [12]	2.14 $\pm$ n/a	66.11%	72.00%	77.63%	87.42%
	Zhong et al. [26]	1.42 $\pm$ 0.84	**76.00%**	**82.90%**	**88.74%**	94.32%
	Chen et al. [4]	1.48 $\pm$ n/a	75.05%	82.84%	88.53%	**95.05%**
	(Σ-target, $\hat{\Sigma}$-fit)	**1.38 $\pm$ 1.33**	75.11%	82.53%	88.26%	94.58%
CV jun.	Lindner et al. [13]	1.20 $\pm$ n/a	84.70%	89.38%	92.62%	96.30%
	Zhong et al. [26]	1.22 $\pm$ 2.45	86.06%	90.84%	94.04%	97.28%
	(σ-target, max)	1.02 $\pm$ 1.13	88.72%	92.55%	94.83%	97.42%
	(σ-target, $\hat{\sigma}$-fit)	1.00 $\pm$ 1.08	89.64%	93.32%	95.66%	97.91%
	(σ-target, $\hat{\Sigma}$-fit)	1.00 $\pm$ 1.07	**89.78%**	93.58%	95.80%	**97.95%**
	(Σ-target, $\hat{\sigma}$-fit)	**0.99 $\pm$ 1.08**	89.63%	93.55%	95.66%	97.83%
	(Σ-target, $\hat{\Sigma}$-fit)	**0.99 $\pm$ 1.07**	89.76%	**93.74%**	**95.83%**	97.82%

5   Results and Discussion

Comparison with Other Methods: While the main focus of our paper lies on evaluating the uncertainty measures, we validate our method by comparing to the state-of-the-art in terms of landmark localization error in Table 1. The reported metrics and values are taken from the respective publications.

On a three-fold cross-validation (CV) of the dataset of left hand radiographs, our proposed method outperforms all previous results. When comparing the different fitting strategies, we can see that defining the landmark coordinate as the maximum value of the heatmap generated from the network with isotropic target heatmaps (σ-target, max) leads to the smallest improvements as compared to the state-of-the-art. When using either isotropic or anisotropic Gaussians during training and fitting isotropic ones during inference, the results increase slightly (σ-target, $\hat{\sigma}$-fit and Σ-target, $\hat{\sigma}$-fit). Finally, fitting anisotropic Gaussians leads to better results (σ-target, $\hat{\Sigma}$-fit and Σ-target, $\hat{\Sigma}$-fit), while also using anisotropic Gaussians during training leads to the overall best results (Σ-target, $\hat{\Sigma}$-fit).

We compare to other methods on both test sets *Test1* and *Test2* of the lateral cephalograms, where we trained and evaluated networks with the average coordinate from both radiologist annotations. Here, the methods using CNNs have similar results, while our method is the most accurate with the smallest PE. In terms of SDR, our method performs in-line with other methods, while Chen et al. [4] perform slightly better in *Test1* and Zhong et al. [26] in *Test2*, respectively.

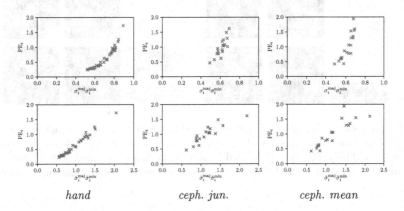

hand   *ceph. jun.*   *ceph. mean*

Fig. 2. Correlation of the mean learned target Gaussian sizes (top) and fitted Gaussian sizes (bottom) of all landmarks L_i to the mean localization error PE_i for all images of the CV of hand radiographs (left), cephalograms with junior annotations (center), and mean of senior and junior (right) in mm.

As we show in later experiments, there exist systematic shifts for some landmarks in *Test1* and *Test2* as compared to the annotations of the training data. To mitigate this, we follow previous work [13,26] and perform a four-fold CV experiment trained and evaluated on the junior annotations only. Similar to the hand radiographs, learning and fitting anisotropic Gaussian functions (Σ-target, $\hat{\Sigma}$-fit) leads to the best results, outperforming all other methods.

Uncertainty Estimation of the Landmark Distributions: Our proposed method models a *dataset-based uncertainty* during training as parameters of the target Gaussian heatmaps (see Sect. 2), as well as an *image-based uncertainty* during inference by fitting a Gaussian function to the predicted heatmaps (see Sect. 3). For evaluating whether the parameters of the target and fitted Gaussians represent uncertainty measures, we compare the sizes of the Gaussians for each landmark L_i with the average PE_i in Fig. 2. We evaluate the CV of the hand dataset, as well as CVs of the cephalograms trained on either the junior annotations only, or the mean of both junior and senior. We can see that both the target and fitted heatmap parameters correlate with the PE, thus representing valid uncertainty measures. We want to highlight that the *dataset-based uncertainty* is obtained during network training without requiring validation images. Thus, it can make use of all annotations of the training dataset and allows identification of difficult to annotate landmarks, even with only a few annotated images.

Moreover, our proposed method is also able to model directional uncertainties, which we visualize in Fig. 3 for selected landmarks (for all landmarks, see the supplementary materials). Here, while both target and predicted heatmaps

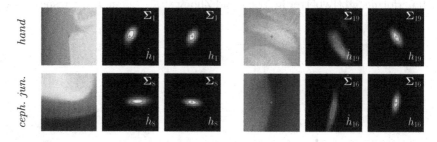

Fig. 3. Input (left), heatmap predictions (middle) and target heatmaps (right) for selected landmarks. Images show 15×15 mm patches around groundtruth annotation (green cross). The target and predicted heatmaps are superimposed with ellipses representing the target and fitted Gaussian parameters, respectively. (Color figure online)

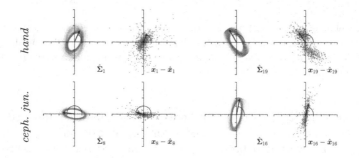

Fig. 4. Gaussian functions fitted to the predicted heatmaps (left) and offsets of the groundtruth coordinate to the predictions (right) for selected landmarks. For all images of the datasets, the fitted Gaussian parameters are shown as blue ellipses, the offsets as red dots. The average major axis of the fitted Gaussian parameter, as well as the major axis of a Gaussian distribution fitted to the offsets, are shown as black arrows. Each tick on the axis lines marks one mm.

are smaller for landmarks on distinct corners as compared to landmarks on edges, the heatmaps are also rotated in direction of the underlying edges, as this is the main source for ambiguities. Interestingly, for landmark L_{19} of the hand dataset and landmark L_{16} of the cephalograms, the predicted heatmap has a larger extent as compared to the target heatmap. Landmark L_{19} of the hand dataset lies on the base of the proximal phalanx of the thumb, which is often wrongly annotated as the head of the metacarpal. For landmark L_{16} of the cephalogram dataset, the predicted heatmaps have a larger extent, as this landmark is difficult to annotate unambiguously, which can also be seen in a large inter-observer variability as shown in later evaluations. Our method is able to detect such ambiguous landmarks by predicting a larger uncertainty expressed as more disperse distributions of landmark locations.

To show that the fitted heatmap parameters $\hat{\Sigma}_i$ represent the same distribution as the expected prediction-groundtruth offsets $x_i - \hat{x}_i$, we visualize all fitted heatmaps and offsets for all images of the dataset in Fig. 4 for some example landmarks. Here we can see that the fitted heatmap parameters have the same distribution as the expected groundtruth-prediction offsets. For landmark L_{19} of the hand radiograph dataset, we can see two clusters of offsets, showing well the misannotations as described previously. Overall, these results further show that the fitted parameters $\hat{\Sigma}_i$ model an image-based landmark location uncertainty.

Uncertainty Estimation for Modeling the Inter-observer Variability: As a final experiment, we evaluate how well our proposed method models the inter-observer variability on the dataset of cephalograms. In Fig. 5, we show the predicted fitted Gaussian parameters, the groundtruth-prediction offsets, as well as groundtruth-senior and groundtruth-junior offsets for the CV trained on the mean of both junior and senior annotations. The plots show that our proposed method models well the inter-observer variability, leading to fitted Gaussian parameters $\hat{\Sigma}_i$ that are similar to the expected offsets $x_i - \hat{x}_i$. On these plots we can also see that there may exist a systematic offset between junior (green) and senior (yellow) annotations, leading to two distinct point clusters as compared to their mean x_i. For landmark L_{16}, which is difficult to annotate unambiguously, the disagreement of junior and senior is very large on the training

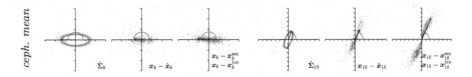

Fig. 5. Gaussian parameters fitted to the predicted heatmaps (left), offsets of the groundtruth coordinate to the predictions (middle), and groundtruth-senior and groundtruth-junior offsets (right) for selected landmarks. The visualization is the same as in Fig. 4, while the offsets of senior and junior annotation to their mean are shown as green and orange dots, respectively. (Color figure online)

dataset. Interestingly, in *Test2* their disagreement reduced from more 5 mm to $\approx$2 mm. This systematic shift of the landmark groundtruth locations for L_{16} can explain the reduced performance of all compared methods in Table 1 for *Test2*. In conclusion, these results show that the fitted heatmap parameters $\hat{\boldsymbol{\Sigma}}_i$ model also the landmark location uncertainty in terms of inter-observer variability.

6   Conclusion

We have shown that CNNs using heatmap regression may be used for predicting location uncertainties. By learning Gaussian parameters of the target heatmaps and fitting Gaussian functions to the predicted heatmaps, our method is able to predict distributions of possible landmark locations. While showing state-of-the-art performance in two datasets, the predicted landmark distributions correlate with the landmark localization error as well as inter-observer variabilities. In future work, we plan to extend our method to three dimensional data.

References

1. Beichel, R., Bischof, H., Leberl, F., Sonka, M.: Robust active appearance models and their application to medical image analysis. IEEE Trans. Med. Imaging **24**(9), 1151–1169 (2005)
2. Bier, B., et al.: Learning to detect anatomical landmarks of the pelvis in X-rays from arbitrary views. Int. J. Comput. Assist. Radiol. Surg. **14**(9), 1463–1473 (2019)
3. Branch, M.A., Coleman, T.F., Li, Y.: A subspace, interior, and conjugate gradient method for large-scale bound-constrained minimization problems. SIAM J. Sci. Comput. **21**(1), 1–23 (1999)
4. Chen, R., Ma, Y., Chen, N., Lee, D., Wang, W.: Cephalometric landmark detection by attentive feature pyramid fusion and regression-voting. In: Shen, D., et al. (eds.) MICCAI 2019. LNCS, vol. 11766, pp. 873–881. Springer, Cham (2019). https://doi.org/10.1007/978-3-030-32248-9_97
5. Cootes, T.F., Ionita, M.C., Lindner, C., Sauer, P.: Robust and accurate shape model fitting using random forest regression voting. In: Fitzgibbon, A., Lazebnik, S., Perona, P., Sato, Y., Schmid, C. (eds.) ECCV 2012. LNCS, vol. 7578, pp. 278–291. Springer, Heidelberg (2012). https://doi.org/10.1007/978-3-642-33786-4_21
6. Gal, Y., Ghahramani, Z.: Dropout as a Bayesian approximation: representing model uncertainty in deep learning. In: Proceedings of the International Conference on Machine Learning, pp. 1050–1059 (2016)
7. Gertych, A., Zhang, A., Sayre, J., Pospiech-Kurkowska, S., Huang, H.: Bone age assessment of children using a digital hand atlas. Comput. Med. Imaging Graph. **31**(4–5), 322–331 (2007)
8. Gunning, D., Stefik, M., Choi, J., Miller, T., Stumpf, S., Yang, G.Z.: XAI–explainable artificial intelligence. Sci. Robot. **4**(37), eaay7120 (2019)
9. Heimann, T., Meinzer, H.P.: Statistical shape models for 3D medical image segmentation: a review. Med. Image Anal. **13**(4), 543–563 (2009)
10. Ibragimov, B., Likar, B., Pernuš, F., Vrtovec, T.: Shape representation for efficient landmark-based segmentation in 3-D. IEEE Trans. Med. Imaging **33**(4), 861–874 (2014)

11. Johnson, H.J., Christensen, G.E.: Consistent landmark and intensity-based image registration. IEEE Trans. Med. Imaging **21**(5), 450–461 (2002)

12. Lindner, C., Bromiley, P.A., Ionita, M.C., Cootes, T.F.: Robust and accurate shape model matching using random forest regression-voting. IEEE Trans. Pattern Anal. Mach. Intell. **37**(9), 1862–1874 (2015)

13. Lindner, C., Wang, C.W., Huang, C.T., Li, C.H., Chang, S.W., Cootes, T.F.: Fully automatic system for accurate localisation and analysis of cephalometric landmarks in lateral cephalograms. Sci. Rep. **6**, 33581 (2016)

14. Nair, T., Precup, D., Arnold, D.L., Arbel, T.: Exploring uncertainty measures in deep networks for Multiple sclerosis lesion detection and segmentation. Med. Image Anal. **59**, 101557 (2020)

15. Payer, C., Štern, D., Bischof, H., Urschler, M.: Regressing heatmaps for multiple landmark localization using CNNs. In: Ourselin, S., Joskowicz, L., Sabuncu, M.R., Unal, G., Wells, W. (eds.) MICCAI 2016. LNCS, vol. 9901, pp. 230–238. Springer, Cham (2016). https://doi.org/10.1007/978-3-319-46723-8_27

16. Payer, C., Štern, D., Bischof, H., Urschler, M.: Integrating spatial configuration into heatmap regression based CNNs for landmark localization. Med. Image Anal. **54**, 207–219 (2019)

17. Tompson, J., Jain, A., LeCun, Y., Bregler, C.: Joint training of a convolutional network and a graphical model for human pose estimation. In: Advances in Neural Information Processing Systems, pp. 1799–1807 (2014)

18. Urschler, M., Ebner, T., Štern, D.: Integrating geometric configuration and appearance information into a unified framework for anatomical landmark localization. Med. Image Anal. **43**, 23–36 (2018)

19. Urschler, M., Zach, C., Ditt, H., Bischof, H.: Automatic point landmark matching for regularizing nonlinear intensity registration: application to thoracic CT images. In: Larsen, R., Nielsen, M., Sporring, J. (eds.) MICCAI 2006. LNCS, vol. 4191, pp. 710–717. Springer, Heidelberg (2006). https://doi.org/10.1007/11866763_87

20. Vrtovec, T., Pernuš, F., Likar, B.: A review of methods for quantitative evaluation of spinal curvature. Eur. Spine J. **18**(5), 593–607 (2009)

21. Wang, C.W., et al.: A benchmark for comparison of dental radiography analysis algorithms. Med. Image Anal. **31**, 63–76 (2016)

22. Wang, G., Li, W., Ourselin, S., Vercauteren, T.: Automatic brain tumor segmentation based on cascaded convolutional neural networks with uncertainty estimation. Front. Comput. Neurosci. **13**, 56 (2019)

23. Wickstrøm, K., Kampffmeyer, M., Jenssen, R.: Uncertainty and interpretability in convolutional neural networks for semantic segmentation of colorectal polyps. Med. Image Anal. **60**, 101619 (2020)

24. Yang, D., et al.: Automatic vertebra labeling in large-scale 3D CT using deep image-to-image network with message passing and sparsity regularization. In: Niethammer, M., et al. (eds.) IPMI 2017. LNCS, vol. 10265, pp. 633–644. Springer, Cham (2017). https://doi.org/10.1007/978-3-319-59050-9_50

25. Zhang, A., Sayre, J.W., Vachon, L., Liu, B.J., Huang, H.K.: Racial differences in growth patterns of children assessed on the basis of bone age. Radiology **250**(1), 228–235 (2009)

26. Zhong, Z., Li, J., Zhang, Z., Jiao, Z., Gao, X.: An attention-guided deep regression model for landmark detection in cephalograms. In: Shen, D., et al. (eds.) MICCAI 2019. LNCS, vol. 11769, pp. 540–548. Springer, Cham (2019). https://doi.org/10.1007/978-3-030-32226-7_60

Weight Averaging Impact on the Uncertainty of Retinal Artery-Venous Segmentation

Markus Lindén, Azat Garifullin$^{(\boxtimes)}$ ⓘ, and Lasse Lensu ⓘ

LUT University, P.O. Box 20, 53851 Lappeenranta, Finland
{markus.linden,azat.garifullin,lasse.lensu}@lut.fi

Abstract. By examining the vessel structure of the eye through retinal imaging, a variety of abnormalities can be identified. Owing to this, retinal images have an important role in the diagnosis of ocular diseases. The possibility of performing computer aided artery-vein segmentation has been the focus of several studies during the recent years and deep neural networks have become the most popular tool used in artery-vein segmentation. In this work, a Bayesian deep neural network is used for artery-vein segmentation. Two algorithms, that is, stochastic weight averaging and stochastic weight averaging Gaussian are studied to improve the performance of the neural network. The experiments, conducted on the RITE and DRIVE data sets, and results are provided along side uncertainty quantification analysis. Based on the experiments, weight averaging techniques improve the performance of the network.

Keywords: Uncertainty quantification · Bayesian deep learning · Artery-vein segmentation · Blood vessel segmentation · Weight averaging

1 Introduction

Eye diseases have become a rapidly increasing health threat worldwide. Retinal images are a great tool for detecting some of the many ocular disease and diseases such as diabetic retinopathy and glaucoma can be detected from retinal images [12]. Ocular diseases are typically detected from retinal images by analyzing the vessel structure. The use of retinal images enables the diagnosis of ocular diseases in their early stages. The task of analyzing the vessel structure has been traditionally left to medical experts. The attention required by the medical experts in this tasks is, however, great and the task is very consuming and expensive. Studying the possibilities in making this process faster is for that reason important, as it would enable wider screenings for ocular diseases from retinal images. Automated image processing methods are a well-motivated possibility in solving this problem [3].

The possibility to use computers in performing artery-vein segmentation has been the focus of a number of studies during the recent years.

© Springer Nature Switzerland AG 2020
C. H. Sudre et al. (Eds.): UNSURE 2020/GRAIL 2020, LNCS 12443, pp. 52–60, 2020.
https://doi.org/10.1007/978-3-030-60365-6_6

However, artery-vein segmentation still remains a challenging tasks for both humans and machines alike. Some of the difficulties in artery-vein segmentation are related to the imaging conditions in which the retinal images are taken. The images tend to suffer from low contrast and changing lighting conditions, both of which make the segmentation process harder.

The deep convolutional neural network (DCNN) has recently become the most common tool used in artery-vein segmentation of retinal images, due to the DCNNs ability to automatically learn meaningful features from images. In a paper by Welikala et al., a convolutional neural network (CNN) was used in artery-vein segmentation. The CNN managed to achieve a 82.26% classification rate using UK Biobanks' retinal image database [13]. Hemelings et al. proposed the usage of U-Net architecture for artery-vein classification [5]. In the paper, Hemeling et al. considered the task as a multi-class classification problem with the goal of labeling pixels into four classes: background, vein, artery and unknown. The problem was solved using the retinal images found in DRIVE data set [6] and it achieved classification rates of 94,42% and 94.11% for arteries and veins. Girard et al. [3] modified the U-Net for artery-vein segmentation and found out that using likelihood score in the minimum spanning tree it was possible to improve the performance of the network in the case of smaller vessels. The method was tested using DRIVE data set, achieving an accuracy of 94.93%. Zhang et al. proposed cascade refined U-net to be used in artery-vein classification [14]. The cascade refined U-net consisted of three sub-networks. The task of the first sub-net (A-net in their paper) was to detect all the vessels from the input image, B-net segmented veins from the predicted vessels from the A-net, and finally the C-net segmented the arterioles from the outputs of the previous nets. In the paper, a classification rate of 97.27% was achieved using the automatically detected vessels from the RITE data set. In a paper by Garifullin et al., a dense fully convolutional neural network (Desne-FCN) was used in the task of artery-vein classification [2]. Using the Dense-FCN architecture and the RITE data the authors were able to achieve classification rates of 96%, 97% and 97% for vessels, arteries and veins respectively. In addition to that the authors performed uncertainty quantification on the results obtained using Monte-Carlo dropout [1] for variational approximation. In the aforementioned article, however, the authors did not illustrate the model calibration and the experiments were conducted with one training setup for different labelling strategies. Thus, the question of reliability of the shown uncertainty estimates arises.

This work illustrates how stochastic weight averaging affects the estimated uncertainties. In addition, differences between two epistemic uncertainty estimation techniques are illustrated. Both more traditional binary classification metrics as well as uncertainty quantification metrics are used to evaluate the algorithms.

2 Data

The retinal image data set chosen to be used in this work was the DRIVE data set [6]. The DRIVE data set contains 20 RGB images for testing and 20 for training. The images are of size 584 × 565.

The AV references standard used in this work is the RITE data set [7]. The RITE data set extends the DRIVE data set with references for arteries, veins, overlapping vessels and uncertain vessels. Red labels in the DRIVE data set stand for arteries, blue labels for veins, green for overlapping vessels and white ones for uncertain vessels. An example of a retinal image from the DRIVE data set as well as the corresponding data labels from the RITE data set can be seen in Fig. 1. During the training the labels for crossings were replaced by labels for both arteries and veins simultaneously and the uncertain labels were omitted for arteries and veins and left for the vessels.

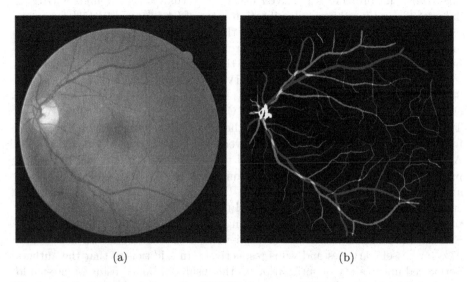

(a)   (b)

Fig. 1. (a) Retinal image from the DRIVE data set. (b) Retinal image labels from RITE dataset. (Color figure online)

3 Bayesian AV Classification

3.1 Baseline

Garifullin et al. followed a standard approach for deep Bayesian classification. First, a neural network f is used to estimate the distribution of logits parametrized through the estimate of the mean $\hat{\mathbf{y}}$ and variance $\boldsymbol{\sigma}$ of logits for arteries and veins:

$$[\hat{\mathbf{y}}, \boldsymbol{\sigma}] = f(\mathbf{x}, \boldsymbol{\theta}). \tag{1}$$

The probability vector $\mathbf{p} = [p_{\text{artery}} \; p_{\text{vein}}]$ of the labels can then be calculated as follows:

$$\hat{\mathbf{p}} = \text{sigmoid}\,(\hat{\mathbf{y}} + \boldsymbol{\sigma} \odot \boldsymbol{\epsilon})\,, \quad \boldsymbol{\epsilon} \sim \mathcal{N}\,(\mathbf{0}, \mathbf{I})\,. \tag{2}$$

Given the probability vector for arteries and veins the probability for the vessels can be inferred based on the addition law of probability:

$$p_{\text{vessel}} = p_{\text{artery}} + p_{\text{vein}} - p_{\text{artery}}p_{\text{vein}}. \tag{3}$$

The resulting optimisation objective is a sum of binary cross-entropy functions for all three labels over all produced aleatoric samples.

The formulae (1)–(3) take into account heteroscedastic aleatoric uncertainty which is a type of uncertainty dependent on the data capturing imperfect imaging conditions, labeling and image noise. The second kind of uncertainty is epistemic uncertainty representing the model's ignorance. By considering the parameters of the model as a random variable with the posterior $p\,(\boldsymbol{\theta} \mid \mathcal{D})$ the posterior predictive distribution over logits can be calculated as follows:

$$p\,(\mathbf{y} \mid \mathbf{x}, \mathcal{D}) = \int p\,(\mathbf{y} \mid \mathbf{x}, \boldsymbol{\theta})\,p\,(\boldsymbol{\theta} \mid \mathcal{D})\,\mathrm{d}\boldsymbol{\theta}. \tag{4}$$

Typically, the integral (4) is intractable and stochastic approximations are used in order to estimate the posterior predictive. One of the most common techniques is to use stochastic variational approximation called MC-Dropout [1] which employs dropout as a Monte Carlo sampling technique in order to obtain samples from the model's posterior. Another widely used method is stochastic weight averaging Gaussian [11] where the model's posterior is approximated by a normal distribution the moments of which are estimated during the training procedure.

3.2 Stochastic Weight Averaging

Izmailov et al. found out that the values traversed by SGD would be around the flat regions of the loss surface, without actually reaching the center of this area [9]. By equally averaging these points traversed by SGD, Izmailov et al. found out that points that are inside this more desirable part of the loss surface would be achieved. They named this method stochastic weight averaging (SWA) and it was shown to improve the results and generalization of networks on a variety of architectures and in multiple applications. Given initial pre-trained weights SWA can be implemented as a running average of the weights calculated while continuing training with an additional computation of batch normalization statistics after (see [9] for more details).

3.3 Stochastic Weight Averaging Gaussian

SWAG was first introduced by Maddox et al. [11] for model averaging and uncertainty estimation. The main idea behind is to use SWA to calculate the mean of the model's parameters and at the same time to estimate a diagonal approxima-tion of the covariance matrix. Thus, the approximated posterior of the model's parameters is a normal distribution:

$$p\left(\boldsymbol{\theta} \mid \mathcal{D}\right) = \mathcal{N}\left(\boldsymbol{\theta}_{\mathrm{SWA}}, \boldsymbol{\Sigma}_{\mathrm{SWAG}}\right), \tag{5}$$

where $\boldsymbol{\theta}_{\mathrm{SWA}}$ is a parameter vector estimated with SWA and $\boldsymbol{\Sigma}_{\mathrm{SWAG}}$ is a corre-sponding diagonal covariance matrix.

4   Experiments and Results

4.1   Description of Experiments

The parameters and methodologies presented here were selected so that the baseline model used in this work would be as similar as possible to [2]. The utilized architecture is Dense-FCN-103 [10]. The baseline model was, however, re-implemented and the experiments reproduced to some degree in this work.

In all the experiments, the network was first pre-trained on RITE dataset with random patches of the input images of size 224×224. The batch size used in the pre-training was 5 and the network was pre-trained with 100 epochs and 1000 steps per epoch.

After the pre-training, the networks were fine-tuned with full-size images that were padded to size of 608×608 so that they could be properly compressed by the downsampling part of the network. The main optimizer used in all of the experiments was Adadelta with learning rate of 1 and decay rate of 0.95. The use of either SWA or SWAG would start on a later epochs of full resolution training.

To increase the diversity of the data set data augmentation techniques were used. The augmentation was performed by applying rotation, flipping, and scal-ing to the input data. The rotation angles used were 90, 180 and 270 degrees and the scaling rates were 0.8, 0.9, 1.0, 1.1 and 1.2.

The aleatoric and epistemic uncertainties were estimated using formulae from [8]. The uncertainties are estimated as an average sum standard deviations per image $S_p = \sum_i \sum_j \sigma_j / N_{\mathrm{test}}$, where i is an index of the image, j is an index of the pixel, and N_{test} is the total number of test images (Table 4).

Baseline. The fine-tuning of the network used as baseline was done using 50 epochs with 500 steps per epoch to match the hyperparameters used in [2]. The batch size used in the fine-tuning of the baseline selected to be 1. MC-Dropout was used to quantify epistemic uncertainty.

SWA. The SWA implementation also had 50 epochs with 500 steps in each epoch in the full resolution training. Like in the baseline the batch size used was 1. The starting epoch for SWA was selected to be 10 and it was only used in the fine-tuning of the network. The starting epoch was selected through empirical experimentation. MC-Dropout was used to quantify epistemic uncertainty.

SWAG. The hyperparameters used in the SWAG implementation were 500 epochs with 50 steps per epoch. This was done so that the Gaussian posteriori approximation formed by SWAG would be generated from a higher number of epochs. Like in the baseline the batch size used was 1. The SWAG starting epoch was selected to be 100. The epistemic uncertainty was quantified by sampling the model's parameters from Gaussian distribution (5). Whereas the sampling is performed from the posterior estimated with SWAG, dropout is still used during the training phase.

4.2 Performance of the Networks

Due to the fact that artery-vein classification was considered a multilabel problem, the performance metrics used in were calculated for arteries, veins and vessels separately. The selected classification metrics were accuracy, sensitivity, specificity, Area Under the Receiver Operating Characteristic Curve (ROC-AUC) and Estimated Calibration Error (ECE) [4].

By examining the performance metrics presented in Tables 1, 2 and 3, it can be seen that SWA improved the network performance overall compared to the baseline and SWAG models including the model calibration.

Table 1. Network performance in artery classification (the best accuracy and calibration are in bold)

Method	Accuracy	Sensitivity	Specificity	ECE	ROC-AUC
Baseline	0.970	0.642	0.990	0.00988	0.974
SWA	**0.975**	0.690	0.992	0.00943	0.981
SWAG	0.973	0.706	0.989	**0.00871**	0.966

Table 2. Network performance in vein classification (the best accuracy and calibration are in bold)

Method	Accuracy	Sensitivity	Specificity	ECE	ROC-AUC
Baseline	0.971	0.655	0.994	0.0169	0.980
SWA	**0.974**	0.742	0.991	0.0120	0.991
SWAG	0.971	0.804	0.983	**0.0107**	0.980

Table 3. Network performance in vessel classification (the best accuracy and calibration are in bold)

Method	Accuracy	Sensitivity	Specificity	ECE	ROC-AUC
Baseline	0.957	0.723	0.989	0.0221	0.980
SWA	**0.961**	0.782	0.986	**0.0208**	0.983
SWAG	**0.961**	0.836	0.978	0.0338	0.984

The example of the segmentation results for SWAG is given in Fig. 2. The segmentation examples for the baseline and SWA look similar. The uncertainties of the results were visualized and example figures can be seen in Fig. 3. In the figure, the intensities of the colors describe the uncertainty in that region as standard deviations of the predicted probabilities: the higher intensity the higher the uncertainty.

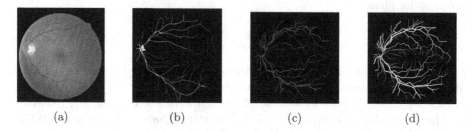

(a)   (b)   (c)   (d)

Fig. 2. (a) The input image; (b) ground truth; (c) mean predicted AV probabilities; (d) mean predicted vessels probabilities. The results are obtained using SWAG.

From the tables and figures, it can be concluded that the aleatoric uncertainty of the baseline is much higher than those of SWA and SWAG. It can also be concluded that sampling the network weights from the Gaussian posterior generated by SWAG to create the variational approximation, rather than using Monte-Carlo dropout, has a reducing effect on the levels of epistemic uncertainty present in the predictions. This could probably be explained by the fact that the variance is estimated only around a local optimum during the late stages of the training, whereas MC-Dropout is enabled during the whole training process. From the estimated performance metrics, however, it is difficult to conclude whether it is a positive or negative effect. One noticeable pattern is the high epistemic uncertainty near the optic disc when estimated with MC-Dropout. On the other hand, sampling from Gaussian distribution leads to the high uncertainties mostly near the end points of the blood vessels and the areas after the crossings which is also present in the case of MC-Dropout.

At the same time one can see that aleatoric uncertainties change when SWA or SWAG are utilized. Kendall et al. [1] describe the aleatoric uncertainty as a loss attenuation mechanism allowing the model to adapt the loss dependent on the data and labelling. While the aleatoric uncertainty is meant to be data dependent, the changes to the training procedure affecting the model's convergence and the parameters of the layers predicting variances also affect the predicted aleatoric uncertainties. For the baseline and SWAG, we can see a similar pattern of the higher aleatoric uncertainty levels near the optic disc and borders of the vasculature, whereas the aleatoric uncertainties almost vanish when estimated using MC-Dropout trained with SWA.

Table 4. Mean sums of estimated aleatoric and epistemic uncertainties per image.

Method	Aleatoric			Epistemic		
	Arteries	Veins	Vessels	Arteries	Veins	Vessels
Baseline	1276.2	1159.5	1807.5	4853.6	4066.4	5069.7
SWA	3.3	3.5	5.3	4038.6	3882.3	4659.7
SWAG	31.1	38.9	57.3	997.8	1104.3	1396.1

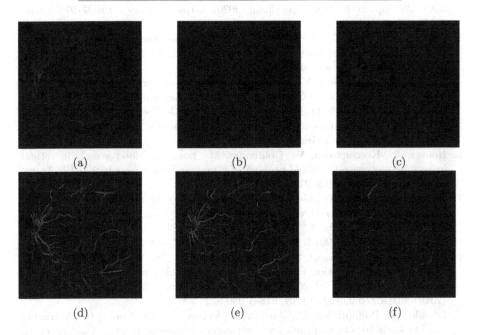

Fig. 3. Aleatoric uncertainties calculated using (a) the baseline, (b) SWA, and (c) SWAG. Epistemic uncertainties calculated using (d) the baseline, (e) SWA, and (f) SWAG.

4.3 Conclusions

In this work, the focus was on blood vessel segmentation from retinal images and on artery-vein classification by using a deep neural network. More specifically, two algorithms were studied to improve the classification performance and help in the model calibration. SWA and SWAG algorithms were implemented on top of the baseline and experimented with the DRIVE and RITE data sets.

The use of SWA improved the performance of the deep neural network on most of the binary classifications as well as the calibration metrics. SWAG showed slight improvements in the vessels and artery classification tasks. The weight averaging as a process significantly affecting the model's convergence seems to lead to diminishing aleatoric uncertainties and sampling from the normal distribution captures less epistemic uncertainty.

References

1. Gal, Y., Ghahramani, Z.: Dropout as a Bayesian approximation: representing model uncertainty in deep learning. In: International Conference on Machine Learning, pp. 1050–1059 (2016)
2. Garifullin, A., Lensu, L., Uusitalo, H.: On the uncertainty of retinal artery-vein classification with dense fully-convolutional neural networks. In: Blanc-Talon, J., Delmas, P., Philips, W., Popescu, D., Scheunders, P. (eds.) ACIVS 2020. LNCS, vol. 12002, pp. 87–98. Springer, Cham (2020). https://doi.org/10.1007/978-3-030-40605-9_8
3. Girard, F., Kavalec, C., Cheriet, F.: Joint segmentation and classification of retinal arteries/veins from fundus images. Artif. Intell. Med. **94**, 96–109 (2019). https://doi.org/10.1016/j.artmed.2019.02.004
4. Guo, C., Pleiss, G., Sun, Y., Weinberger, K.Q.: On calibration of modern neural networks. In: International Conference on Machine Learning, pp. 1321–1330 (2017)
5. Hemelings, R., Elen, B., Stalmans, I., Van Keer, K., De Boever, P., Blaschko, M.B.: Artery-vein segmentation in fundus images using a fully convolutional network. Comput. Med. Imaging Graph. **76**, 101636 (2019)
6. Hoover, A., Kouznetsova, V., Goldbaum, M.: Locating blood vessels in retinal images by piecewise threshold probing of a matched filter response. IEEE Trans. Med. Imaging **19**(3), 203–210 (2000)
7. Hu, Q., Abràmoff, M.D., Garvin, M.K.: Automated separation of binary overlapping trees in low-contrast color retinal images. In: Mori, K., Sakuma, I., Sato, Y., Barillot, C., Navab, N. (eds.) MICCAI 2013. LNCS, vol. 8150, pp. 436–443. Springer, Heidelberg (2013). https://doi.org/10.1007/978-3-642-40763-5_54
8. Hu, S., Worrall, D., Knegt, S., Veeling, B., Huisman, H., Welling, M.: Supervised uncertainty quantification for segmentation with multiple annotations. In: Shen, D., et al. (eds.) MICCAI 2019. LNCS, vol. 11765, pp. 137–145. Springer, Cham (2019). https://doi.org/10.1007/978-3-030-32245-8_16
9. Izmailov, P., Podoprikhin, D., Garipov, T., Vetrov, D.P., Wilson, A.G.: Averaging weights leads to wider optima and better generalization. In: The Conference on Uncertainty in Artificial Intelligence (2018)
10. Jégou, S., Drozdzal, M., Vazquez, D., Romero, A., Bengio, Y.: The one hundred layers tiramisu: fully convolutional densenets for semantic segmentation. In: 2017 IEEE Conference on Computer Vision and Pattern Recognition Workshops (CVPRW), pp. 1175–1183. IEEE (2017)
11. Maddox, W., Garipov, T., Izmailov, P., Vetrov, D.P., Wilson, A.G.: A simple baseline for Bayesian uncertainty in deep learning. In: NeurIPS (2019)
12. Miri, M., Amini, Z., Rabbani, H., Kafieh, R.: A comprehensive study of retinal vessel classification methods in fundus images. J. Med. Signals Sens. **7**(2), 59 (2017)
13. Welikala, R., et al.: Automated arteriole and venule classification using deep learning for retinal images from the UK biobank cohort. Comput. Biol. Med. **90**, 23–32 (2017). https://doi.org/10.1016/j.compbiomed.2017.09.005
14. Zhang, S., et al.: Simultaneous arteriole and venule segmentation of dual-modal fundus images using a multi-task cascade network. IEEE Access **7**, 57561–57573 (2019). https://doi.org/10.1109/ACCESS.2019.2914319

Improving Pathological Distribution Measurements with Bayesian Uncertainty

Ka Ho Tam[1]([✉]), Korsuk Sirinukunwattana[1], Maria F. Soares[2], Maria Kaisar[3], Rutger Ploeg[3], and Jens Rittscher[1]

[1] Institute of Biomedical Engineering, University of Oxford, Oxford, UK
kaho.tam@hertford.ox.ac.uk
[2] Department of Cellular Pathology, Oxford University Hospitals NHS Foundation Trust, John Radcliffe Hospital, Oxford, UK
[3] Oxford Transplant Centre, Nuffield Department of Surgical Sciences, University of Oxford, Oxford, UK

Abstract. Deep learning assisted histopathology has the potential to extract reproducible and accurate measurements from digitised slides in a scalable fashion. A typical workflow of such analysis may involve instance segmentation of relevant tissues followed by feature measurements. Inherent segmentation uncertainties produced by these deep models, however, could propagate to the downstream measurements, causing biased distribution estimate of the whole slide. One challenging aspect when handling ambiguous tissues is that the number of instances could differ as the instance segmentation step may not generalise well to these tissues. As an attempt to address this problem, we propose to derive a confidence score from the segmentation uncertainties obtained from Bayesian Neural Networks (BNNs) and utilise these as weights to improve the distribution estimate. We generate a synthetic dataset that mimics the diverse and varying visual features of the original data to enable systematic experiments. With this dataset we demonstrate the robustness of the method by extracting several clinically relevant measurements with two different BNNs. Our results indicate that the distribution estimates are consistently improved when the instances are weighted by the entropy-derived confidence measure. In addition, we provide results on applying the method to the original data.

Keywords: Bayesian Neural Network · Uncertainty propagation · Digital pathology

KHT is funded by the EPSRC and MRC grant number EP/L016052/1. JR and KS are supported by the Oxford NIHR Biomedical Research Centre and the PathLAKE consortium (Innovate UK App. Nr. 18181).

Electronic supplementary material The online version of this chapter (https://doi.org/10.1007/978-3-030-60365-6_7) contains supplementary material, which is available to authorized users.

C. H. Sudre et al. (Eds.): UNSURE 2020/GRAIL 2020, LNCS 12443, pp. 61–70, 2020.
https://doi.org/10.1007/978-3-030-60365-6_7

1   Introduction

The core goal of computational pathology is to extract clinically relevant information from digitised slides that will support the work of human experts. Examples of such measurements include the size and shape of certain tissue architecture components (e.g. glands, tubules, and cells) as well as their colour and texture. Accurate evaluation of these measurements is crucial but could also be very challenging for a number of reasons. Firstly, pathological changes are often subtle and could easily be overwhelmed by the biopsies' preparation artefacts. Secondly, colour and morphological appearances could vary greatly between different datasets which leads to overfitting errors. Thirdly, the quality and number of annotations could be imbalanced between the easy examples and tissues with ambiguity. Many measurement errors are the result of downstream propagation of the segmentation errors of different tissue instances. As segmentation uncertainties are often heteroscedastic, erroneously segmented instances could lead to systematic errors in the estimated distributions.

As neural networks are now commonly used to perform segmentation tasks, uncertainty quantification of these black-box models have become particularly important. To date, a number of Bayesian Neural Networks (BNNs) have successfully demonstrated quantification of semantic segmentation errors on everyday images [7,20] as well as on medical images [4,11,12,21,23]. On the other hand, uncertainty quantification in object detection task is more challenging and not as well studied as it involves identifying separate objects in an image. In this regard, Miller et al. [17,18] employed Monte Carlo (MC) dropout in a single shot detector and cluster boxes from multiple forward passes based on spatial and semantic similarities. Instance segmentation is yet more challenging as it involves delineating the mask of each instance. For this task, Morrison [19] extended Miller's implementation to work with MaskRCNNs. Clustering detection boxes, however, could be a slow process. It may also be difficult to train the aforementioned end-to-end instance segmentation networks as medical image datasets are typically very small.

While all the above mentioned focused on the evaluation of segmentation errors, there has been little discussion on how they can be put to practical use for risk management or to improve inference. In this paper, we propose to use confidence measures derived from BNNs to refine the distribution estimate of our data. Here, instances are weighted by the confidence of their associated segmentation mask when calculating the distribution. But unlike Nketia and colleagues [22] who studied cellular segmentation, the confidence scores we use are derived from a deep BNNs rather than handcrafted.

For our dataset, we initially speculated that domain shift might be the main source of segmentation errors. Hence we design an experiment to test how our method performs on images that gradually differ from the training data. We synthesise a dataset based on a VAE-BicycleGAN pipeline [9,14,31] and perform tissue area, colour distribution, and major axis measurements on different subsets of the synthetic data and the real test images. We find that the confidence-weighted measurements consistently perform better than the unweighted measurements.

2   Method

In this section we summarise the theoretical underpinnings of our methodology and design an experiment to validate the proposed approach. Firstly, We elaborate three exemplary histopathological measurements derived from renal proximal tubules. After that, we describe methods of obtaining confidence scores from BNNs. Next, we would like to test whether confidence-weighted instances can improve measurements on slides that contain ambiguous tissue instances. To achieve this, we generate a synthetic dataset where subsets of images differ gradually from the original training data. Finally, we measure the distance between various confidence-weighted and non-weighted distributions against the ground truth.

2.1   Histopathological Measurements

A quantitative histology pipeline typically involves segmentation of relevant tissue components, followed by extraction of features developed based on domain knowledge. Many of these features and downstream measurements, however, are sensitive to uncertainties in the segmentation masks.

The simplest of these features would be tissue area measurements, obtained by summing up the pixels that belongs to an instance. If the predictions are over-confident, we may end up with fewer, larger instances. A network that produces under-confident predictions may produce more small instances than a properly calibrated network.

Another useful clinical feature that could be extracted from the renal biopsies is the thickness of the proximal tubules' epithelial cells that outlines the tubules. If the cells are damaged, they could vacuolate and expand, causing the epithelial lining to appear thickened. However, in damaged tissue it is often difficult to determine the boundaries of the epithelial cell lining. Hence, a workaround is to measure the distribution of H&E/PAS stain with respect to the mask's distance transform. We name this measurement y^γ and is calculated as follows:

$$y^\gamma = \frac{\sum_{m \in M} d_m x_m}{\sum_{m \in M} d_m \sum_{m \in M} x_m} \, , \tag{1}$$

where d_m is the distance transform of an instance's mask measured from the edge; x_m is the pixel value of the image bounded by mask M of the instance. The two terms in the denominator are normalisation terms that reduces the dependency of y^γ on the size and mean pixel values of the tissue.

As we are measuring the 2D cross section of 3D objects, area measurements of the tissue structures on its own may not be a very informative pathological feature. To augment to such limitations, we can also measure the tissue's aspect ratio. This could help us estimate the direction on how the tissue is cut. This measurement could be determined from the major and minor axis of the minimum-area rectangle fitted to the segmentation mask. We present measurements of instance area, y^γ, and major axis in the following experiment.

2.2   Uncertainty Estimation

Sample averaged BNNs could produce confidence values that scales more linearly with the probability the model makes a correct prediction. However, interpretation of the statistical distribution of BNN's output is important as it would allow us to better understand to what extent the model can be improved. Given a BNN has been sampled N iterations during test time, one possible measure to quantify uncertainty is the predictive entropy H [13]:

$$H = -\frac{1}{N} \sum_{i=1}^{N} \sum_{j=1}^{C} \hat{y}_{ij} log(\hat{y}_{ij}) \,, \tag{2}$$

where C are the classes output by the model; $\hat{y}_{ij}$ is the probability for each class j and sample i predicted by a network stochastically initialised based on some variational parameters $\hat{\theta}$. From H, we can derive a normalised confidence measure for instance k over the pixels m in the segmentation mask M_k as follows:

$$g_k^H = 1 - \frac{1}{|M_k|log(C)} \sum_{m \in M_k} H_m \,. \tag{3}$$

Kendall [8] proposed another measure to quantify uncertainty by decomposing the predictive variance from neural networks into aleatoric and epistemic terms. Aleatoric variance measures uncertainty as a result of inherent ambiguity or noise of the data whereas epistemic variance measures uncertainty due to limitations of the model. From these standard errors we can derive the following confidence measure for instance k:

$$g_k^\sigma = max\left(1 - \frac{1}{|M_k|} \sum_{m \in M_k} \sigma_m(w), 0\right) \,, \tag{4}$$

where σ_m is either the aleatoric or epistemic standard error at a given pixel m. We use Kwon $et\ al.$'s [12] implementation to evaluate σ_m in our experiment.

2.3   Datasets

The dataset we use for training originated from an organ reperfusion experiment [28,29]. The slides were obtained from kidneys deemed unsuitable for transplantation and most samples suffered from significant cold ischemic damage. The tissues were stained with H&E but had been computationally converted to PAS stain using a CycleGAN [30] with image quality largely indiscernible by our collaborating pathologist. The training dataset consists of 1642 patches from 169 kidneys containing 13,103 manually annotated tubules.

Our test dataset consists of 144 PAS-stained slides obtained from the QUOD Oxford biobank from kidneys that had been transplanted. We annotated 30 patches with a total of 1741 tubules in this dataset.

For the purpose of our experiment, we also synthesise a dataset that deviates progressively from the training data. We would like the data to fulfill three requirements. Firstly, the images need to contain tissue structures that exhibit diverse morphological, textural, and colour variations. Secondly, the images need to be accompanied by a corresponding segmentation mask to be used as the ground truth. Thirdly, to simplify how these images are generated we would like to control these visual changes using a single parameter. While the simplest way to generate controlled morphological changes is to deform the images and masks simultaneously, this would provide only limited morphological variations. Consequently, we build a pipeline to generate synthetic images that fulfils the above requirements using a Variational AutoEncoder (VAE) [9,14] and a BicycleGAN [31]. A simple schematic and some examples of the synthetic images are shown in Fig. 1. The VAE learns the underlying morphological variations of the relevant renal tissues, whereas the BicycleGAN is used to convert masks from the VAE to a diverse set of realistic-looking images. To obtain images that progressively differ from the real data, we sample the VAE 10 times with a latent vector $\sigma_{VAE} \in [0.0, 1.8]$. This produces masks with varying morphological changes. Next, the BicycleGAN is used generate 6 images from each mask, one of which is generated from the encoded vector from the real image (BGAN0), the other 5 are generated from a sampled latent vector (BGAN1). A total of 98,400 synthetic images are produced but a large number of images do not resemble the mask, so we select 39,400 images based on the resemblance between the reconstructed image-mask pair. Details on the synthetic data are described in Supplementary Material S1.

2.4   Tissue Segmentation

To demonstrate that our method is robust to the choice of hyperparameters, we perform the experiment on two different networks. We train a UNet [25] with Monte Carlo Dropout [5] of 0.2 in all but the first and last layer, and another UNet with Bayes by Backprop and local reparameterisation trick (BBB_LRT) [1,10,26] using a unit Gaussian prior to replace the dropout layers. The number of trainable parameters for both networks are set to approximately 50.3 M for fair comparison. We train the networks with 3-fold cross validation while ensuring that tiles from the same slide are not split. After that, for each network we obtain 5 Bayesian samples over each of the 3 cross validation models and take the mean softmax over the 15 predictions. We obtain instances using max-flow min-cut graph algorithm [2] and classical morphological operations. Instances smaller than 400 pixels are discarded. More details on the neural networks and how the tissue instances are obtained can be found in Supplementary Material S2 and S3 respectively.

3   Experiment Results

The tubule instances' area, y^γ, and major axis measurements are obtained as described in Sect. 2.1 on the synthetic and the real test datasets. We evaluate

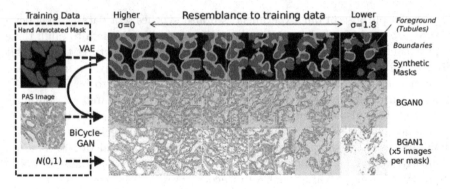

Fig. 1. Generation of synthetic images and examples. We train a VAE to generate synthetic masks at varying σ_{VAE} based on the encoded embedding (1st row). The $2 - 3^{rd}$ rows show examples generated by the BicycleGAN based on the mask above. We generate 6 images per mask, including 1 generated using the encoded vector from the real image (BGAN0); the other 5 are generated from a sampled vector (BGAN1) to produce images with diverse tissue texture and background.

the performance of different versions of our proposed method by comparing the various weighted and unweighted estimated measurements against the ground truth. Here, we present comparisons of probability distributions (PDF) using the first Wasserstein distance (WD) [24]. Other metrics such as Kullback–Leibler (KL) and Jensen-Shannon (JS) distance could also be used and would result in similar conclusion of the experiment. But we find WD to be most suitable as it takes into account the metric space and does not approach infinity where the PDFs are disjoint.

We initially expected WD to be higher for the harder examples. However, in our results WD tends to decrease with increasing σ_{VAE}. To understand this counter-intuitive trend we inspect the images and observe that instances tend to shrink in size as σ_{VAE} increases. Although the instances become morphologically less plausible, having fewer touching instances may reduce ambiguity of the segmentation. Thus we conclude that UNets when trained on our data generalises to this unseen morphology. An example of this observation is illustrated on the top row masks in Fig. 1. Next, we define an evaluation metric ΔWD as follows:

$$\Delta WD = WD(\tilde{P}(Y), P(Y)) - WD(\tilde{P}_{Baseline}(Y), P(Y)) , \qquad (5)$$

where WD is the function for calculating the Wasserstein metric; $\tilde{P}(Y)$ is the estimated PDF of interest; $P(Y)$ is the ground truth PDF; $\tilde{P}_{Baseline}(Y)$ is the baseline estimated PDF derived from instances segmented by the UNets without MC Dropout. We plot ΔWD values in Fig. 2. Each plot shows the results of a different measurement by the UNet with either MC Dropout or BBB_LRT. The x-axes show the different subsets of the synthetic data ($\sigma_{VAE} \in [0, 1.8]$) and the real test data (*real*). A more negative ΔWD represents greater improvement.

For the confidence-weighted ($CW1$) measurements, we weight each instance by confidence derived from entropy (Eq. 3), aleatoric, and epistemic uncertainty

(Eq. 4) to obtain the estimated PDF. We also split our synthetic dataset by quality - *BGAN0* denotes synthetic encoded images and are better quality than those generated using a sampled vector with the BicycleGAN (*BGAN1*). For both networks, the weighted measurements always appear better than the unweighted (*CW0*). Instances weighted by entropy generally perform the best, followed by those weighted by aleatoric uncertainty. Instances weighted by epistemic uncertainty receive the least improvement because the dominant uncertainty in our dataset is aleatoric.

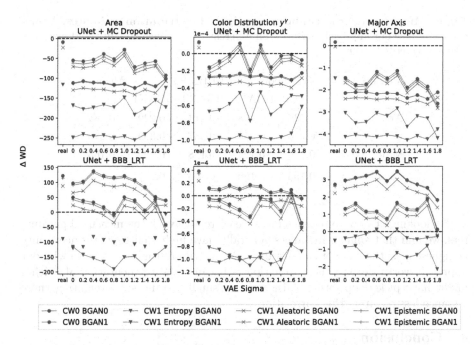

Fig. 2. Comparison of Measurements. Wasserstein metric comparing distributions between measurements derived from the predicted instances vs derived from the ground truth masks. The x-axes show how the improvement changes as the instances differ from the training data at varying σ_{VAE}. The test data (real) is also added to the plot for comparison. Values are relative to the baseline. Lower ΔWD means greater improvement. *CW1/0* stands for confidence weighted/unweighted respectively; *BGAN1/0* stands for images with/without BicycleGAN resampling respectively.

In order to compare improvement between different measurements we normalise the WD metric as follows:

$$WD_{norm} = (WD_{CW1} - WD_{CW0})/WD_{CW0} , \qquad (6)$$

where WD_{CW1} is the confidence-weighted WD; WD_{CW0} is the unweighted WD. Table 1 shows the entropy-weighted normalised WD averaged over different σ_{VAE}. It can be seen that improvement is greater on the image subset with poorer quality (BGAN1) than better quality (BGAN0). A similar trend can be seen in Fig. 2 where greater improvement can be seen on the synthetic dataset than on the real data. These results suggest our approach becomes more useful the more different the test data deviates from the training data. We also notice that improvement is the smallest on major axis measurements. We reason that major axis measurements are generally more robust to segmentation errors as it requires a lot of misclassified pixels to change the size of an instance's bounding box so the other measurements benefit more from confidence weighting.

Table 1. Improvement in confidence-weighted distribution estimates. A comparison of how our approach performs on different BNNs, image quality, and measurements. (Lower is better)

Measurement	MC Dropout		BBB_LRT		Mean
	BGAN0	BGAN1	BGAN0	BGAN1	
Area	−0.136	−0.158	−0.214	−0.229	−0.184
y^{γ}	−0.246	−0.288	−0.337	−0.369	−0.310
Major axis	−0.106	−0.124	−0.188	−0.202	−0.155
Mean	−0.163	−0.190	−0.246	−0.267	

By looking at how confidence measure correlates with the measured parameters, we find that smaller instances generally have higher entropy as uncertainty is highest near the edge of the instances. We attribute the reason as to why our approach works despite the correlation is because the segmentation algorithm might have picked up lots of false positive small instances so weighting these instance less counters this correlation.

4   Conclusion

We proposed a method to improve pathological measurements by weighting tissue instances by confidence measures derived from BNNs without the need to find a hyperparameter to discard instances with high uncertainty.

To demonstrate the performance of our method, we generated synthetic data with an embedding that progressively differs from the original images. Confidence-weighted measurements were obtained on both real and synthetic images using uncertainty derived from UNets with either MC Dropout or Bayes by Backprop. The weighted distribution improved for all pathological measurements, suggesting that our proposal is robust to the choice of BNN and measurement. We also notice that the improvement is greater over analysis of data with lesser resemblance to the training data, suggesting that our approach could be particularly useful for cross-domain datasets. For future work, we will investigate whether decorrelating pathological parameters with confidence measures could help to further improve metric estimation.

Our synthetic dataset is available at https://tinyurl.com/vaebicycleganpas.

References

1. Blundell, C., Cornebise, J., Kavukcuoglu, K., Wierstra, D.: Weight uncertainty in neural networks. arXiv preprint arXiv:1505.05424 (2015)
2. Boykov, Y., Funka-Lea, G.: Graph cuts and efficient ND image segmentation. Int. J. Comput. Vis. **70**(2), 109–131 (2006). https://doi.org/10.1007/s11263-006-7934-5
3. Chatrian, A., Sirinukunwattana, K., Verrill, C., Rittscher, J.: Towards the identification of histology based subtypes in prostate cancer. In: 2019 IEEE 16th International Symposium on Biomedical Imaging (ISBI 2019), pp. 948–952. IEEE (2019)
4. DeVries, T., Taylor, G.W.: Leveraging uncertainty estimates for predicting segmentation quality. arXiv preprint arXiv:1807.00502 (2018)
5. Gal, Y., Ghahramani, Z.: Dropout as a Bayesian approximation: representing model uncertainty in deep learning. In: International Conference on Machine Learning, pp. 1050–1059 (2016)
6. Isola, P., Zhu, J.Y., Zhou, T., Efros, A.A.: Image-to-image translation with conditional adversarial networks. In: Proceedings of the IEEE conference on computer vision and pattern recognition, pp. 1125–1134 (2017)
7. Kendall, A., Badrinarayanan, V., Cipolla, R.: Bayesian SegNet: model uncertainty in deep convolutional encoder-decoder architectures for scene understanding. arXiv preprint arXiv:1511.02680 (2015)
8. Kendall, A., Gal, Y.: What uncertainties do we need in Bayesian deep learning for computer vision? In: Advances in Neural Information Processing Systems, pp. 5574–5584 (2017)
9. Kingma, D.P., Welling, M.: Auto-encoding variational bayes. arXiv preprint arXiv:1312.6114 (2013)
10. Kingma, D.P., Salimans, T., Welling, M.: Variational dropout and the local reparameterization trick. In: Advances in Neural Information Processing Systems, pp. 2575–2583 (2015)
11. Kohl, S., et al.: A probabilistic U-Net for segmentation of ambiguous images. In: Advances in Neural Information Processing Systems, pp. 6965–6975 (2018)
12. Kwon, Y., Won, J.H., Kim, B.J., Paik, M.C.: Uncertainty quantification using Bayesian neural networks in classification: application to biomedical image segmentation. Comput. Stat. Data Anal. **142**, 106816 (2020)
13. Lakshminarayanan, B., Pritzel, A., Blundell, C.: Simple and scalable predictive uncertainty estimation using deep ensembles. In: Advances in Neural Information Processing Systems, pp. 6402–6413 (2017)
14. Larsen, A.B.L., Sønderby, S.K., Larochelle, H., Winther, O.: Autoencoding beyond pixels using a learned similarity metric. In: International Conference on Machine Learning, pp. 1558–1566 (2016)
15. Lin, T.Y., Goyal, P., Girshick, R., He, K., Dollár, P.: Focal loss for dense object detection. In: Proceedings of the IEEE International Conference on Computer Vision, pp. 2980–2988 (2017)
16. Maas, A.L., Hannun, A.Y., Ng, A.Y.: Rectifier nonlinearities improve neural network acoustic models. In: Proceedings of the ICML, vol. 30, no. 1, p. 3 (2013)
17. Miller, D., Dayoub, F., Milford, M., Sünderhauf, N.: Evaluating merging strategies for sampling-based uncertainty techniques in object detection. In: 2019 International Conference on Robotics and Automation (ICRA), pp. 2348–2354. IEEE (2019)

18. Miller, D., Nicholson, L., Dayoub, F., Sünderhauf, N.: Dropout sampling for robust object detection in open-set conditions. In: 2018 IEEE International Conference on Robotics and Automation (ICRA), pp. 1–7. IEEE (2018)
19. Morrison, D., Milan, A., Antonakos, E.: Uncertainty-aware instance segmentation using dropout sampling. Technical report, CVPR Robotic Vision Probabilistic Object Detection Challenge (2019)
20. Mukhoti, J., Gal, Y.: Evaluating Bayesian deep learning methods for semantic segmentation. arXiv preprint arXiv:1811.12709 (2018)
21. Ng, M., Guo, F., Biswas, L., Wright, G.A.: Estimating uncertainty in neuralnetworks for segmentation quality control. Technical report (2018). https://www.doc.ic.ac.uk/~bglocker/public/mednips2018/med-nips_2018_paper_105.pdf
22. Nketia, T.A., Noble, J.A., Rittscher, J.: Towards quantifying the impact of cell boundary estimation on morphometric analysis for phenotypic screening. In: 2015 IEEE 12th International Symposium on Biomedical Imaging (ISBI), pp. 781–784. IEEE (2015)
23. Orlando, J.I., et al.: U2-Net: a Bayesian U-Net model with epistemic uncertainty feedback for photoreceptor layer segmentation in pathological oct scans. In: 2019 IEEE 16th International Symposium on Biomedical Imaging (ISBI 2019), pp. 1441–1445. IEEE (2019)
24. Ramdas, A., Trillos, N.G., Cuturi, M.: On wasserstein two-sample testing and related families of nonparametric tests. Entropy **19**(2), 47 (2017)
25. Ronneberger, O., Fischer, P., Brox, T.: U-Net: convolutional networks for biomedical image segmentation. In: Navab, N., Hornegger, J., Wells, W.M., Frangi, A.F. (eds.) MICCAI 2015. LNCS, vol. 9351, pp. 234–241. Springer, Cham (2015). https://doi.org/10.1007/978-3-319-24574-4_28
26. Shridhar, K., Laumann, F., Liwicki, M.: A comprehensive guide to Bayesian convolutional neural network with variational inference. arXiv preprint arXiv:1901.02731 (2019)
27. Wang, Z., Bovik, A.C., Sheikh, H.R., Simoncelli, E.P.: Image quality assessment: from error visibility to structural similarity. IEEE Trans. Image Process. **13**(4), 600–612 (2004)
28. Weissenbacher, A.: Normothermic kidney preservation. Ph.D. thesis, University of Oxford (2018)
29. Weissenbacher, A., Lo Faro, L., Boubriak, O., Soares, M.F., Roberts, I.S., Hunter, J.P., Voyce, D., Mikov, N., Cook, A., Ploeg, R.J., et al.: Twenty-four-hour normothermic perfusion of discarded human kidneys with urine recirculation. Am. J. Transplant. **19**(1), 178–192 (2019)
30. Zhu, J.Y., Park, T., Isola, P., Efros, A.A.: Unpaired image-to-image translation using cycle-consistent adversarial networks. In: Proceedings of the IEEE International Conference on Computer Vision, pp. 2223–2232 (2017)
31. Zhu, J.Y., et al.: Toward multimodal image-to-image translation. In: Advances in neural information processing systems, pp. 465–476 (2017)

Improving Reliability of Clinical Models Using Prediction Calibration

Jayaraman J. Thiagarajan[1], Bindya Venkatesh[2(✉)], Deepta Rajan[3],
and Prasanna Sattigeri[3]

[1] Lawrence Livermore National Labs, Livermore, USA
[2] Arizona State University, Tempe, USA
[3] IBM Research AI, New York city, USA

Abstract. The wide-spread adoption of representation learning technologies in clinical decision making strongly emphasizes the need for characterizing model reliability and enabling rigorous introspection of model behavior. In supervised and semi-supervised learning, prediction calibration has emerged as a key technique to achieve improved generalization and to promote trust in learned models. In this paper, we investigate the effectiveness of different prediction calibration techniques in improving the reliability of clinical models. First, we introduce *reliability plots*, which measures the trade-off between model autonomy and generalization, to quantify model reliability. Second, we propose to utilize an interval calibration objective in lieu of the standard cross entropy loss to build classification models. Finally, using a lesion classification problem with dermoscopy images, we evaluate the proposed prediction calibration approach against both uncalibrated models as well as existing prediction calibration techniques such as mixup and single-shot calibration.

Keywords: Prediction calibration · Deep learning · Uncertainty quantification · Reliability

1 Introduction

Artificial intelligence methods such as deep learning have achieved unprecedented success with critical decision-making, from diagnosing diseases to prescribing treatments, in healthcare [4,11,17]. However, to prioritize patient safety, one must ensure such methods are accurate and reliable [2]. For example, a neural network model can produce highly concentrated softmax probabilities – suggesting a reliable class assignment – even for out-of-distribution test samples, which indicates that the confidences are not well-calibrated. This strongly emphasizes the need to both reliably assess model's confidences [8,16], and enable rigorous introspection of model behavior [1,2,23]. As a result, a large class of methods

J.J. Thiagarajan—This work was performed under the auspices of the U.S. Department of Energy by Lawrence Livermore National Laboratory under Contract DE-AC52-07NA27344.

C. H. Sudre et al. (Eds.): UNSURE 2020/GRAIL 2020, LNCS 12443, pp. 71–80, 2020.
https://doi.org/10.1007/978-3-030-60365-6_8

that characterize prediction uncertainties in deep models to evaluate their reliability have emerged [5,7,8,10]. A number of studies based on these uncertainty estimation methods have reported that predictions from deep models are often poorly calibrated [5,10]. A widely adopted solution to address this limitation is to incorporate *prediction calibration* strategies into the learning process [21,22].

In this paper, we propose to study the role of prediction calibration in improving the reliability of clinical models. To this end, we first introduce *reliability plots*, which measure the trade-off between model autonomy and expected generalization performance by including experts in the loop during inference, as a holistic evaluation mechanism of model reliability. Using this tool, we study the effectiveness of existing approaches including standard deep models (uncalibrated) and state-of-the-art prediction calibration techniques such as *mixup* regularization [22] and single-shot confidence calibration [18]. Next, we propose a new prediction calibration technique for classification models based on interval calibration, which has been found to be highly effective for regression tasks [21]. Finally, using a lesion classification problem with dermoscopy images, we demonstrate the effectiveness of the proposed approach over existing calibration techniques.

2   Prediction Calibration in Deep Models

Formally, the goal of predictive modeling is to build a functional relationship between observed *input* data x (image or a vector representation from a pretrained feature extractor) and a *response* variable y. Without loss of generality, we consider a K–way classification problem where $y \in \mathcal{Y} = \{1, 2, \cdots, K\}$. This is typically solved using supervised learning, where the expected discrepancy between y and $f(x)$, typically measured using a loss function $\mathcal{L}(y, f(x))$, is minimized over the joint distribution $p(x, y)$. The predictive modeling process amounts to estimating the tuple $(\hat{y}, \hat{p})$, where $\hat{y}$ is the predicted label and $\hat{p}$ is the likelihood of the prediction. Note, $\hat{p}$ is a sample from the unknown likelihood $p(y|x)$, which represents the associated uncertainties in the prediction.

The intricate interactions between data sampling, model selection and the inherent stochasticity strongly emphasize the need for a rigorous characterization of ML algorithms. In conventional statistics, uncertainty quantification (UQ) provides this characterization by measuring how accurately a model reflects the physical reality and by studying the impact of different error sources on the prediction [9,10,19]. Consequently, several recent efforts have proposed to utilize prediction uncertainties in deep models to shed light onto when and how much to trust the predictions [2,6,15,20]. However, it has been reported in several studies that these estimators are not inherently well calibrated [12], i.e., the confidences of a model in its predictions are not correlated to its accuracy. Consequently, approaches that are aimed at producing well-calibrated predictions have gained interest. For example, in a fully supervised setting, one might expect a reliable predictive model not to be overconfident while making wrong predictions [18]. In practice, these requirements are incorporated as regularization strategies to systematically adjust the predictions during training, most often leading to better performing models. Though a large class of methods exist for obtaining calibrated predictions [10,13], we focus on two state-of-the-art approaches:

(i) **Mixup**: This is a popular augmentation strategy [25] that generates additional synthetic training samples by convexly combining random pairs of images and their corresponding labels, in order to temper overconfidence in predictions. Recently, in [22], it was found that mixup regularization led to improved calibration in the resulting model. Formally, mixup training is designed based on Vicinal Risk Minimization, wherein the model is trained not only on the training data, but also using samples in the vicinity of each training sample:

$$x = \lambda x_i + (1 - \lambda)x_j; \quad y = \lambda y_i + (1 - \lambda)y_j, \tag{1}$$

where x_i and x_j are randomly chosen samples with labels y_i and y_j. The parameter λ, drawn from a symmetric Beta distribution, determines the mixing ratio.

(ii) **Single-shot Confidence Calibration (SSC)**: Seo et al. [18] proposed to augment a confidence-calibration term to the standard cross-entropy loss and the two terms are weighted using the variance measured via multiple stochastic inferences. Mathematically, this can be written as:

$$\frac{1}{N} \sum_{i=1}^{N} -(1 - \alpha_i) \log(p(\hat{y}_i|x_i)) + \alpha_i D_{KL}(\mathcal{U}(y)\|p(\hat{y}_i|x_i)). \tag{2}$$

Here the first term denotes the cross-entropy loss, and the predictions $p(\hat{y}_i|x_i)$ are inferred using stochastic inferences for x_i, while the variance (α_i) in the predictions is used to balance the loss terms. More specifically, we perform T forward passes with dropout in the network and promote the softmax probabilities to be closer to an uniform distribution, i.e. high uncertainty, when the variance is large. The normalized variance α_i is given by the mean of the Bhattacharyya coefficients between each of the T predictions and the mean prediction.

3   Model Evaluation Using Reliability Plots

While metrics such as accuracy and area under ROC have been widely adopted for evaluating model performance, we argue that it is critical to understand how calibrated the confidences of a model are, in order to quantify its reliability. In practice, metrics such as the empirical calibration error and Brier score are used to quantify the reliability of classification models. However, these metrics are known to be insufficient when estimated using smaller datasets and more importantly are not readily interpretable to a practitioner. Hence, we introduce reliability plots to study the trade-off between model autonomy and performance - i.e. by allowing a model to defer from making predictions when its confidence is low, we can effectively characterize how well the model is calibrated. On one extreme, the model can defer every decision to the expert thus being not useful in practice, while on the other hand, by making predictions even in regimes of large uncertainty, an over-confident model can be unfavorable in clinical settings.

A *reliability plot* quantifies this trade-off between model autonomy and expected test-time performance by including experts (virtually) in the loop during inference. We use the held-out validation set to construct a *reliability plot* as follows: We first measure the model's confidence on a prediction for each sample, e.g. using the entropy of the softmax probabilities from a neural network, $\mathcal{H}(\rho) = \sum_{k=1}^{K} -\rho[k] \log \rho[k]$ where $\rho = \texttt{Softmax}(\hat{y})$. Subsequently, we rank the samples based on their confidences, and hypothesize that one can use the model's predictions for the most confident cases and engage the expert to label less confident samples (i.e. use the true labels from the validation set). The overall performance is obtained by combining the predictions from both the model and the expert. In an ideal scenario, one would expect high validation accuracies for the model, while requiring minimal expert involvement. A *reliability plot* summarizes this trade-off by varying the % Samples deferred by the model to an expert and measuring the validation accuracy in each case.

4   A New Prediction Calibration Objective

We now present the proposed prediction calibration approach for classification problems. Subsequently, we will introduce a simple confidence estimation strategy for our approach, which can be used for assessing the reliability of predictions.

Interval Calibration. The notion of interval calibration comes from the uncertainty quantification literature and is used to evaluate uncertainty estimates in continuous-valued regression problems. Assuming that a model f produces prediction intervals, in lieu of simple point estimates, for the response y, i.e., $[\hat{y} - \delta, \hat{y} + \delta]$. Here, δ is used to define the interval. While the point estimate is a random variable, an interval estimate is a random interval which has a certain probability of containing a value. Suppose that the likelihood for the true response y to be contained in the prediction interval is $p(\hat{y} - \delta \leq y \leq \hat{y} + \delta)$, the intervals are considered to be well calibrated if the likelihood matches the expected confidence level. For a confidence level α, we expect the interval to contain the true response for $100 \times \alpha\%$ of realizations from $p(\mathbf{x})$. Recently, in [21], it was showed that interval calibration can be used to design a loss function to create well-calibrated deep regression models. In this paper, we propose to leverage interval calibration to obtain well-calibrated predictions in clinical problems.

Algorithm. Our model is comprised of two modules f and g, implemented as neural networks, to produce estimates $\hat{y} = f(\mathbf{x})$ and $\delta = g(\mathbf{x})$ respectively. Here, $\hat{y} \in \mathbb{R}^K$ is a vector of predicted logits for each of the K classes. Since the interval calibration process is defined for continuous-valued targets, we define the loss function for training on the logits directly. In other words, our models are trained solely on the interval calibration objective without including standard loss functions like the cross-entropy or the focal loss. To this end, we first transform the ground truth labels into logits. More specifically, we found that smoothing the labels led to improved convergence. For example, in our experiments, we consider a 7-way classification problem and for a training sample belonging to class 1 we assigned the logits $[+2, -2, -2, -2, -2, -2, -2]$. This assignment allows a small non-zero probability (≈ 0.015) to each of the other 6 classes. As discussed earlier, suppose that the likelihood for the true $y[k], k \in (1, \cdots, K)$ ($K = 7$ in our experiments) to be contained in the interval is $p(\hat{y}[k] = -\delta[k] \leq y[k] \leq \hat{y}[k] + \delta[k])$, the intervals are considered to be well calibrated if the likelihood matches the expected confidence level. Here, the index k indicates the kth output unit.

Denoting the parameters of the models f and g by θ and ϕ respectively, we design an alternating optimization strategy based on interval calibration to infer the parameters using the labeled data $\{(x_i, y_i)\}_{i=1}^{N}$. In order to update the parameters of g, we use an empirical interval calibration error, similar to [21], evaluated using mini-batches:

$$\phi^* = \arg\min_{\phi} \sum_{k=1}^{K} \left| \alpha - \frac{1}{N} \sum_{i=1}^{N} \mathbb{1}\left[(\hat{y}_i[k] - \delta_i[k]) \leq y_i[k] \leq (\hat{y}_i[k] + \delta_i[k]) \right] \right|, \quad (3)$$

where $\delta_i = g(x_i; \phi)$, $y_i[k]$ is the kth element of the vector y_i and the desired confidence level α is an input to the algorithm. When updating the parameters ϕ, we assume that the estimator $f(.; \theta)$ is known and fixed. Now, given the updated ϕ, we learn the parameters θ using the following hinge-loss objective:

$$\theta^* = \arg\min_{\theta} \sum_{k=1}^{K} \frac{1}{N} \sum_{i=1}^{N} \left[\max\left(0, (\hat{y}_i[k] - \delta_i[k]) - y_i[k] + \tau \right) \right.$$
$$\left. + \max\left(0, y_i[k] - (\hat{y}_i[k] + \delta_i[k]) + \tau \right) \right], \quad (4)$$

where $\hat{y}_i = f(x; \theta)$ and τ is a threshold set to 0.05 in our experiments. Intuitively, for a fixed ϕ, obtaining improved estimates for $\hat{y}$ can increase the empirical calibration error in (3) by achieving higher likelihoods even for lower confidence levels. However, in the subsequent step of updating ϕ, we expect $\delta's$ to become sharper in order to reduce the calibration error. This collaborative optimization process thus leads to superior quality point estimates and highly calibrated intervals. We repeat the two steps (Eqs. (3) and (4)) until convergence.

Measuring Confidences. In order to construct reliability plots for models trained using the proposed approach, we define a confidence estimation strategy. For a test sample x, we first use the predictor f to estimate the logits $\hat{y}$ and the corresponding class label $\ell = \arg\max_k \hat{y}[k]$. The confidence for the prediction is computed using the interval estimator g as follows:

$$\text{Conf}(x) = \frac{\delta[\ell]}{\max_{k \neq \ell} \delta[k]}; \delta = g(x), \ell = \arg\max_k \hat{y}[k]. \quad (5)$$

While the numerator indicates the uncertainty in accepting the positive class, the denominator indicates the worst-case uncertainty in rejecting a negative class. When this confidence measure is larger than 1, the model effectively avoids confusion with other classes. On the other hand, for samples near the decision boundary, the confidence score will be lesser than 1.

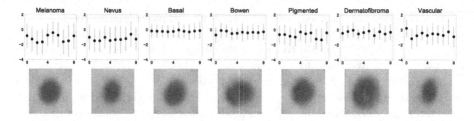

Fig. 1. Distribution of latent features in each class obtained using DIP-VAE [14]. We show the decoder reconstruction for the average latent vector in each of the classes. Furthermore, we illustrate the distribution for each latent dimension obtained using images from all 7 classes. We observe that these generative factors in addition to enabling reliable model design, they can provide interpretable signatures that are useful for discriminating between different lesion types.

5   Experiments

5.1   Dataset and Problem Description

In this paper, we use the ISIC 2018 lesion diagnosis challenge dataset [3, 24], which contains a total of $10,015$ dermoscopic lesion images (corresponding to the labeled training set) from the HAM10000 database [24]. The images were acquired with a variety of dermatoscope types from a historical sample of patients presented for skin cancer screening from multiple institutions. Each image is associated with one out of 7 disease states: Melanoma, Melanocytic nevus, Basal cell carcinoma, Actinic keratosis, Benign keratosis, Dermatofibroma and Vascular lesion. The goal is to build a classifier to predict the disease type from the image, while satisfying the key design objectives of improved model reliability and being interpretable. Dermatologists use rules of thumb when initially investigating a skin lesion, for example the widely adopted ABCD signatures: asymmetry, border, color, and diameter. This naturally motivates the use of representation learning approaches that can automatically infer latent concepts to effectively describe the distribution of images in different classes.

5.2   Model Design

Pre-training. Supervised models built upon representations that align well with true generative factors of data are found to be robust and interpretable. Most real-world problems involve raw observations without any supervision about the generative factors. Consequently, the use of latent generative models with *disentanglement* has become popular, wherein the goal is to recover a latent space with statistically independent dimensions – a small change in one of the dimensions often produces interpretable change in the generated data sample.

Table 1. Comparing prediction performance obtained by including prediction calibration during model design. We show the weighted area under ROC and the accuracy scores. The results reported were obtained via 3-fold cross validation and the best performance is highlited in bold.

Method	W-AUC	Accuracy
FCNN	0.8 ± 0.003	0.66 ± 0.008
SSC	0.77 ± 0.007	0.66 ± 0.003
Mixup	0.79 ± 0.011	0.69 ± 0.005
Proposed	$\mathbf{0.83 \pm 0.004}$	$\mathbf{0.72 \pm 0.005}$

In our approach, we use DIP-VAE [14], a variant of Variational Autoencoders (VAE), which has been shown to be effective on standard disentanglement benchmarks. The conventional VAE works with a relatively simple and disentangled prior $p(z)$ with no explicit interaction among the latent dimensions (e.g., the standard normal $\mathcal{N}(0, I)$). The complexity of the observed data x, modeled by the decoder, is absorbed in the conditional distribution $p(x|z)$ which infers the interactions among latent dimensions. Even though the prior is disentangled, it is possible that the variational distribution $q(z) = \int q(z|x)p(x)dx$ (*aggregated-posterior*), induced over the latent space, modeled by the encoder, is not disentangled. DIP-VAE encourages a disentangled aggregated-posterior by matching the covariance of the two distributions $q(\mathbf{z})$ and $p(\mathbf{z})$. This amounts to decorrelating the dimensions of the inferred latent space. Figure 1 shows the distribution of latent features obtained using DIP-VAE (10 latent dimensions) for each of the 7 classes. We also show the decoder reconstruction for the average latent representation in each class.

Predictive Model. Given the latent representations for the images from the pre-trained DIP-VAE model, we then construct a fully connected network to predict the lesion type. The architectures for both models, f and g, were designed as 5–layer fully connected networks with hidden sizes $[64, 128, 256, 64, 7]$ and *ReLU* activation. In our experiments, we set the desired confidence level $\alpha = 0.9$. We used the Adam optimizer with learning rates $3e-4$ and $1e-4$ for the two models, and performed the alternating optimization for 200 iterations.

Baselines. We consider the following baselines that were also trained using the pre-trained representations from DIP-VAE: (i) a standard fully connected neural network (FCNN) with the same architecture as described earlier; (ii) a fully connected network trained using the single-shot calibration technique [18] (SSC); (iii) fully connected network trained with mixup regularization [22] (Mixup).

5.3   Results

In Table 1, we report the performance of different modeling approaches obtained using 3–fold cross validation of the proposed approach. As discussed earlier, we

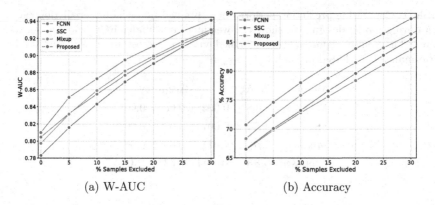

(a) W-AUC   (b) Accuracy

Fig. 2. Reliability plots obtained using the different prediction calibration techniques. We find that, in both metrics considered, the proposed approach achieves improved accuracy (in the case of 0% samples excluded) and calibration.

used only the labeled training set from the ISIC 2018 dataset for our evaluation and all models were trained using representations from a pre-trained DIP-VAE. Furthermore, in Fig. 2, we show the reliability plots for both the uncalibrated neural network baseline as well as the different prediction calibration strategies. When compared to standard cross-entropy based training (uncalibrated), our confidence estimates are highly effective. For instance, our approach achieves 81% accuracy on this challenging benchmark with only 15% samples being deferred to the expert, in contrast to the 75% accuracy of an uncalibrated neural network. Even though the *SSC* baseline enforces prediction calibration, it performs poorly when compared to other approaches. This can be attributed to the sensitivity of the choice of the layer-wise dropout parameter, particularly in smaller datasets. Similarly, the performance of *Mixup* strongly depends on the choice of mixing hyperparameter. In contrast, our approach does not require hyperparameter tuning, and can consistently produce reliable and safe models.

6   Conclusions

In this work, we demonstrated the importance of calibration strategies in building reliable models for clinical decision making. We used reliability plots to simulate the interventional decision making process in safety-critical applications, thereby enabling effective validation of the model reliability. In addition, we presented a novel prediction calibration technique, based on interval calibration, for training classifiers. Using empirical study with a challenging lesion classification dataset, we showed that the proposed approach consistently outperforms standard cross-entropy based neural networks, as well as existing prediction calibration strategies such as mixup and single-shot calibration. Future work includes a rigorous analysis of the uncertainty estimates obtained using our approach, and investigating if this approach can be an effective solution for similar small-data problems commonly encountered in clinical settings.

References

1. Cabitza, F., Campagner, A.: Who wants accurate models? arguing for a different metrics to take classification models seriously. arXiv preprint arXiv:1910.09246 (2019)
2. Ching, T., et al.: Opportunities and obstacles for deep learning in biology and medicine. J. R. Soc. Interface **15**(141), 20170387 (2018)
3. Codella, N., et al.: Skin lesion analysis toward melanoma detection 2018: a challenge hosted by the international skin imaging collaboration (ISIC). arXiv preprint arXiv:1902.03368 (2019)
4. Faust, O., Hagiwara, Y., Hong, T.J., Lih, O.S., Acharya, U.R.: Deep learning for healthcare applications based on physiological signals: a review. Comput. Methods Programs Biomed. **161**, 1–13 (2018)
5. Gal, Y.: Uncertainty in deep learning. University of Cambridge, vol. 1, p. 3 (2016)
6. Gal, Y., Ghahramani, Z.: Dropout as a Bayesian approximation: representing model uncertainty in deep learning. In: International Conference on Machine Learning, pp. 1050–1059 (2016)
7. Ghahramani, Z.: Probabilistic machine learning and artificial intelligence. Nature **521**(7553), 452–459 (2015)
8. Guo, C., Pleiss, G., Sun, Y., Weinberger, K.Q.: On calibration of modern neural networks. In: Proceedings of the 34th International Conference on Machine Learning, vol. 70, pp. 1321–1330. JMLR. org (2017)
9. Heskes, T.: Practical confidence and prediction intervals. In: Advances in Neural Information Processing Systems, pp. 176–182 (1997)
10. Kendall, A., Gal, Y.: What uncertainties do we need in Bayesian deep learning for computer vision? In: Advances in Neural Information Processing Systems, pp. 5574–5584 (2017)
11. Kononenko, I.: Machine learning for medical diagnosis: history, state of the art and perspective. Artif. Intell. Med. **23**(1), 89–109 (2001)
12. Kuleshov, V., Fenner, N., Ermon, S.: Accurate uncertainties for deep learning using calibrated regression. arXiv preprint arXiv:1807.00263 (2018)
13. Kuleshov, V., Liang, P.S.: Calibrated structured prediction. In: Advances in Neural Information Processing Systems, pp. 3474–3482 (2015)
14. Kumar, A., Sattigeri, P., Balakrishnan, A.: Variational inference of disentangled latent concepts from unlabeled observations. arXiv preprint arXiv:1711.00848 (2017)
15. Lakshminarayanan, B., Pritzel, A., Blundell, C.: Simple and scalable predictive uncertainty estimation using deep ensembles. In: Advances in Neural Information Processing Systems, pp. 6402–6413 (2017)
16. Leibig, C., Allken, V., Ayhan, M.S., Berens, P., Wahl, S.: Leveraging uncertainty information from deep neural networks for disease detection. Sci. Rep. **7**(1), 1–14 (2017)
17. Miotto, R., Wang, F., Wang, S., Jiang, X., Dudley, J.T.: Deep learning for healthcare: review, opportunities and challenges. Brief. Bioinform. **19**(6), 1236–1246 (2018)
18. Seo, S., Seo, P.H., Han, B.: Learning for single-shot confidence calibration in deep neural networks through stochastic inferences. In: Proceedings of the IEEE Conference on Computer Vision and Pattern Recognition, pp. 9030–9038 (2019)
19. Smith, R.C.: Uncertainty quantification: theory, implementation, and applications, vol. 12. SIAM (2013)

20. Thiagarajan, J.J., Kim, I., Anirudh, R., Bremer, P.T.: Understanding deep neural networks through input uncertainties. In: ICASSP 2019–2019 IEEE International Conference on Acoustics, Speech and Signal Processing (ICASSP), pp. 2812–2816. IEEE (2019)
21. Thiagarajan, J.J., Venkatesh, B., Sattigeri, P., Bremer, P.T.: Building calibrated deep models via uncertainty matching with auxiliary interval predictors. AAAI Conference on Artificial Intelligence (2019)
22. Thulasidasan, S., Chennupati, G., Bilmes, J.A., Bhattacharya, T., Michalak, S.: On mixup training: improved calibration and predictive uncertainty for deep neural networks. In: Advances in Neural Information Processing Systems, pp. 13888–13899 (2019)
23. Tonekaboni, S., Joshi, S., McCradden, M.D., Goldenberg, A.: What clinicians want: contextualizing explainable machine learning for clinical end use. arXiv preprint arXiv:1905.05134 (2019)
24. Tschandl, P., Rosendahl, C., Kittler, H.: The ham10000 dataset, a large collection of multi-source dermatoscopic images of common pigmented skin lesions. Sci. Data **5**, 180161 (2018)
25. Zhang, H., Cisse, M., Dauphin, Y.N., Lopez-Paz, D.: mixup: Beyond empirical risk minimization. arXiv preprint arXiv:1710.09412 (2017)

Uncertainty Estimation in Medical Image Denoising with Bayesian Deep Image Prior

Max-Heinrich Laves$^{(\boxtimes)}$, Malte Tölle, and Tobias Ortmaier

Leibniz Universität Hannover, Hanover, Germany
{laves,ortmaier}@imes.uni-hannover.de, malte.toelle@gmail.com

Abstract. Uncertainty quantification in inverse medical imaging tasks with deep learning has received little attention. However, deep models trained on large data sets tend to hallucinate and create artifacts in the reconstructed output that are not anatomically present. We use a randomly initialized convolutional network as parameterization of the reconstructed image and perform gradient descent to match the observation, which is known as deep image prior. In this case, the reconstruction does not suffer from hallucinations as no prior training is performed. We extend this to a Bayesian approach with Monte Carlo dropout to quantify both aleatoric and epistemic uncertainty. The presented method is evaluated on the task of denoising different medical imaging modalities. The experimental results show that our approach yields well-calibrated uncertainty. That is, the predictive uncertainty correlates with the predictive error. This allows for reliable uncertainty estimates and can tackle the problem of hallucinations and artifacts in inverse medical imaging tasks.

Keywords: Variational inference · Hallucination · Deep learning

1 Introduction

Noise in medical imaging affects all modalities, including X-ray, magnetic resonance imaging (MRI), computed tomography (CT), ultrasound (US) or optical coherence tomography (OCT) and can obstruct important details for medical diagnosis [1,7,16]. Besides "classical" approaches with linear and non-linear filters, such as the Wiener filter, or wavelet-denoising [3,22], convolutional neural networks (CNN) have proven to yield superior performance in denoising of natural and medical images [16,28].

The task of denoising is an inverse image problem and aims at reconstructing a clean image $\hat{\boldsymbol{x}}$ from a noisy observation $\tilde{\boldsymbol{x}} = \boldsymbol{c} \circ \boldsymbol{x}$. A common assumption of the noise model $\boldsymbol{c}$ of the image $\tilde{\boldsymbol{x}}$ is additive white Gaussian noise with zero mean and standard deviation σ [23,28]. Given a noisy image $\tilde{\boldsymbol{x}}$, the denoising can be expressed as optimization problem of the form

$$\hat{\boldsymbol{x}} = \arg \min \left\{ \mathcal{L}(\tilde{\boldsymbol{x}}, \hat{\boldsymbol{x}}) + \lambda \mathcal{R}(\hat{\boldsymbol{x}}) \right\} . \tag{1}$$

© Springer Nature Switzerland AG 2020
C. H. Sudre et al. (Eds.): UNSURE 2020/GRAIL 2020, LNCS 12443, pp. 81–96, 2020.
https://doi.org/10.1007/978-3-030-60365-6_9

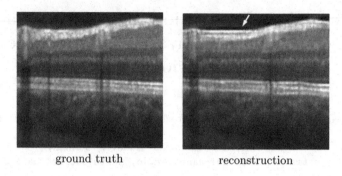

ground truth   reconstruction

Fig. 1. Hallucinations in reconstructed retinal OCT scan from supervisely trained CNN. (Left) Ground truth OCT scan. (Right) The white arrow denotes a hallucinated retinal layer that is anatomically incorrect. Hallucinations are the result of reconstructing an unseen noisy input using previously learned image statistics.

The reconstruction $\hat{x}$ should be close to $\tilde{x}$ by means of a similarity metric $\mathcal{L}$, but with substantially less noise. The regularizer $\mathcal{R}$ expresses a prior on the reconstructed images, which leads to $\hat{x}$ having less noise than $\tilde{x}$. One usually imposes a smoothness constrain by penalizing first or higher order spatial derivatives of the image [24]. More recently, denoising autoencoders have successfully been used to implicitly learn a regularization prior from a data set with corrupted and uncorrupted data samples [11]. Autoencoders are usually composed of an encoding and decoding part with a data bottleneck in between. The encoder extracts important visual features from the noisy input image and the decoder reconstructs the input from the extracted features using learned image statistics.

This, however, creates the root problem of medical image denoising with deep learning that is addressed in this paper. The reconstruction is in accordance with the expectation of the denoising autoencoder based on previously learned information. At worst, the reconstruction can contain false image features, that look like valid features, but are not actually present in the input image. Due to the excellent denoising performance of autoencoders, those false features can be indistinguishable from valid features to a layperson and are embedded in an otherwise visually appealing image. This phenomenon is known as *hallucination* and, while acceptable in the reconstruction of natural images [25], must be avoided at all costs in medical imaging (see Fig. 1). Hallucinations can lead to false diagnoses and thus severely compromise patient safety.

To further increase the reliability in the denoised medical images, the reconstruction uncertainty has to be considered. Bayesian autoencoders provide the mathematical framework to quantify a per-pixel reconstruction uncertainty [2,4,14]. This allows the detection of hallucinations and other artifacts, given that the uncertainty is well-calibrated; i. e. the uncertainty corresponds well with the reconstruction error [15].

In this work, we employ *deep image prior* [18] to cope with hallucinations in medical image denoising and provide a Bayesian approach with Monte Carlo (MC) dropout [6] that yields well-calibrated reconstruction uncertainty. We present experimental results on denoising images from low-dose X-ray, ultrasound and OCT. Compared to previous work, our approach leads to better uncertainty estimates and is less prone to overfitting of the noisy image. Our code is publicly available at github.com/mlaves/uncertainty-deep-image-prior.

2   Related Work

Image Priors. Besides manually crafted priors such as 3D collaborative filtering [5], convolutional denoising autoencoders have been used to implicitly learn an image prior from data [7,11]. Lempitsky et al. have recently shown that the excellent performance of deep networks for inverse image tasks, such as denoising, is based not only on their ability to learn image priors from data, but also on the structure of a convolutional image generator itself [18]. An image generator network $\hat{x} = f_\theta(z)$ with randomly-initialized parameters θ is interpreted as parameterization of the image. The parameters θ of the network are found by minimizing the pixel-wise squared error $\|\tilde{x} - f_\theta(z)\|$ with stochastic gradient descent (SGD). The input z is sampled from a uniform distribution with additional perturbations by normally distributed noise in every iteration. This is referred to as deep image prior (DIP). They provided empirical evidence that the structure of a CNN alone is sufficient to capture enough image statistics to provide state-of-the-art performance in inverse imaging tasks. During the process of SGD, low-frequency image features are reconstructed first, followed by higher frequencies, which makes human supervision necessary to retrieve the optimal denoised image. Therefore, this approach heavily relies on early stopping in order to not overfit the noise. However, a key advantage of deep image prior is the absence of hallucinations, since there is no prior learning. A Bayesian approach could alleviate overfitting and additionally provide reconstruction uncertainty.

Bayesian Deep Learning. Bayesian neural networks allow estimation of predictive uncertainty [2] and we generally differentiate between aleatoric and epistemic uncertainty [12]. Aleatoric uncertainty results from noise in the data (e. g. speckle noise in US or OCT). It is derived from the conditional log-likelihood under the maximum likelihood estimation (MLE) or maximum posterior (MAP) framework and can be captured directly by a deep network (i. e. by subdividing the last layer of an image generator network). Epistemic uncertainty is caused by uncertainty in the model parameters. In deep learning, we usually perform MLE or MAP inference to find a single best estimate $\hat{\theta}$ for the network parameters. This does not allow estimation of epistemic uncertainty and we therefore place distributions over the parameters. In Bayesian inference, we want to consider all possible parameter configurations, weighted by their posterior. Computing the posterior predictive distribution involves marginalization of the parameters θ, which is intractable. A common approximation of the posterior distribution is variational inference with Monte Carlo dropout [6]. It allows estimation of epistemic uncertainty by Monte Carlo sampling from the posterior of a network, that has been trained with dropout.

Bayesian Deep Image Prior. Cheng et al. recently provided a Bayesian perspective on the deep image prior in the context of natural images, which is most related to our work [4]. They interpret the convolutional network as spatial random process over the image coordinate space and use stochastic gradient Langevin dynamics (SGLD) as Bayesian approximation [26] to sample from the posterior. In SGLD, an MC sampler is derived from SGD by injecting Gaussian noise into the gradients after each backward pass. The authors claim to have solved the overfitting issue with DIP and to be able to provide uncertainty estimates. In the following, we will show that this is not the case for medical image denoising, even when using the code provided by the authors. Further, the uncertainty estimates from SGLD do not reflect the predictive error with respect to the noise-free ground truth image.

3   Methods

3.1   Aleatoric Uncertainty with Deep Image Prior

We first revisit the concept of deep image prior for denoising and subsequently extend it to a Bayesian approach with Monte Carlo dropout to estimate both aleatoric and epistemic uncertainty. Let $\tilde{x}$ be a noisy image, x the true but generally unknown noise-free image and f_θ an image generator network with parameter set θ, that outputs the denoised image $\hat{x}$. In deep image prior, the optimal parameter point estimate $\hat{\theta}$ is found by maximum likelihood estimation with gradient descent, which results in minimizing the squared error

$$\hat{\theta} = \arg \min \|\tilde{x} - f_\theta(z)\|^2 \tag{2}$$

between the generated image f_θ and the noisy image $\tilde{x}$. The input $z \sim \mathcal{U}(0, 0.1)$ of the neural network has the same spatial dimensions as $\tilde{x}$ and is sampled from a uniform distribution. To ensure that $\hat{x}$ has less noise, carefully chosen early stopping must be applied (see Sect. 5).

To quantify aleatoric uncertainty, we assume that the image signal $\tilde{x}$ is sampled from a spatial random process and that each pixel i follows a Gaussian distribution $\mathcal{N}(\tilde{x}_i; \hat{x}_i, \hat{\sigma}_i^2)$ with mean $\hat{x}_i$ and variance $\hat{\sigma}_i^2$. We split the last layer such that the network outputs these values for each pixel

$$f_\theta = [\hat{x}, \hat{\sigma}^2] \ . \tag{3}$$

Now, MLE is performed by minimizing the full negative log-likelihood, which leads to the following optimization criterion [12,15]

$$\mathcal{L}(\theta) = \frac{1}{N} \sum_{i=1}^{N} \hat{\sigma}_i^{-2} \|\tilde{x}_i - \hat{x}_i\|^2 + \log \hat{\sigma}_i^2 \ , \tag{4}$$

where N is the number of pixels per image. In this case, $\hat{\sigma}^2$ captures the pixel-wise aleatoric uncertainty and is jointly estimated with $\hat{x}$ by finding θ that minimizes Eq. (4) with SGD. For numerical stability, Eq. (4) is implemented such that the network directly outputs $-\log\hat{\sigma}^2$.

3.2 Epistemic Uncertainty with Bayesian Deep Image Prior

Next, we move towards a Bayesian view to additionally quantify the epistemic uncertainty. The image generator f_θ is extended into a Bayesian neural network under the variational inference framework with MC dropout [6]. A prior distribution $p(\theta) \sim \mathcal{N}(0, \lambda^{-1}I)$ is placed over the parameters and the network $f_{\hat{\theta}}$ is trained with dropout by minimizing Eq. (4) with added weight decay. For inference, T stochastic forward passes with applied dropout are performed to sample from the approximate Bayesian posterior $\tilde{\theta} \sim q(\theta)$. This allows us to approximate the posterior predictive distribution

$$p(\hat{x}|\tilde{x}) = \int p(\hat{x}|\theta, \tilde{x})p(\theta|\tilde{x})\,\mathrm{d}\theta \;, \tag{5}$$

which is wider than the distribution from MLE or MAP, as it accounts for uncertainty in θ. We use Monte Carlo integration to estimate the predictive mean

$$\hat{x} = \frac{1}{T}\sum_{t=1}^{T}\hat{x}_t \tag{6}$$

and predictive variance [12,15]

$$\hat{\sigma}^2 = \underbrace{\frac{1}{T}\sum_{t=1}^{T}\left(\hat{x}_t - \frac{1}{T}\sum_{t=1}^{T}\hat{x}_t\right)^2}_{\text{epistemic}} + \underbrace{\frac{1}{T}\sum_{t=1}^{T}\hat{\sigma}_t^2}_{\text{aleatoric}} \tag{7}$$

with $f_{\hat{\theta}_t} = [\hat{x}_t, \hat{\sigma}_t^2]$. In this work, we use $T = 25$ MC samples with dropout probability of $p = 0.3$. The resulting $\hat{x}$ is used as estimation of the noise-free image and $\hat{\sigma}^2$ is used as uncertainty map. We use the mean over the pixel coordinates as scalar uncertainty value U.

3.3 Calibration of Uncertainty

Following recent literature, we define predictive uncertainty to be well-calibrated if it correlates linearly with the predictive error [8,15,19]. More formally, miscalibration is quantified with

$$\mathbb{E}_{\hat{\sigma}^2}\left[\left|\left(\|\tilde{x} - \hat{x}\|^2 \,\big|\, \hat{\sigma}^2 = \sigma^2\right) - \sigma^2\right|\right] \quad \forall\left\{\sigma^2 \in \mathbb{R}\,|\,\sigma^2 \geq 0\right\} \;. \tag{8}$$

That is, if all pixels in a batch were estimated with uncertainty of 0.2, we expect the predictive error (MSE) to also equal 0.2. To approximate Eq. (8) on an image with finite pixels, we use the uncertainty calibration error (UCE) metric presented in [15], which involves binning the uncertainty values and computing a weighted average of absolute differences between MSE and uncertainty per bin.

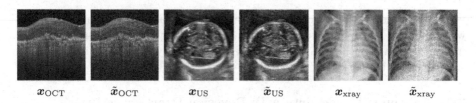

x_{OCT} $\quad\quad$ $\tilde{x}_{\mathrm{OCT}}$ $\quad\quad$ x_{US} $\quad\quad$ $\tilde{x}_{\mathrm{US}}$ $\quad\quad$ x_{xray} $\quad\quad$ $\tilde{x}_{\mathrm{xray}}$

Fig. 2. Images used to evaluate the denoising performance. The task is to reconstruct a noise-free image from $\tilde{x}$ without having access to x. OCT and US images are characterized by speckle noise which can be simulated by additive Gaussian noise. Low-dose X-ray shows uneven photon density that can be simulated by Poisson noise.

4 Experiments

We refer to the presented Bayesian approach to deep image prior with Monte Carlo dropout as MCDIP and evaluate its denoising performance and the calibration of uncertainty on three different medical imaging modalities (see Fig. 2). The first test image x_{OCT} shows an OCT scan of a retina affected by choroidal neovascularization. Next, x_{US} shows an ultrasound of a fetal head for gestational age estimation. The third test image x_{xray} shows a chest x-ray for pneumonia assessment. All test images are arbitrarily sampled from public data sets [9,13] and have a resolution of 512×512 pixel.

Images from optical coherence tomography and ultrasound are prone to speckle noise due to interference phenomena [21]. Speckle noise can obscure small anatomical details and reduce image contrast. It is worth mentioning that speckle patterns also contain information about the microstructure of the tissue. However, this information is not perceptible to a human observer, therefore the denoising of such images is desirable. Noise in low-dose X-ray originates from an uneven photon density and can be modeled with Poisson noise [17,27]. In this work, we approximate the Poisson noise with Gaussian noise since $\mathsf{Poisson}(\lambda)$ approaches a Normal distribution as $\lambda \to \infty$ (see Appendix A.5). We first create a low-noise image x by smoothing and downsampling the original image from public data sets using the ANTIALIAS filter from the Python Imaging Library (PIL) to 256×256 pixel. Downsampling involves averaging over highly correlated neighboring pixels affected by uncorrelated noise. This decreases the observation noise by sacrificing image resolution (see Appendix A.4). The downsampled image acts as ground truth to which we compute the peak signal-to-noise ratio (PSNR) and the structural similarity (SSIM) of the denoised image $\hat{x}$. Further, we compute the UCE and provide calibration diagrams (MSE vs. uncertainty) to show the (mis-)calibration of the uncertainty estimates.

We compare the results from MCDIP to standard DIP and to DIP with SGLD from Cheng et al. [4]. SGLD posterior inference is performed by averaging over T posterior samples $\hat{x} = \frac{1}{T}\sum_{t=1}^{T}\hat{x}_t$ after a "burn in" phase. The posterior variance is used as an estimator of the epistemic uncertainty $\frac{1}{T}\sum_{t=1}^{T}(\hat{x} - \hat{x}_t)^2$. Cheng et al. claim that their approach does not require early stopping and yields

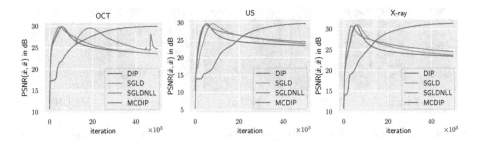

Fig. 3. Peak signal-to-noise ratio between denoised image $\hat{x}$ and ground truth x vs. number of optimizer iterations. DIP and SGLD(+NLL) quickly overfit the noisy image. MCDIP converges to its highest PSNR value and does not overfit $\tilde{x}$. The plots show means from 3 runs with different random initialization.

better denoising performance. Additionally, we train the SGLD approach with the loss function from Eq. (7) to consider aleatoric uncertainty and denote this with SGLD+NLL. We implement SGLD using the Adam optimizer, which works better in practice and is more related to preconditioned SGLD [20].

5   Results

The results are presented threefold: We show (1) possible overfitting in Fig. 3 by plotting the PSNR between the reconstruction $\hat{x}$ and the ground truth image x; (2) denoising performance by providing the denoised images in Fig. 4 and PSNR in Table 1 after convergence (i. e. after 50k optimizer steps); and (3) goodness of uncertainty in Fig. 5 by providing calibration diagrams and uncertainty maps.

Our experiments confirm what is already known: The non-Bayesian DIP quickly overfits the noisy image. The narrow peaks in PSNR values during optimization show that manually performed early stopping is essential to obtain a reconstructed image with less noise (see Fig. 3). The PSNR between $\hat{x}$ and the ground truth x approaches the value of the PSNR between the noisy image $\tilde{x}$ and the ground truth, thus reconstructing the noise as well. However, the SGLD approach shows almost identical overfitting behavior in our experiments. This is in contrast to what is stated by Chen et al., even when using the original implementation of SGLD provided by the authors [4]. SGLD+NLL additionally considers aleatoric uncertainty and converges to a higher PSNR level. This indicates that SGLD+NLL does not overfit the noisy image completely. MCDIP on the other hand does not show a sharp peak in Fig. 3 and safely converges to its highest PSNR value. This requires no manual early stopping to obtain a denoised image. The reconstructed X-ray images after convergence in Fig. 4 underline this: MCDIP does not reconstruct the noise. The PSNR values in Table 1 confirm these observations. Although it was not the intention of this work to reach highest-possible PSNR values, MCDIP even outperforms the other methods with early-stopping applied (see Appendix A.2).

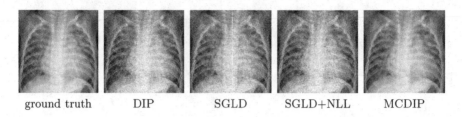

ground truth   DIP   SGLD   SGLD+NLL   MCDIP

Fig. 4. Denoised X-ray images after convergence. Only MCDIP does not show overfitted noise. Additional reconstructions can be found in Appendix A.1.

Table 1. PSNR values after convergence (at least 50k iterations). Note that our goal was not to reach highest possible PSNR, but to show overfitting in convergence.

PSNR	DIP	SGLD	SGLD+NLL	MCDIP
OCT	23.64 ± 0.19	23.58 ± 0.12	24.82 ± 0.12	$\mathbf{29.88 \pm 0.03}$
US	23.55 ± 0.11	23.81 ± 0.15	24.55 ± 0.08	$\mathbf{29.67 \pm 0.07}$
X-ray	23.28 ± 0.08	23.50 ± 0.12	24.60 ± 0.04	$\mathbf{31.19 \pm 0.10}$

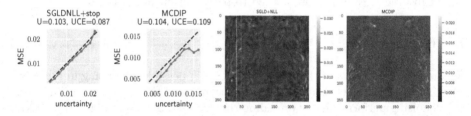

Fig. 5. Calibration diagrams and uncertainty maps for SGLD+NLL with early stopping and MCDIP after convergence on the X-ray image (best viewed with digital zoom). (Left) The calibration diagrams show MSE vs. uncertainty and provide mean uncertainty (U) and UCE values. (Right) Uncertainty maps show per-pixel uncertainty.

The calibration diagrams and corresponding UCE values in Fig. 5 suggest that SGLD+NLL is better calibrated than MCDIP. However, due to overfitting the noisy image without early stopping, the MSE from SGLD+NLL concentrates around 0.0, which results in low UCE values. On the US and OCT image, the uncertainty from SGLD+NLL collapses to a single bin in the calibration diagram and does not allow to reason about the validness of the reconstructed image (see Fig. 9 in Appendix A.1). The uncertainty map from MCDIP shows high uncertainty at edges in the image and the mean uncertainty value (denoted by U) is close to the noise level in all three test images.

6   Discussion and Conclusion

In this paper, we provided a new Bayesian approach to the deep image prior. We used variational inference with Monte Carlo dropout and the full negative log-likelihood to both quantify epistemic and aleatoric uncertainty. The presented approach is applied to medical image denoising of three different modalities and provides state-of-the-art performance in denoising with deep image prior. Our Bayesian treatment does not need carefully applied early stopping and yields well-calibrated uncertainty. We observe the estimated mean uncertainty value to be close to the noise level of the images.

The question remains why Bayesian deep image prior with SGLD does not work as well as expected and is outperformed by MC dropout. First, SGLD as described by Welling et al. requires a strong decay of the step size to ensure convergence to a mode of the posterior [26]. Cheng et al. did not implement this and we followed their approach [4]. After implementing the described step size decay, SGLD did not overfit the noisy image (see Appendix A.3). However, this requires a carefully chosen step size decay which is equivalent to early stopping.

The deep image prior framework is especially interesting in medical imaging as it does not require supervised training and thus does not suffer from hallucinations and other artifacts. The presented approach can further be applied to deformable registration or other inverse image tasks in the medical domain.

A   Appendix

A.1   Additional Figures

(See Figs. 6, 7, 8 and 10)

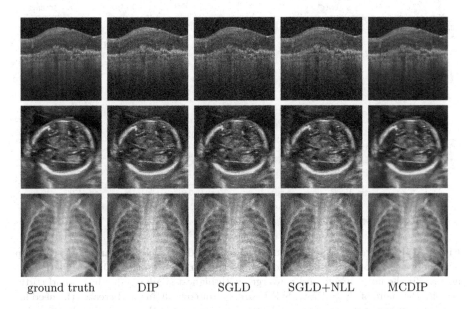

ground truth   DIP   SGLD   SGLD+NLL   MCDIP

Fig. 6. Denoised images after convergence.

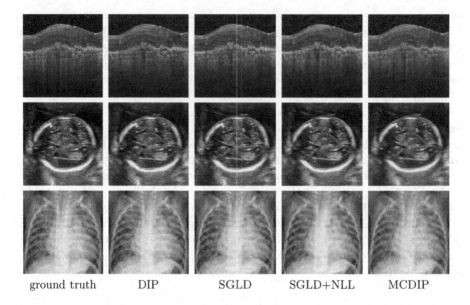

ground truth   DIP   SGLD   SGLD+NLL   MCDIP

Fig. 7. Denoised images with early-stopping applied.

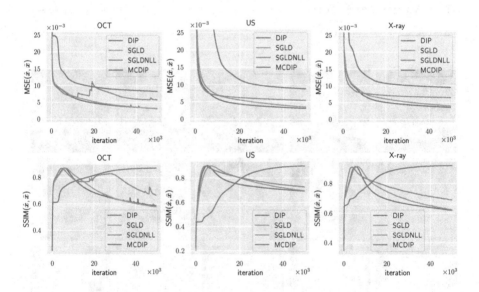

Fig. 8. MSE (top row) between denoised $\hat{x}$ image and noisy image $\tilde{x}$ and SSIM (bottom row) between denoised $\hat{x}$ image and ground truth x vs. iteration. Only MCDIP does not overfit the noisy image and converges with highest similarity to the ground truth. Despite the claim of the authors, SGLD suffers from overfitting and creates the need for carefully applied early stopping [4]. Note: We compared both our own implementation of SGLD and the original code provided by the authors. The plots show means from 3 runs with different random initialization.

A.2   Additional Tables

(See Table 2, 3 and 4)

Table 2. PSNR with early-stopping.

PSNR	DIP	SGLD	SGLD+NLL	MCDIP
OCT	29.88 ± 0.02	29.89 ± 0.05	29.77 ± 0.07	$\mathbf{29.92 \pm 0.03}$
US	29.74 ± 0.05	$\mathbf{29.78 \pm 0.02}$	29.54 ± 0.03	29.7 ± 0.07
X-ray	30.91 ± 0.05	30.98 ± 0.09	30.74 ± 0.03	$\mathbf{31.22 \pm 0.1}$

Table 3. SSIM after convergence.

SSIM	DIP	SGLD	SGLD+NLL	MCDIP
OCT	0.582 ± 0.0	0.574 ± 0.0	0.66 ± 0.0	$\mathbf{0.872 \pm 0.0}$
US	0.687 ± 0.0	0.703 ± 0.0	0.723 ± 0.0	$\mathbf{0.902 \pm 0.0}$
X-ray	0.625 ± 0.0	0.631 ± 0.0	0.686 ± 0.0	$\mathbf{0.922 \pm 0.0}$

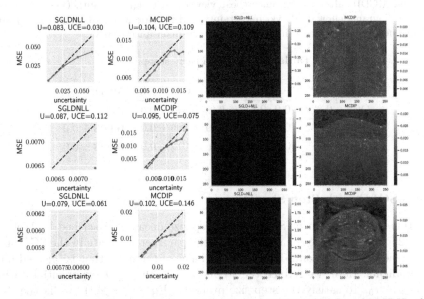

Fig. 9. Calibration diagrams and uncertainty maps for SGLD+NLL and MCDIP after convergence (best viewed with digital zoom). (Left) The calibration diagrams show MSE vs. uncertainty and provide mean uncertainty (U) and UCE values. (Right) Uncertainty maps show per-pixel uncertainty. Due to overfitting, the MSE and uncertainty from SGLD+NLL concentrates around 0.0.

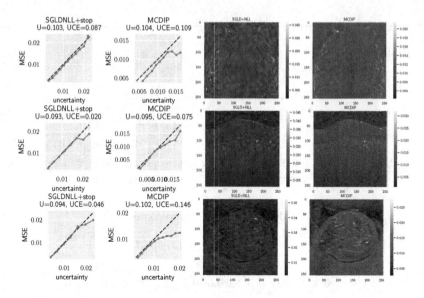

Fig. 10. Calibration diagrams and uncertainty maps for SGLD+NLL after early stopping and MCDIP after convergence (best viewed with digital zoom). (Left) The calibration diagrams show MSE vs. uncertainty and provide mean uncertainty (U) and UCE values. (Right) Uncertainty maps show per-pixel uncertainty.

Table 4. SSIM with early-stopping.

SSIM	DIP	SGLD	SGLD+NLL	MCDIP
OCT	0.872 ± 0.0	0.872 ± 0.0	0.872 ± 0.0	0.872 ± 0.0
US	0.902 ± 0.0	$\mathbf{0.903} \pm 0.0$	0.899 ± 0.0	$\mathbf{0.903} \pm 0.0$
X-ray	0.915 ± 0.0	0.917 ± 0.0	0.912 ± 0.0	$\mathbf{0.923} \pm 0.0$

A.3   SGLD with Step Size Decay

Additionall, we implement SGLD with step size decay as described by Welling et al. [26]. The step size ϵ is used to scale the parameter update in the SGD step (i.e. the learning rate) and defines the variance of the noise that is injected into the gradients. Here, we reduce the step size at each step t exponentially with $\epsilon_t = 0.999^t \epsilon_0$. To satisfy the step size property (Eq. (2) in [26]), we fix the step size once it decreases below 1e-8. We observe no overfitting of the noisy image with step size decay (see Fig. 11). However, the quality of the resulting denoised image is very sensitive to the decay scheme. Choosing a decrease that is too low (i.e. $\epsilon_t = 0.9999^t \epsilon_0$) results in overfitting; a decrease that is too high (i.e. $\epsilon_t = 0.99^t \epsilon_0$) results in convergence to a subpar reconstruction. This is equivalent to carefully applied early stopping and therefore nullifies the advantage of SGLD for denoising of medical images.

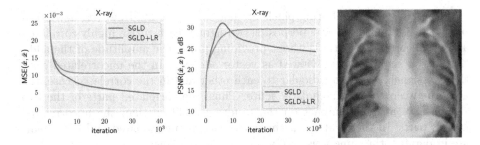

Fig. 11. Comparison of SGLD and SGLD+LR (with step size decay). Carefully chosen step size decay impedes overfitting the noisy image. (Right) Reconstruction of SGLD+LR after convergence (no early stopping applied).

A.4 Downsampling

Here, we provide justification why downsampling of an image by averaging neighboring pixels reduces the noise level and can be used as an approximation to a ground truth noise-free image (by sacrificing image resolution).

Proposition 1. *Downsampling of an image reduces the observation noise.*

Proof. Let $X = \mu_x + \varepsilon_x$ and $Y = \mu_y + \varepsilon_y$ be two neighboring pixels affected by additive i.i.d. noise $\varepsilon_x, \varepsilon_y \sim \mathcal{N}(0, \sigma^2)$. The pixels are assumed to be uncorrelated to noise. Pixels in a local neighborhood are highly correlated and assumed to be of high similarity $\mu_x \approx \mu_y = \mu$. Let $Z = \frac{1}{2}(X + Y)$ be the average of two neighboring pixels (i.e. the result of downsampling). The expectation is given by

$$\mathbb{E}[Z] = \frac{1}{2}\left(\mathbb{E}[X] + \mathbb{E}[Y]\right) \tag{9}$$

$$= \frac{1}{2}2\,\mathbb{E}[X] \tag{10}$$

$$= \mu \tag{11}$$

and the variance is given by

$$\mathrm{Var}\,[Z] = \mathrm{Var}\left[\frac{1}{2}(X + Y)\right] \tag{12}$$

$$= \frac{1}{2^2}\left(\mathrm{Var}\,[X] + \mathrm{Var}\,[Y]\right) \tag{13}$$

$$= \frac{1}{2^2}2\mathrm{Var}\,[X] \tag{14}$$

$$= \frac{1}{2}\sigma^2 . \tag{15}$$

Thus, if the similarity of neighboring pixels is sufficiently high, downsampling reduces the variance of average pixel Z by a factor of 2.   □

Naturally, two neighboring pixels are not exactly equal. However, downsampling can also be viewed as superposing two signals, each with a highly correlated and an uncorrelated part. Without providing proof, the amplitude of the addition of two signals can be viewed as vector addition. In the uncorrelated case, the two signals are perpendicular to each other and in the correlated case, the angle between the two signals is acute. Thus, the correlated parts of the two signals have a higher impact on the resulting addition than the uncorrelated (noise) parts. In the ideal case, where the noise is uncorrelated and the signals are in parallel, the same noise reduction as above follows.

A.5   Link Between Poisson Distribution and Normal Distribution

We approximate the Poisson noise to simulate a low-dose X-ray image with a Normal distribution. It is well-known that the limiting distribution of $\mathsf{Poisson}(\lambda)$ is Normal as $\lambda \to \infty$ [10]. For completeness, we list a common proof using the moment generating function of a standardized Poisson random variable:

Theorem 1. *The Poisson(λ) distribution can be approximated with a Normal distribution as $\lambda \to \infty$.*

Proof. Let $X_\lambda \sim \mathsf{Poisson}(\lambda)$, $\lambda \in \{1, 2, \ldots\}$. The probability mass function of X_λ is given by

$$f_{X_\lambda}(x) = \frac{\lambda^x e^{-\lambda}}{x!} \quad x \in \{0, 1, 2, \ldots\} \, . \tag{16}$$

The moment generating function is given by [10]

$$M_{X_\lambda}(t) = \mathbb{E}[e^{tX_\lambda}] = e^{\lambda(e^t - 1)} \, . \tag{17}$$

The standardized Poisson random variable

$$Z = \frac{X_\lambda - \lambda}{\sqrt{\lambda}} \tag{18}$$

has the limiting moment generating function

$$\lim_{\lambda \to \infty} M_Z(t) = \lim_{\lambda \to \infty} \mathbb{E}\left[\exp\left(t \cdot \frac{X_\lambda - \lambda}{\sqrt{\lambda}}\right)\right] \tag{19}$$

$$= \lim_{\lambda \to \infty} \exp\left(-t\sqrt{\lambda}\right) \mathbb{E}\left[\exp\left(\frac{tX_\lambda}{\sqrt{\lambda}}\right)\right] \tag{20}$$

$$= \lim_{\lambda \to \infty} \exp\left(-t\sqrt{\lambda}\right) \exp\left(\lambda\left(e^{t/\sqrt{\lambda}} - 1\right)\right) \tag{21}$$

$$= \lim_{\lambda \to \infty} \exp\left(-t\sqrt{\lambda} + \lambda\left(t\lambda^{-1/2} + t^2\lambda^{-1}/2 + t^3\lambda^{-3/2}/6 + \ldots\right)\right) \tag{22}$$

$$= \lim_{\lambda \to \infty} \exp\left(t^2/2 + t^3\lambda^{-1/2}/6 + \ldots\right) \tag{23}$$

$$= \exp\left(t^2/2\right) \tag{24}$$

which is the moment generating function of a standard normal random variable. $\qquad\square$

References

1. Agostinelli, F., Anderson, M.R., Lee, H.: Adaptive multi-column deep neural networks with application to robust image denoising. In: Advances in Neural Information Processing Systems, pp. 1493–1501 (2013)
2. Bishop, C.M.: Pattern Recognition and Machine Learning. Springer, Boston (2006). https://doi.org/10.1007/978-1-4615-7566-5
3. Chang, S.G., Yu, B., Vetterli, M.: Adaptive wavelet thresholding for image denoising and compression. IEEE Trans. Image Process. **9**(9), 1532–1546 (2000). https://doi.org/10.1109/83.862633
4. Cheng, Z., Gadelha, M., Maji, S., Sheldon, D.: A Bayesian perspective on the deep image prior. In: IEEE/CVF Conference on Computer Vision and Pattern Recognition, pp. 5443–5451 (2019)
5. Dabov, K., Foi, A., Katkovnik, V., Egiazarian, K.: Image denoising by sparse 3-D transform-domain collaborative filtering. Trans. Image Process. **16**(8), 2080–2095 (2007). https://doi.org/10.1109/TIP.2007.901238
6. Gal, Y., Ghahramani, Z.: Dropout as a Bayesian approximation: Representing model uncertainty in deep learning. In: ICML, pp. 1050–1059 (2016)
7. Gondara, L.: Medical image denoising using convolutional denoising autoencoders. In: International Conference on Data Mining Workshops, pp. 241–246 (2016). https://doi.org/10.1109/ICDMW.2016.0041
8. Guo, C., Pleiss, G., Sun, Y., Weinberger, K.Q.: On calibration of modern neural networks. In: ICML, pp. 1321–1330 (2017)
9. van den Heuvel, T.L., de Bruijn, D., de Korte, C.L., Ginneken, B.v.: Automated measurement of fetal head circumference using 2D ultrasound images. PloS One **13**(8), e0200412 (2018). https://doi.org/10.1371/journal.pone.0200412. US dataset source
10. Hogg, R.V., McKean, J., Craig, A.T.: Introduction to Mathematical Statistics, 8th edn. Pearson, New York (2018)
11. Jain, V., Seung, S.: Natural image denoising with convolutional networks. In: Advances in Neural Information Processing Systems, pp. 769–776 (2009)
12. Kendall, A., Gal, Y.: What uncertainties do we need in Bayesian deep learning for computer vision? In: NeurIPS, pp. 5574–5584 (2017)
13. Kermany, D.S., et al.: Identifying medical diagnoses and treatable diseases by image-based deep learning. Cell **172**(5), 1122–1131 (2018). https://doi.org/10.1016/j.cell.2018.02.010
14. Kingma, D.P., Welling, M.: Auto-encoding variational Bayes. In: ICLR (2014)
15. Laves, M.H., Ihler, S., Fast, J.F., Kahrs, L.A., Ortmaier, T.: Well-calibrated regression uncertainty in medical imaging with deep learning. In: Medical Imaging with Deep Learning (2020)
16. Laves, M.H., Ihler, S., Kahrs, L.A., Ortmaier, T.: Semantic denoising autoencoders for retinal optical coherence tomography. In: SPIE/OSA European Conference on Biomedical Optics, vol. 11078, pp. 86–89 (2019). https://doi.org/10.1117/12.2526936
17. Lee, S., Lee, M.S., Kang, M.G.: Poisson-gaussian noise analysis and estimation for low-dose x-ray images in the NSCT domain. Sensors **18**(4), 1019 (2018)
18. Lempitsky, V., Vedaldi, A., Ulyanov, D.: Deep Image Prior. In: IEEE/CVF Conference on Computer Vision and Pattern Recognition, pp. 9446–9454 (2018). https://doi.org/10.1109/CVPR.2018.00984

19. Levi, D., Gispan, L., Giladi, N., Fetaya, E.: Evaluating and calibrating uncertainty prediction in regression tasks. arXiv arXiv:1905.11659 (2019)
20. Li, C., Chen, C., Carlson, D., Carin, L.: Preconditioned stochastic gradient Langevin dynamics for deep neural networks. In: Proceedings of the Thirtieth AAAI Conference on Artificial Intelligence, pp. 1788–1794 (2016)
21. Michailovich, O.V., Tannenbaum, A.: Despeckling of medical ultrasound images. Trans. Ultrason. Ferroelectr. Freq. Control 53(1), 64–78 (2006). https://doi.org/10.1109/TUFFC.2006.1588392
22. Rabbani, H., Nezafat, R., Gazor, S.: Wavelet-domain medical image denoising using bivariate Laplacian mixture model. Trans. Biomed. Eng. 56(12), 2826–2837 (2009). https://doi.org/10.1109/TBME.2009.2028876
23. Salinas, H.M., Fernandez, D.C.: Comparison of PDE-based nonlinear diffusion approaches for image enhancement and denoising in optical coherence tomography. IEEE Trans. Med. Imaging 26(6), 761–771 (2007). https://doi.org/10.1109/TMI.2006.887375
24. Sotiras, A., Davatzikos, C., Paragios, N.: Deformable medical image registration: a survey. IEEE Trans. Med. Imaging 32(7), 1153–1190 (2013). https://doi.org/10.1109/TMI.2013.2265603
25. Wang, N., Tao, D., Gao, X., Li, X., Li, J.: A comprehensive survey to face hallucination. Int. J. Comput. Vis. 106(1), 9–30 (2014). https://doi.org/10.1007/s11263-013-0645-9
26. Welling, M., Teh, Y.W.: Bayesian learning via stochastic gradient Langevin dynamics. In: ICML, pp. 681–688 (2011)
27. Žabić, S., Wang, Q., Morton, T., Brown, K.M.: A low dose simulation tool for CT systems with energy integrating detectors. Med. Phys. 40(3), 031102 (2013). https://doi.org/10.1118/1.4789628
28. Zhang, K., Zuo, W., Chen, Y., Meng, D., Zhang, L.: Beyond a Gaussian denoiser: residual learning of deep CNN for image denoising. IEEE Trans. Image Process. 26(7), 3142–3155 (2017). https://doi.org/10.1109/TIP.2017.2662206

Uncertainty Estimation for Assessment of 3D US Scan Adequacy and DDH Metric Reliability

Arunkumar Kannan[1]($\boxtimes$), Antony Hodgson[2], Kishore Mulpuri[3], and Rafeef Garbi[1]

[1] Department of Electrical and Computer Engineering, University of British Columbia, Vancouver, BC, Canada
arunk@ece.ubc.ca
[2] Department of Mechanical Engineering, University of British Columbia, Vancouver, BC, Canada
[3] Department of Orthopaedic Surgery, BC Children's Hospital, Vancouver, BC, Canada

Abstract. Developmental Dysplasia of the Hip (DDH) is the most common paediatric hip disorder and a major cause of early hip replacement and osteoarthritis (OA) in young adults. Clinical practice for diagnosis remains reliant on manual measurement of pediatric hip joint features from 2D Ultrasound (US) scans, a process plagued with high inter/intra operator and scan variability. Recently, 3D US was shown to be markedly more reliable with deeply-learned image features effectively used to localize and measure anatomical bone landmarks. However, opaqueness of neural-net based analysis provides no means for assessing the reliability of computed results, a limitation that hampers deployment in clinical settings. We propose using interpretable uncertainty measures that can simultaneously measure bone segmentation reliability and quantify scan adequacy in clinical DDH assessment from 3D US. Our approach measures the variability of estimates generated from an encoder-decoder type CNN optimized for hip joint localization using random dropout. We quantitatively evaluate our proposed uncertainty estimates on a clinical dataset comprising 118 neonates. Results demonstrate smaller variability in dysplasia metrics to be markedly correlated with higher Dice scores for repeated segmentation estimates. Further, we observe that US scans with lower dysplasia metric variability are strongly associated with those labelled as clinically adequate by a human expert. Findings suggest that our uncertainty estimation may improve clinical workflow acting as a quality control check on deep learning based analysis. This in turn may improve overall reliability of the diagnostic process and the prospects of adoption in clinical settings.

Keywords: Developmental Dysplasia of the Hip (DDH) · Uncertainty · Bone segmentation · US scan adequacy classification · 3D Ultrasound

© Springer Nature Switzerland AG 2020
C. H. Sudre et al. (Eds.): UNSURE 2020/GRAIL 2020, LNCS 12443, pp. 97–105, 2020.
https://doi.org/10.1007/978-3-030-60365-6_10

1   Introduction

Developmental Dysplasia of the Hip (DDH) - a condition characterized by hip joint instability, is one of the most common orthopaedic congenital disorders estimated to affect up to 2.85% of all newborns [5]. Accurate early clinical diagnosis of DDH is key for effective treatment [1]. Current clinical practice for DDH diagnosis relies on 2D Ultrasound (US) imaging of the neonatal hip, owing to its safety, low-cost, portability and ability to image yet-to-ossify bone structures. In a typical diagnostic procedure, a sonographer will scan an infant's hip looking for relevant anatomical landmarks including the femoral head, ilium and acetabulum. Once judged to be adequate for conducting measurements, the US scan is saved for quantitative analysis. Later, the sonographer will manually delineate the bone surfaces and extract metrics like the alpha angle and femoral head coverage (FHC) to report the dysplastic condition of the infant. However, in a meta-analysis study [10], Quader et al. reported 2D US to have very low inter-exam and inter-observer intraclass correlation coefficient (ICC) for alpha angle and FHC (23% and 2%). This significant variability motivated the exploration of 3D US as a possibly better alternative for diagnosing DDH.

Quader et al. [9] proposed hand-engineered features including confidence-weighted local phase symmetry (CSPS) of 3D US images to segment the femoral head and pelvic bone. In [7], Quader et al. used a 3D alpha angle based on the hand-engineered features reporting 75% reduction in test-retest variability compared to standard 2D alpha angle, demonstrating 3D US to be a far more reproducible alternative than conventional 2D US. More recently, Hariri et al. [3] proposed using deep-learned features, which were shown to perform better in bone localization of the hip joint than hand-engineered features, with the latter having poorer robustness/generalizability to new data. In related work, Paserin et al. [6] developed an automated deep-learning based scan adequacy assessment method to aid the human operator in classifying US volumes as 'adequate' or 'inadequate' for subsequent DDH metric extraction, reporting a classification Area under the Receiver Operating Characteristic curve (AROC) of 83%. Despite these recent significant contributions towards deployment of 3D US for DDH assessment, several limitations remain, the most important of which is model opacity of neural network models. The black-box nature of deep-learning frameworks present generalizability and interpretability complications to clinical adoption.

In this work, we propose an interpretable uncertainty measure that quantifies a U-Net-like architecture's reliability in segmenting the hip joint. We deploy this measure to augment extracted DDH metrics with an estimated uncertainty in the network's prediction. In addition to segmentation reliability estimation, we demonstrate the utility of the uncertainty measure in assessing scan adequacy, which can provide a more accurate approach to assessing the suitability of the 3D US images for subsequent quantitative analysis in real time during patient scanning. Our method is based on Gal et al. approach to uncertainty estimation, which deploys dropout as a simplified bayesian approximation for representing model uncertainty while maintaining low computational cost [4].

2   Methods

We propose estimating an interpretable uncertainty measure for clinical use of automated deep learning-based US image analysis for hip dysplasia diagnosis. Our measure captures the variability in DDH metric values and 3D US scan quality as inferred by a CNN. More specifically, we deploy a 3D U-Net-like CNN for segmenting pelvic bone surfaces that integrates dropout layers at the end of each encoder-decoder block to approximate the architecture of a Bayesian neural network by generating Monte-Carlo (MC) samples [4]. We extract diagnostic DDH metrics including 3D alpha angle [7] and 3D FHC [8] from said MC segmentation samples to estimate uncertainty.

2.1   Materials and Experimental Setup

With required research ethics approvals in place, we collected 3D B-mode US images of the hip from 118 newborns with mean age of 6 weeks using the Ultrasonix 4DL14-5/38 3D US probe with transducer centre frequency kept at 7.5 MHz, image depth of 3.8-5 cm and resolution of 0.16 mm/voxel. A specialized US technician acquired multiple sweeps of both hips for each participant following a static assessment protocol with no force applied to the hip. In this study, we used a subset of the collected data totalling 133 volumes for training and testing.

2.2   Bone Segmentation and Metric Extraction

We use a 3D U-Net-like architecture as shown in Fig. 1 comprising 4 encoder and 3 decoder blocks which we optimize for segmenting the femoral head, ilium and acetabulum surfaces of the hip joint area. Each encoder-decoder block extracts features using a conv3x3 ReLU conv3x3 ReLU arrangement.

Segmentation Network Training: A user who was closely mentored by an expert radiologist manually traced the iliac bone and femoral head in 64 US image volumes that we use to train our bone segmentation network. In addition to manual tracing of relevant anatomical structures, the user labelled the adequacy of each US volume with a 'yes', 'no' or 'maybe' label, where 'yes' signified that all needed bone structures (femoral head, ilium and acetabulum) are adequately visualized in the US volume, 'no' reflected absence of some or all of these structures, and 'maybe' denoted border line scans where the user could not make a clear designation. Our training used 16 (of the 64) volumes for validation. Due to the limited amount of available labelled training data, we heavily augmented this dataset including translation, rotation, flipping in medial and lateral directions, non-uniform zooming, as well as applying elastic deformations. As per the standard configuration deployed in [3], we used stride 1 for the 3D convolutions in the expanding and contracting path. We performed max-pooling of stride 2 with a kernel size of 2×2 in the contracting path and transposed convolution in

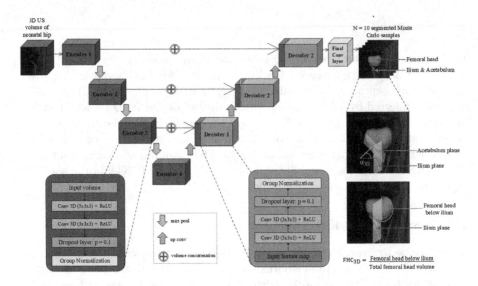

Fig. 1. Architecture used for segmenting the femoral head, ilium and acetabulum surfaces of the hip joint area from 3D US scans of infant hips.

the expanding path. A dropout layer with a probability rate of 0.1 was appended at the end of each block (except for the final convolutional layer) to produce an MC sample distribution. We trained our network to optimize the Binary Cross Entropy (BCE) loss for 90 epochs with a batch-size of 1. Network features were further optimized using stochastic gradient descent with a learning rate of 0.001 and a multi-step learning rate scheduler that decreased the learning rate by a gamma factor of 0.1 at the 50th and 75th epochs. At inference time, a test US volume was fed forward into the trained network N times to produce N MC sample segmentations. We restricted the number of MC samples to 10 at test time (<1 min) to reduce computational cost, as our training experiments showed the resulting variance estimates were relatively insensitive to the number of processing runs used; a marginal improvement of less than 0.006% when 100 MC samples were generated instead of 10.

Extraction of DDH Metrics: Using the bone segmentations, we extracted the 3D alpha angle [7] and 3D FHC [8], as their 2D counterparts are most commonly reported in clinical practice. The 3D alpha(α_{3D}) measured the shallowness of the hip socket and was defined as the angle between unit normal vectors to planar surfaces fitted to the ilium and acetabulum in the segmented hip joint (Fig. 1). A lower alpha angle dipping below normal range signifies increased DDH severity. The 3D femoral head coverage (FHC_{3D}) measures the percentage of the femoral head capped by the acetabulum, and is defined as the ratio of the volume of femoral head contained medial to the ilium plane to total femoral head volume in the neonatal hip (Fig. 1). Lower FHC_{3D} signifies increased DDH severity.

2.3   Uncertainty Estimation

Model or epistemic uncertainty signifies the network's confidence in the prediction. Interpreted as a naive Bayesian approach [2], 3D U-Net can be approximated as a probabilistic model $p(y|x, w)$ with x as input 3D US volume, y as the corresponding class label and w as the parameters of the network. As w stores features of training data, the model's uncertainty can be evaluated by placing a prior distribution over the parameter w, denoted by $p(w|x, y)$. However, such analytical calculation of the function is impractical due to associated heavy computational cost and extensive training time required. Instead, we use Gal et al. tractable approach to approximate the distribution using MC sampling. To estimate the variance in extracted DDH metrics on test data, we estimate the MC distribution of the samples by enabling dropout activation at test time to calculate the predictive standard deviation (SD):

$$SD_{DDH\,metric} = \sqrt{\frac{1}{N}\sum_{n=1}^{N}(y_n - y)^2} \qquad (1)$$

where y_n denotes the DDH metric calculated from each of N MC sample and y is the average of the metric given by $y = \frac{1}{N}\sum_n (y_n)$.

Having calculated our uncertainty estimate (SD) for each DDH metric per volume, we further calculate a structure-wise uncertainty measure similar to Roy et al. [11]. The structure-wise uncertainty measure is based on the pair-wise Dice scores of all combinations of MC samples and is evaluated as the average of Dice scores per test data, for the ilium and acetabulum surface segmentations d_{IA}^{MC}, and the femoral head segmentations d_{F}^{MC}.

$$d_{IA}^{MC} = \frac{1}{N}\sum_{i,j=1}^{N} Dice(IA_i, IA_j)_{i\neq j} \qquad (2)$$

$$d_{F}^{MC} = \frac{1}{N}\sum_{i,j=1}^{N} Dice(F_i, F_j)_{i\neq j} \qquad (3)$$

where N - number of MC samples, IA - ilium acetabulum segmentation mask, F - femoral head segmentation mask and i,j - ith and jth MC sample.

3   Results and Discussion

We first evaluated the accuracy of our network comparing to Hariri et al. architecture [3] by calculating the Dice scores on 69 test volumes. Results demonstrate that our addition of dropout layers did not result in any sacrifice in network accuracy, achieving almost the same average Dice score of 85%.

In Fig. 2 we present the scatter plot between our estimated SD in DDH metrics and the corresponding structure-wise uncertainty measure (average Dice

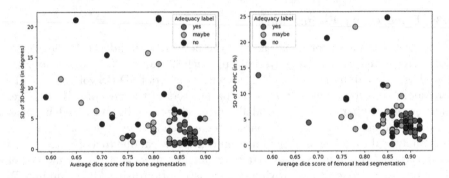

Fig. 2. Scatter plot between structure-wise uncertainty measure in segmented regions and corresponding deviation estimated in DDH metrics

score of MC samples on the same test data). We observed that SD in 3D alpha score is negatively correlated with average Dice score of ilium and acetabulum segmentations, with a correlation value of −0.64. Similar observations were made for femoral head coverage measurements; SD in 3D FHC was negatively correlated with average Dice score estimated for femoral head segmentations with a correlation value of −0.67. This confirms that accurate and stable segmentation of the ilium, acetabulum, and femoral head is necessary for robust alpha angle and FHC metric extraction. It is worth mentioning that certain outlier cases in the scatter plots were observed, with concurrent low SD values and low average Dice scores. This suggests that a combination of high average Dice scores and low SD may be a better indication of uncertainty, compared to low SD on its own.

Figure 2 also shows almost all scans with adequacy 'yes' labels have low SD and 'no'/'maybe' labels have high SD. Figure 3 shows qualitative examples of low and high certainty cases for each of the scan adequacy labels (yes, no, maybe). We evaluate our proposed uncertainty measure for adequacy classification by testing for statistical significance between the 'yes' and 'no'/'maybe' labels. The calculated variance in DDH metrics was tested for skewness and found to be not normally distributed. Hence a non-parametric 2-independent sample test was performed between the two adequacy groups 'yes' and 'no/maybe' labels. We observed a statistically significant difference in SD for 3D alpha between the two adequacy groups with a p-value of 0.001; similarly for 3D FHC, with a p-value of 0.0015. This suggests that our proposed uncertainty may be quite valuable as a tool for sonographers to decide on the inclusion of scans for diagnosis in real time while scanning a patient: if the calculated variance of DDH metric is low, the scan can be used for further analysis, otherwise is discarded and a better scan is pursued. Figure 2 shows that certain 'yes' labels were associated with high SD, and some 'no' labels with low SD. These scans are shown in Fig. 4. We expect that this mislabelling of scan adequacy is related to user error.

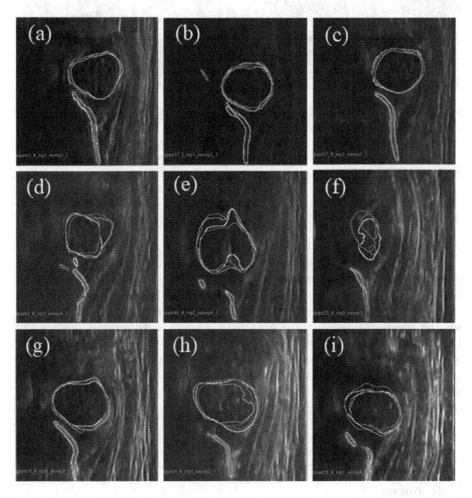

Fig. 3. Qualitative results to show examples of high/low certainty in predictions (bone segmentation and scan adequacy classification) (a) Yes label with low uncertainty (SD in $\alpha_{3D} = 2.65°$, $FHC_{3D} = 3.03\%$), (b) Yes label with low uncertainty (SD in $\alpha_{3D} = 1.67°$, $FHC_{3D} = 1.67\%$), (c) Yes label with low uncertainty (SD in $\alpha_{3D} = 1.15°$, $FHC_{3D} = 1.72\%$), (d) No label with high uncertainty (SD in $\alpha_{3D} = 21.34°$, $FHC_{3D} = 20.74\%$), (e) No label with high uncertainty (SD in $\alpha_{3D} = 15.32°$, $FHC_{3D} = 6.60\%$), (f) No label with high uncertainty (SD in $\alpha_{3D} = 21.07°$, $FHC_{3D} = 9.11\%$), (g) Maybe label with low uncertainty (SD in $\alpha_{3D} = 1.25°$, $FHC_{3D} = 2.86\%$), (h) Maybe label with high uncertainty (SD in $\alpha_{3D} = 15.62°$, $FHC_{3D} = 11.5\%$), (i) Maybe label with high uncertainty (SD in $\alpha_{3D} = 10.05°$, $FHC_{3D} = 5.42\%$). Each colour represents each of the MC sample generated per US volume.

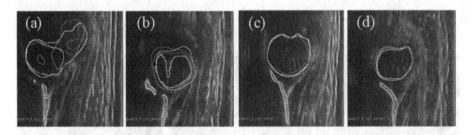

Fig. 4. Visualization of mislabelled adequacy volumes (a) Yes label with high uncertainty (SD in $\alpha_{3D} = 5.59°$, $FHC_{3D} = 13.59\%$), (b) Yes label with high uncertainty (SD in $\alpha_{3D} = 2.86°$, $FHC_{3D} = 8.88\%$), (a) No label with low uncertainty (SD in $\alpha_{3D} = 0.30°$, $FHC_{3D} = 3.48\%$), (a) No label with low uncertainty (SD in $\alpha_{3D} = 1.79°$, $FHC_{3D} = 3.32\%$),

4   Conclusions

We proposed the use of an interpretable model uncertainty measure to augment a DL framework for DDH assessment. The proposed uncertainty measures help quantify the network's reliability in segmenting pelvic bone and femoral head surfaces in 3D US scans of the neonatal hip and reliability of the DDH metrics extracted from those segmentation. The measures can be also be used to classify the adequacy/inadequacy of acquired US scans for subsequent diagnosis of DDH. Such capabilities have the potential to facilitate and accelerate adoption of opaque deep learning based DDH analyses in clinical settings. Our future work will focus on assessing our method's generalizability to US data collected at multi-institutional pediatric orthopedic centres evaluating DDH across the world.

Acknowledgement. We would like to thank NVIDIA Corporation and Compute Canada for supporting our research through their GPU grant program.

References

1. Cox, P., Woodacre, T.: The costs of late detection of developmental dysplasia of the hip. Orthop. Proc. **95-B**(SUPP_18), 14–14 (2013). https://doi.org/10.1302/1358-992X.95BSUPP_18.SWOC2012-014
2. Denker, J.S., LeCun, Y.: Transforming neural-net output levels to probability distributions. In: NIPS (1990)
3. El-Hariri, H., Mulpuri, K., Hodgson, A., Garbi, R.: Comparative Evaluation of Hand-Engineered and Deep-Learned Features for Neonatal Hip Bone Segmentation in Ultrasound. In: Shen, D., Liu, T., Peters, T.M., Staib, L.H., Essert, C., Zhou, S., Yap, P.-T., Khan, A. (eds.) MICCAI 2019. LNCS, vol. 11765, pp. 12–20. Springer, Cham (2019). https://doi.org/10.1007/978-3-030-32245-8_2
4. Gal, Y., Ghahramani, Z.: Dropout as a Bayesian approximation: representing model uncertainty in deep learning. In: International Conference on Machine Learning, pp. 1050–1059 (2016)

5. Loder, R.T., Skopelja, E.N.: The epidemiology and demographics of hip dysplasia. ISRN Orthop. **2011**, 46 (2011)
6. Paserin, O., Mulpuri, K., Cooper, A., Hodgson, A.J., Garbi, R.: Real Time RNN Based 3D Ultrasound Scan Adequacy for Developmental Dysplasia of the Hip. In: Frangi, A.F., Schnabel, J.A., Davatzikos, C., Alberola-López, C., Fichtinger, G. (eds.) MICCAI 2018. LNCS, vol. 11070, pp. 365–373. Springer, Cham (2018). https://doi.org/10.1007/978-3-030-00928-1_42
7. Quader, N., Hodgson, A., Mulpuri, K., Cooper, A., Abugharbieh, R.: Towards Reliable Automatic Characterization of Neonatal Hip Dysplasia from 3D Ultrasound Images. In: Ourselin, S., Joskowicz, L., Sabuncu, M.R., Unal, G., Wells, W. (eds.) MICCAI 2016. LNCS, vol. 9900, pp. 602–609. Springer, Cham (2016). https://doi.org/10.1007/978-3-319-46720-7_70
8. Quader, N., Hodgson, A.J., Mulpuri, K., Cooper, A., Abugharbieh, R.: A 3D femoral head coverage metric for enhanced reliability in diagnosing hip dysplasia. In: Descoteaux, M., Maier-Hein, L., Franz, A., Jannin, P., Collins, D.L., Duchesne, S. (eds.) MICCAI 2017. LNCS, vol. 10433, pp. 100–107. Springer, Cham (2017). https://doi.org/10.1007/978-3-319-66182-7_12
9. Quader, N., Hodgson, A.J., Mulpuri, K., Schaeffer, E., Abugharbieh, R.: Automatic evaluation of scan adequacy and dysplasia metrics in 2-D ultrasound images of the neonatal hip. Ultrasound Med. Biol. **43**(6), 1252–1262 (2017)
10. Quader, N., Schaeffer, E.K., Hodgson, A.J., Abugharbieh, R., Mulpuri, K.: A systematic review and meta-analysis on the reproducibility of ultrasound-based metrics for assessing developmental dysplasia of the hip. J. Pediatr. Orthop. **38**(6), e305–e311 (2018)
11. Roy, A.G., Conjeti, S., Navab, N., Wachinger, C.: Inherent brain segmentation quality control from fully ConvNet Monte Carlo sampling. In: Frangi, A.F., Schnabel, J.A., Davatzikos, C., Alberola-López, C., Fichtinger, G. (eds.) MICCAI 2018. LNCS, vol. 11070, pp. 664–672. Springer, Cham (2018). https://doi.org/10.1007/978-3-030-00928-1_75

GRAIL 2020

Clustering-Based Deep Brain MultiGraph Integrator Network for Learning Connectional Brain Templates

Uğur Demir[1], Mohammed Amine Gharsallaoui[1,2], and Islem Rekik[1(✉)] (iD)

[1] BASIRA Laboratory, Faculty of Computer and Informatics,
Istanbul Technical University, Istanbul, Turkey
irekik@itu.edu.tr
[2] Ecole Polytechnique de Tunisie (EPT), Tunis, Tunisia
http://basira-lab.com

Abstract. Recently, the use of connectional brain templates (CBTs) has revolutionized the field of neurological disorder diagnosis through providing integral representation maps of a population-driven brain connectivity and effective identification of atypical changes in brain connectivity. Ideally, a reliable CBT should satisfy the following criteria: (1) centeredness as it occupies the center of the brain network population, and (2) discriminativeness as it allows to identify differences in brain connectivity between populations with different brain states (e.g., healthy and disordered). Existing state-of-the-art methods for connectional brain template (CBT) estimation from a population of multi-view brain networks (also called brain multigraphs) learn the integration process in a *dichotomized* manner, where different learning steps are pieced in together independently. Hence, such frameworks are inherently agnostic to the cumulative estimation error from step to step. This is a key limitation that we addressed by capitalizing on the power of deep learning frameworks residing in learning an *end-to-end* deep mapping using a single objective function to optimize to transform input data into target output data. In this paper, we propose to learn a *many-to-one* deep learning mapping by designing a clustering-based multi-graph integrator network (MGINet). Our MGINet inputs population of brain multigraphs (many) and outputs a single CBT graph (one). We first propose to tease apart brain multigraph data heterogeneity by first clustering similar samples together using multi-kernel manifold learning. In this way, we are optimally learning to disentangle the heterogeneity of our population and facilitating the integration task for our MGINet. Next, for each cluster, we first integrate the multigraph of each subject into a single graph, then merge the generated graphs into a *cluster-specific* CBT. Finally, we simply average the *cluster-specific* CBTs into a final CBT. Our experimental results show that our MGINet largely outperforms state-of-the-art methods in terms of centeredness and representativeness of the estimated CBT using both autistic and healthy brain multigraph datasets. Our clustering-based MGINet (cMGINet) source code is available at https://github.com/basiralab/cMGINet in Python.

C. H. Sudre et al. (Eds.): UNSURE 2020/GRAIL 2020, LNCS 12443, pp. 109–120, 2020.
https://doi.org/10.1007/978-3-030-60365-6_11

Keywords: Connectional brain template · Multi-view Network Fusion · Multigraph integrator network · Clustering-based learning · Brain connectivity

1 Introduction

The use of image-based brain templates (or atlases) [1–5] has been prevalent in automated brain parcellation and neuroscientific comparative studies –just to name a few applications. The concept of image brain atlas has been recently generalized to brain *graphs* by introducing the network-based brain atlas [6], also called a connectional brain template (CBT), as an average of a population of brain graphs, providing an integral connectional map charting the shared brain connectivities across subjects. In particular, [6] designed a diffusive graph shrinking technique using populations of *unimodal* (i.e. single connectivity type) brain graphs. While this method is able to derive a representative CBT of a population of brain graphs, the multimodal connectional aspect of the brain as *multigraph* is overlooked. In a multigraph representation of the brain wiring, the interaction between two anatomical regions of interest (ROIs), namely the multigraph nodes, is encoded in a set of edges of multiple types. Each edge type is defined using a particular measure for modeling the relationship between brain ROIs such as functional connectivity derived from resting state functional magnetic resonance imaging (MRI) or morphological similarity derived from structural T1-weighted MRI [7].

In the face of the oncoming 'tsunami' of disordered neuroimaging datasets [8,9] on brain graphs, namely the ongoing 14 connectomic brain data collection studies for Connectome Related to Human Disease (CRHD) initiative funded by the National Institutes of Health, there is an urgent need for handling connectomic datasets with unprecedented scale and heterogeneity via developing brain multigraphs integration framework for mapping brain connectivity. Hence, models that capture the multimodal aspect present in the brains connectional construct can build connectional templates that are highly designed for mapping both healthy and disordered populations [10]. To fill this gap, [11] proposed netNorm, a brain multigraph integration framework based on first selecting, for each pair of ROIs, the connectivity weight of most centered subject in the population to generate a representative population tensor stacking centered network views. Next, non-linear similarity fusion is used to integrate the population tensor into a single CBT. So far, existing CBT estimation methods [6,11–13], develop the integration process in dichotomized steps that are unrelated. Hence, such frameworks are inherently agnostic to the cumulative estimation error from step to step.

To address the limitations of such models, we formalize the integration tasks of a set of multigraphs as a deep learning task, where we aim to learn a many-to-one none-linear deep mapping from a population of multigraphs to a target CBT in an end-end-manner using a single objective loss function to optimize. Deep learning techniques such as convolutional neural networks (CNNs) and recurrent neural networks (RNNs) have achieved revolutionary performance results on a wide range of real world problems from different domains (e.g. chemistry, biology, medical imaging) [14]. Despite the indubitable performance of deep learning approaches, they are heavily dependent on the Euclidean properties of the input data which makes these techniques hard to apply on non-Euclidean data (i.e. irregular data shapes) such as graphs. Considering the emergent interest in non-Euclidean data (e.g. graphs) and the abundance of non-Euclidean data in real world problems, many methods have been set under the term *geometric deep learning* to mathematically suit graph structured data. The earliest applications of deep learning on graphs were rooted in [15], which proposed the graph neural network (GNN) architecture as a generalization of neural networks to graph structures. Other early attempts to extend CNN architecture to graphs were due to Bruna *et al.* [16,17], in which a convolution-like operator was defined in the graph spectral domain. Capitalizing on geometric deep learning, we propose a multigraph integrator network (MGINet) for estimating a CBT from a population of multigraphs. The MGINet is a two-stage integration approach that combines a *subject-specific* integration block and a *cluster-specific* integration layer for a given set of graphs. In the first integration block, MGINet integrates the multigraph of a single subject into a single graph. To effectively, extract a characteristic graph representation, MGINet identifies the useful edge types between connected nodes. This identification process results in generating *meta-paths* which are composite edge relations of multiple edge attributes. Meta-paths can be very useful to encapsulate the representative connections of a graph which evidently leads to a dimensionality reduction. The second stage consists in integrating the produced subject-specific graph in a particular cluster into a new graph that is representative of all graphs in that cluster. This second integration involves learning a weighted average vector under the constraint of minimizing the distance between the resulting template and all multigraphs in the populations. Through this end-to-end integration process, we learn a single graph representative of the multigraph population.

Given that brain multigraph data is inherently heterogeneous, we introduce clustering prior to data integration to reduce the heterogeneity and eventually facilitate the integration tasks for the MGINet. For clustering, we use multi-kernel manifold learning introduced in [18] which learns a pairwise similarity matrix between subjects by combining multiple Gaussian kernels with learned weights to better capture the data distribution at multiple scales (i.e., standard deviation of the learned kernels). Next, for each cluster of brain multigraphs, we train a MGINet to generate a cluster-specific connectional brain template. Finally, we use averaging (linear or nonlinear) to generate the final CBT that represents the entire population. We compare our methods performance on both autistic and typical brain multigraph populations against state-of-the-art method netNorm [11] while also experimenting with different cluster numbers.

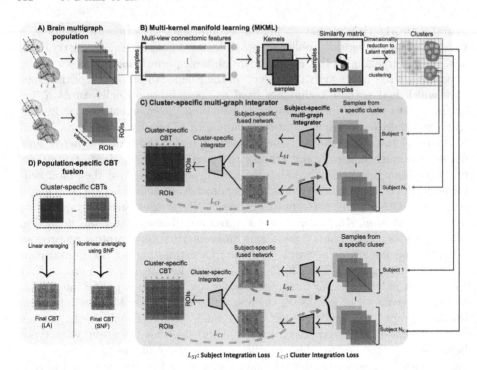

Fig. 1. Overview of the cluster-based multi-graph integrator (cMGINet) pipeline for connectional brain template estimation (CBT) from a population of brain multigraphs.

2   Proposed Method

We denote tensors by bold face Euler script letters, e.g., $\mathcal{T}$. Matrices are denoted by boldface capital letters, e.g., $\mathbf{X}$, and scalars are denoted by lower case letters, e.g., x.

Brain Multigraph Definition. The brain connectivity can be encoded in a graph $G = (V, E)$, where $V = \{v_1, ..., v_N\}$ is a set of $n = |V|$ nodes and $E \subseteq V \times V$ denotes a set of $m = |E|$ edges connecting pairs of nodes. The graph nodes represent brain ROIs while the graph edges represent the connectivity weights between two ROIs. We can describe connectivity weights using many metrics such as similarity in brain morphology or correlation between neural activities. Using multiple measures to capture the interactions between ROIs, we define a brain multigraph as a graph with multiple types of edges by assigning an $\mathbb{R}^p$ vector for each edge with p being the number of edge features (i.e., connectivity weights). Hence, a brain multigraph can be mathematically encoded in a tensor $\mathcal{A} \in \mathbb{R}^{n \times n \times p}$ to represent the edge features of the graph, which can also be viewed as a set of stacked adjacency matrices $\{A_k\}_{k=1}^p$, where $\mathcal{A}_k[i, j]$ is the value of the kth connectivity attribute of the edge connecting the ith and j^{th} nodes.

Problem Definition. Given a population of brain multigraphs $\{\mathcal{A}^s\}_{s=1}^N$ comprising N subjects, we aim to learn how to integrate them into a single brain graph, namely a CBT, that represents the center of the population while satisfying the following criteria: (1) centeredness as it occupies the center of the brain multigraph population, and (2) discriminativeness as it allows to identify differences in brain connectivity between populations with different brain states (e.g., healthy and disordered).

Overall Framework. Figure 1 illustrates the steps of our proposed cluster-based multi-graph integrator network (cMGINet) architecture for connectional brain estimation of a population of brain multigraphs. Our proposed method includes these major steps: **(i)** clustering subjects using MKML [18] to decrease the heterogeneity of the dataset, **(ii)** training a cluster-specific multigraph integrator network to extract a unique CBT for subjects in each cluster, and **(iii)** population-specific CBT fusion to output a more representative CBT at a population level. These steps will be explained in detail in what follows.

Clustering Subjects Using Multi-kernel Manifold Learning (MKML) [18]. Instead of using the whole population to estimate the population CBT, we first cluster similar samples together using MKML algorithm [18] to create a homogeneous data distribution within each cluster for effective MGINet training. MKML takes as input a multi-view connectivity feature matrix of size $N \times (n \times (n-1)/2) \times p)$ where, N is the number of subjects and $n \times (n-1)/2 \times p$ is the connectivity weights in the off-diagonal upper triangular parts of the multigraph tensor. The goal is to estimate similarity matrix S of size $N \times N$ that captures the pairwise similarity between subjects. We extract the multi-view connectomic feature vector $\mathbf{f_s}$ for each brain multigraph tensor $\mathcal{A}^s$ by concatenating the off-diagonal upper triangular parts of its frontal view matrices as follows:

$$\mathbf{f_s} = \|_{k=1}^p A_k^s[i,j]; \ \forall (1 \leq i,j \leq n); \ \text{where } j > i \tag{1}$$

where $\|$ denotes the concatenation operation.

MKML uses multiple Gaussian kernels with learned weights to better capture the sample similarity patterns. Compared to using predefined distance metrics such as the Euclidean distance, this strategy is more effective in capturing nonlinear relationships in our high-dimensional heterogeneous brain multigraph dataset. Gaussian kernels take the form of $\mathbf{K}(\mathbf{f_i}, \mathbf{f_j}) = \frac{1}{\epsilon_{ij}\sqrt{2\pi}} \exp\left(-\frac{\|\mathbf{f_i}-\mathbf{f_j}\|_2^2}{2\epsilon_{ij}^2}\right)$, where $\mathbf{f_i}$ and $\mathbf{f_j}$ denote the multi-view connectomic feature vectors for i^{th} and j^{th} subjects, respectively. The variance ϵ_{ij} is calculated using the mean Euclidean distances between the feature vectors of subjects i and j and their respective k nearest neighbors as follows:

$$\mu_i = \frac{\sum_{p \in \text{KNN}(\mathbf{f_i})} \|\mathbf{f_i}-\mathbf{f_p}\|_2}{k}, \varepsilon_{ij} = \frac{\sigma(\mu_i + \mu_j)}{2} \tag{2}$$

where σ represents the standard deviation of the kernel $\mathbf{K}$. MKML learns the similarity matrix $\mathbf{S} \in \mathbb{R}^{N \times N}$ by optimizing the following objective function:

$$\min_{\mathbf{S},\mathbf{L},\mathbf{w}} \sum_{i,j} -w_l \mathbf{K}_l \left(\mathbf{f}_i, \mathbf{f}_j\right) \mathbf{S}_{ij} + \beta \|\mathbf{S}\|_F^2 + \gamma \mathbf{tr}\left(\mathbf{L}^T \left(\mathbf{I}_n - \mathbf{S}\right) \mathbf{L}\right) + \rho \sum_l w_l \log w_l$$

Subject to: $\sum_l w_l = 1, w_l \geq 0, \mathbf{L}^T \mathbf{L} = \mathbf{I}_c, \sum_j \mathbf{S}_{ij} = 1$, and $\mathbf{S}_{ij} \geq 0$ for all (i,j), where:

$\star$ $\sum_{i,j} -w_l \mathbf{K}_l \left(\mathbf{f}^i, \mathbf{f}^j\right) \mathbf{S}_{ij}$ captures the relationship between the kernel distance and the similarity matrix with the intuition that if the kernel distance between subjects is high the learned similarity should be small.

$\star$ $\beta \|\mathbf{S}\|_F^2$ is the regularization term that prevents over-fitting.

$\star$ $\gamma \mathbf{tr}\left(\mathbf{L}^T \left(\mathbf{I}_n - \mathbf{S}\right) \mathbf{L}\right)$: $\mathbf{L}$ is an auxiliary low-dimensional matrix of size $N \times N_c$ where N is the number of subjects and N_c is the number of clusters, enforcing the low rank constraint on $\mathbf{S}$. The matrix $(\mathbf{I}_n - \mathbf{S})$ is essentially the graph Laplacian.

$\star$ $\rho \sum_l w_l \log w_l$ term enforces the selection of multiple kernels as it prohibits the learned weights from shrinking to 0, which might end up in selecting one kernel or zero kernels.

MKML objective function is non-convex; however, its terms depending on $\mathbf{S}$, w and $\mathbf{L}$ are convex. So an alternating tri-convex optimization method is adopted where we fix two of the variables and optimize for the other one [18]. The learned latent matrix $\mathbf{L}$ of size $\mathbb{R}^{N \times N_c}$ retains the similarities captured in $\mathbf{S}$ in a lower dimensional space which enhances the accuracy of clustering algorithms. K-means clustering is then applied on the latent matrix to group similar samples together.

Cluster-Specific MGINet. The MGINet takes in a set of multigraph tensors $\{\mathcal{A}^s\}_{s=1}^N$ and outputs a single $n \times n$ matrix (i.e. CBT) that is centered in terms of Frobenius distance to all connectivity tensors. The MGINet framework was inspired by graph transformer network introduced in [19], which we have adapted to our goal by introducing a new population-based objective loss function to optimize. In fact, while the original graph transformer network (GTN) [19] was first proposed to solve node classification task, here we adapt it to solve a multigraph integration task. Our MGINet consists of two parts. The first part reduces the dimensionality of the input *subject-specific* tensor $\mathcal{A} \in \mathbb{R}^{n \times n \times p}$ and transforms it into a more representative single graph encoded in a $n \times n$ matrix (**Fig. 1–C**). The second part generates for each cluster the final *cluster-specific* CBT by learning a weighted averaging of the previously produced subject-specific brain graphs. Extraction of single view networks out of multi-view graphs is done by meta-path generation as explained in [19]. Meta-paths can be used to explain relationships between nodes that cannot be characterized by a single edge type. Despite of their specificity, meta-paths are often hard to discover without an automated generation process specially when it comes to relatively complicated graphs. The meta-path generation is done via $(n_l + 1) \times 1 \times 1$ multi-channel convolutions applied on the connectivity tensor $\mathcal{A}$ where n_l is the number of subject graph integration layers. Given the meta-path h describing the relation R between two nodes which are not necessarily connected by a simple edge, we can define the adjacency matrix $\mathbf{A}_h$ as the multiplication of the adjacency matrices of the edge types included in the meta-path h as follows:

$$\mathbf{A}_h = \mathcal{A}_p ... \mathcal{A}_2 \mathcal{A}_1 \qquad (3)$$

where $\mathcal{A}_k$ denotes the adjacency matrix for the kth edge attribute, $(1, 2, ..., p)$ the different edge types of R with the tensor subscript denoting a unique edge type (or connectivity measurement in our scenario). In what follows, we explain how MGINet generates a meta-path adjacency matrix (Fig. 2).

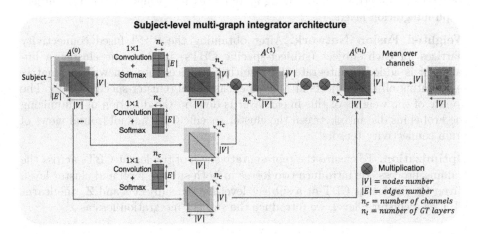

Fig. 2. Architecture of the subject-level integrator block of the proposed MGINet.

The main goal of our MGINet is to learn the dominant connectivity patterns across the multigraph tensor within a given population. In our case, a meta-path allows us to learn deeper relationships between ROIs through capturing the most salient connectivity weights for a brain multigraph with multiple edge types. Therefore, the subject-specific CBT will be generated through the learning of useful meta-paths extracted from subject connectivity tensor. The integration is done via multiplications of convolutions of the connectivity tensor $\mathcal{A}$. The first layer consists in the multiplication of two convolutions of the tensor $\mathcal{A}$. In the second layer, we multiply the resulting tensor from the first layer $\mathcal{A}^{(1)}$ by another convolution of the initial connectivity tensor $\mathcal{A}^{(0)}$. The MGINet consists in the superposition of n_l layers containing the same operations. At the lth layer, the resulting tensor $\mathcal{A}^{(l)}$ containing the softly selected edge types is obtained by:

$$\mathcal{A}^{(l)} = \mathcal{A}^{(0)} \times \text{softmax}(W_{\phi(l)}) \times \mathcal{A}^{(l-1)}, \; l > 1 \qquad (4)$$

Where $W_{\phi(l)} \in \mathbb{R}^{n_c \times p \times 1 \times 1}$ is the weight parameter of the 1×1 convolution layer $\phi_{(l)}$ that softly selects n_c views from the connectivity tensor $\mathcal{A}$ and n_c is the number of channels which is a hyperparameter. The resulting tensor $\mathcal{A}^{(l)} \in \mathbb{R}^{n \times n \times n_c}$ contains the meta-paths generated up until l^{th} graph transformer layer.

After processing the last layer n_l, we calculate the average over the channels of the final subject-specific CBT (i.e. resulting from the stack of n_l subject graph integration layers). This will reduce the tensor to a subject-specific CBT matrix $\mathbf{Q} \in \mathbb{R}^{n \times n}$. Same operations are applied to each subject in the cluster.

To ensure that the CBTs are representative of the initial brain connectivity graphs, we propose a novel loss function of our graph integrator minimizing the Frobenius distance between the fused subject-specific CBT matrix and every view of the connectivity tensors in the same cluster. As such, we are able to create learners that converge towards meta-path matrices that minimize final CBT estimation errors while gaining more representetiveness through n_l subject graph integration layers.

Weighted Fusion Network. After obtaining the $\mathbb{R}^{n \times n}$ fused connectivity matrices for each subject (subject-specific CBTs) in the same cluster, a linear layer is added to integrate the resulting matrices into a new $\mathbb{R}^{n \times n}$ matrix representing all the subjects at a given cluster level (cluster-specific CBT). The update of the weights of this linear layer is done in the direction of minimizing the Frobenius distance between the cluster specific CBT and all frontal views of brain connectivity tensors.

Optimization. To ensure the representativeness of the learnt CBTs across the training process, we introduce two losses in both subject level and cluster level. Given $\mathbf{Q}_s$ the learnt CBT at a subject level for the subject s and $\mathbf{Z}_c$ the learnt CBT at a cluster c level, we introduce the subject integration loss as

$$\mathcal{L}_{SI} = \frac{1}{N_c} \sum_{s=1}^{N_c} \sum_{k=1}^{p} ||\mathbf{Q_s} - \mathcal{A}_k^s||^2 \tag{5}$$

and the cluster integration loss as

$$\mathcal{L}_{CI} = \sum_{s=1}^{N_c} \sum_{k=1}^{p} ||\mathbf{Z_c} - \mathcal{A}_k^s||^2 \tag{6}$$

where N_c is the number of subjects contained in the cluster c. Hence, the global cMGINet loss function is expressed as:

$$\mathcal{L} = \mathcal{L}_{CI} + \lambda \mathcal{L}_{SI} \tag{7}$$

where λ is a hyperparameter used to scale the subject-specific integration loss. Having these losses, the learning process will tend to minimize the distance between the learnt CBT and all the population. As a result, the algorithm will maximize the centeredness of the learnt CBT at a subject level and at a cluster level.

Population-Specific CBT Fusion. In this section we merge the c cluster CBTs that each represent a portion of the population, in order to build the final CBT that represent the entire population. This step will be performed using linear and non-linear fusion methods. In linear averaging, we simply take the average of cluster CBTs while overlooking the possibly complex and nonlinear relationships between different clusters. In nonlinear averaging, we use similarity network fusion (SNF) introduced in [20]. SNF integrates multiple networks of same size into a single network that gathers both local and global similarities between fused networks.

3   Results and Discussion

Evaluation Dataset. For evaluation, we used a subset of the Autism Brain Imaging Data Exchange ABIDE I public dataset[1] comprising 155 autistic spectrum disorder (ASD) subjects (140 male and 15 female) and 186 normal control (NC) subjects (155 male, 31 female). Each subject has a T1-weighted MRI, which was processed using FreeSurfer to extract the right and left hemispheres. Following the parcellation of each hemisphere into 35 cortical regions of interest using Desikan-Killiany cortical atlas, we derive a brain multigraph using the following cortical attributes (i.e., edge types): maximum principal curvature, cortical thickness, sulcal depth, and average curvature. The connectivity strength between two ROIs is defined using the absolute difference of their average cortical attribute as introduced in [21]. For more details about the used cortical brain multigraphs we refer the reader to [11,22].

Parameter Setting. For MKML parameters, in two different runs, the number of clusters is empirically set to $N_c = 2$ and $N_c = 3$, respectively. For both runs, the number of kernels is set to 5, using the following standard deviation values $\sigma = 1.0, 1.25, 1.5, 1.75, 2$. For MGINet we trained the model using 300 epochs with hyperparameters $\lambda = 0.3$ and $n_c = 2$. For SNF, the number of nearest neighbors is set to $q = 20$. These values were empirically set.

Evaluation Measures and Results. The centeredness and representativeness of the estimated CBT is evaluated by measuring the Frobenius distance from the estimated template to each tensor view of each subject in the population. Frobenius distance between two matrices $\mathbf{A}$ and $\mathbf{B}$ is a scalar value and is calculated as: $d_F(\mathbf{A}, \mathbf{B}) = \sqrt{\sum_i \sum_j |a_{ij} - b_{ij}|^2}$. Frobenius distances calculated are normalized using the following formula as in [11] for fair comparison with netNorm : $d'_f = (d_f - mean_i)/(max_i - mean_i) + 1.5$, where $mean_i$ and max_i denote the average and maximum values of the Frobenius distances calculated between a given CBT estimation and its source population, respectively. d_F is a row vector of size $1 \times N$ that contains the distance between CBT and i^{th} view in the population.

For comparative evaluation, we benchmarked cMGINet against (i) state-of-the-art method netNorm introduced in [11], and (ii) MGINet trained on the whole population without clustering. In cMGINet the fusion step of merging resulting cluster CBTs into a single network representing the final CBT is conducted using one of the following merging techniques: linear averaging (average

---

[1] http://fcon_1000.projects.nitrc.org/indi/abide/.

of cluster CBTs) or nonlinear similarity network fusion (SNF), which nonlinearly diffuses graphs to ultimately fuse them [20].

Our cMGINet considerably outperformed netNorm [11] by achieving the minimum average Frobenius distance for all evaluation datasets in both hemispheres as shown in (**Fig.** 3). These results can be explained by comparing the inner workings of both methods. netNorm constructs a population representative tensor using cross-view feature vectors of subjects. For every pairwise connection between ROIs, the most representative feature vector is determined by its average Euclidean distance to the rest of the population multigraphs. In contrast, cMGINet takes into account the data heterogeneity and learns the optimized

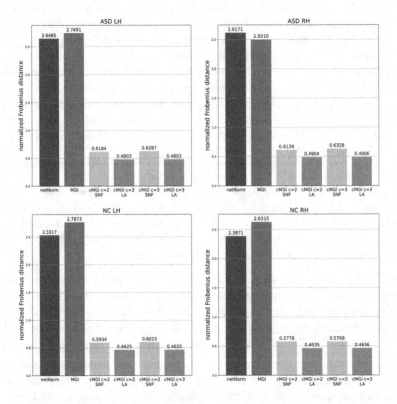

Fig. 3. Evaluation of cMGINet performance in estimating centered and representative connectional brain templates. In order to evaluate the centeredness of the learned connectional brain templates (CBTs), we compute the mean Frobenius distance between the estimated CBTs and the tensor views of all multigraphs in the population for both baseline methods as well as our proposed method for both hemispheres. In addition to netNorm introduced in [11] and MGINet without clustering, we evaluate our cluster-based MGINet on four populations while varying the number of clusters and using linear and non-linear averaging methods in the last integration step of cluster-specific CBTs. ASD: autism spectrum disorder. NC: normal control. RH: right hemisphere. LH: left hemisphere.

integration for each homogeneous set of multigraphs in an *end-to-end* manner. It is quite remarkable the effect that clustering had on MGINet performance. This might be explained by the fact that deep learning models might struggle to learn from heterogeneous data distribution; however, with a homogeneous training set to train on, their performance can be largely boosted.

4 Conclusion

In this paper, we proposed a cluster-based multigraph integrator network for connectional brain template estimation from a population of multi-view brain networks (or multigraphs). We showed that our cMGINet outperforms state-of-the-art methods in generating centered CBTs which better capture distinct connectional patters in brain multigraph populations. Specifically, by learning the manifold space where the mutligraphs are nested, we identified homogeneous clusters. Training our deep integrator on samples with a homogeneous distribution (i.e., belonging to a single cluster) remarkably improved the centeredness and representativeness of the learned CBTs in comparison with benchmarks. In our future work, we will extend the application of our framework to other populations with different neurological disorders. Our deep multigraph integration framework can also be extended to fuse signed and directed multigraphs derived from other MR modalities such as functional or diffusion MRI.

Acknowledgments. I. Rekik is supported by the European Union's Horizon 2020 research and innovation programme under the Marie Sklodowska-Curie Individual Fellowship grant agreement No 101003403 (http://basira-lab.com/normnets/).

References

1. Xue, Z., et al.: Simulating deformations of mr brain images for validation of atlas-based segmentation and registration algorithms. NeuroImage **33**, 855–866 (2006)
2. Rohlfing, T., et al.: The INIA19 template and neuromaps atlas for primate brain image parcellation and spatial normalization. Front. Neuroinf. **6**, 27 (2012)
3. Reuter, M., Schmansky, N.J., Rosas, H.D., Fischl, B.: Within-subject template estimation for unbiased longitudinal image analysis. Neuroimage **61**, 1402–1418 (2012)
4. Shi, F., et al.: Infant brain atlases from neonates to 1-and 2-year-olds. PloS One **6**, e18746 (2011)
5. Wu, G., et al.: Hierarchical multi-atlas label fusion with multi-scale feature representation and label-specific patch partition. NeuroImage **106**, 34–46 (2015)
6. Rekik, I., Li, G., Lin, W., Shen, D.: Estimation of Brain Network Atlases Using Diffusive-Shrinking Graphs: Application to Developing Brains. In: Niethammer, M., Styner, M., Aylward, S., Zhu, H., Oguz, I., Yap, P.-T., Shen, D. (eds.) IPMI 2017. LNCS, vol. 10265, pp. 385–397. Springer, Cham (2017). https://doi.org/10.1007/978-3-319-59050-9_31
7. Bassett, D.S., Sporns, O.: Network neuroscience. Nat. Neurosci. **20**, 353–364 (2017)
8. Pescosolido, B.A., et al.: Linking genes-to-global cultures in public health using network science. In: Handbook of Applied System Science, pp. 25–48 (2016)

9. Holmes, A.J., et al.: Brain genomics superstruct project initial data release with structural, functional, and behavioral measures. Sci. Data **2**, 1–16 (2015)
10. Yuan, L., et al.: Multi-source feature learning for joint analysis of incomplete multiple heterogeneous neuroimaging data. NeuroImage **61**, 622–632 (2012)
11. Dhifallah, S., et al.: Estimation of connectional brain templates using selective multi-view network normalization. Med. Image Anal. **59**, 101567 (2020)
12. Rekik, I., Li, G., Lin, W., Shen, D.: Estimation of shape and growth brain network atlases for connectomic brain mapping in developing infants. In: 2018 IEEE 15th International Symposium on Biomedical Imaging (ISBI 2018), pp. 985–989 (2018)
13. Dhifallah, S., et al.: Clustering-based multi-view network fusion for estimating brain network atlases of healthy and disordered populations. J. Neurosci. Methods **311**, 426–435 (2019)
14. Biswas, M., et al.: State-of-the-art review on deep learning in medical imaging. Front. Biosci. (Landmark Ed.) **24**, 392–426 (2019)
15. Scarselli, F., Gori, M., Tsoi, A.C., Hagenbuchner, M., Monfardini, G.: The graph neural network model. IEEE Trans. Neural Netw. **20**, 61–80 (2008)
16. Bruna, J., Zaremba, W., Szlam, A., LeCun, Y.: Spectral networks and locally connected networks on graphs. arXiv preprint arXiv:1312.6203 (2013)
17. Henaff, M., Bruna, J., LeCun, Y.: Deep convolutional networks on graph-structured data. arXiv preprint arXiv:1506.05163 (2015)
18. Wang, B., et al.: SIMLR: a tool for large-scale genomic analyses by multi-kernel learning. Proteomics **18**, 1700232 (2018)
19. Yun, S., Jeong, M., Kim, R., Kang, J., Kim, H.J.: Graph transformer networks. In: Advances in Neural Information Processing Systems, pp. 11983–11993(2019)
20. Wang, B., et al.: Similarity network fusion for aggregating data types on a genomic scale. Nat. Methods **11**, 333 (2014)
21. Mahjoub, I., Mahjoub, M.A., Rekik, I.: Brain multiplexes reveal morphological connectional biomarkers fingerprinting late brain dementia states. Sci. Rep. **8**, 1–14 (2018)
22. Soussia, M., Rekik, I.: Unsupervised manifold learning using high-order morphological brain networks derived from T1-w MRI for autism diagnosis. Front. Neuroinform. **12**, 70 (2018)

Detection of Discriminative Neurological Circuits Using Hierarchical Graph Convolutional Networks in fMRI Sequences

Xiaodan Xing[1,2], Lili Jin[3], Qinfeng Li[4], Lei Chen[1], Zhong Xue[1], Ziwen Peng[3,5(✉)], Feng Shi[1(✉)], and Dinggang Shen[1]

[1] United-Imaging Intelligence, Shanghai, China
feng.shi@united-imaging.com
[2] Medical Imaging Center, Shanghai Advanced Research Institute, Shanghai, China
[3] Center for the Study of Applied Psychology, South China Normal University, Guangzhou, China
pengzw@email.szu.edu.cn
[4] Laboratory of Psychological Health and Imaging, Shanghai Mental Health Center, Shanghai Jiao Tong University School of Medicine, Shanghai, China
[5] Department of Child Psychiatry, Shenzhen Kangning Hospital, Shenzhen Mental Health Center, Shenzhen, China

Abstract. Graph convolutional network (GCN) has shown its potential on modeling functional MRI connectivity and recognizing neurological disease tasks. However, conventional GCN layers generally inherit the original graph topology, without the modeling of hierarchical graph representation. Besides, although the interpretability of GCN has been widely investigated, such studies only identify several independently affected brain regions instead of forming them as neurological circuits, which are more desirable for disease mechanism investigation. In this paper, we propose a hierarchical dynamic GCN (HD-GCN), which combines the information from both low-order graph composed of brain regions and high-order graph composed of brain region clusters. The algorithm learns a consistent dynamic graph pooling, which helps improve the classification accuracy by hierarchical graph representation learning and could identify the affected neurological circuits. We employed two datasets to evaluate the generalizability of the proposed method: ADNI dataset containing 177 AD patients and 115 controls, and Obsessive-Compulsive Disorder (OCD) dataset including 67 patients and 61 controls. The classification accuracy reaches 89.4% on ADNI dataset and 89.1% on OCD dataset. The affected brain circuits were also identified, which are consistent with previous psychological studies.

Keywords: Graph convolution · Functional connectivity · Circuit detection

© Springer Nature Switzerland AG 2020
C. H. Sudre et al. (Eds.): UNSURE 2020/GRAIL 2020, LNCS 12443, pp. 121–130, 2020.
https://doi.org/10.1007/978-3-030-60365-6_12

1 Introduction

Functional MRI (fMRI) has been investigated to provide representative and discriminant imaging markers for neurological disease diagnosis due to its ability of detecting brain activation. The correlations of fMRI signals between each pair of brain regions form a symmetric functional connectivity matrix and reflect the connections between spatially distinct neurophysiological events. Such a brain connectivity network can be described as a graph, with brain anatomical regions as nodes and functional connectivity as edges. Considering the dynamic property of brain activation, the concept of dynamic functional connectivity is proposed to characterize temporal changes of neurophysiological correlations. Thus, dynamic graph analysis could provide essential insights on the brain connectivity changes in neurological patients.

Graph convolutional networks aim to learn graph representations using a convolutional neural network with a message passing model [4, 7], which updates the representations of every node layer by layer while maintains the graph topology. However, this model does not consider the hierarchical structures of the graph, and its performance of graph classification tasks is thus largely limited. To date, high-order graphical patterns are less explored. Some methods has been proposed to investigate the high order graph structure and graph coarsening algorithms, including Deepwalk [8] and node2vec [6] operations. In the context of graph convolutional networks, Ying et al. [12] proposed a differential pooling (DIFF-POOL) algorithm, which assigns every node into high-order clusters using a cluster assignment matrix. Yet, the dynamic property of brain activation has not been investigated. Also, they failed to produce a group-wise graph pooling for a given neurological disease, given most graph pooling algorithms generate distinctive pooling rules for each graph structure.

Although GCN has demonstrated satisfactory performance on classification tasks, its interpretability is still limited. Current networks use Class Activation Mapping (CAM) [13] or Gradient Guided CAM (Grad-CAM) [9] for interpretation and can only help identify one or two independent regions. These methods are thus limited for explaining neurological diseases because brain regions work together functionally to process information, and such abnormal areas could be one or multiple subnetworks containing multiple regions. However, brain regions usually integrate as groups to account for different cognitive tasks. For example, the Default Mode Network (DMN) was reported to affect AD, composed of posterior cingulate cortex, precuneus, medial prefrontal cortex and angular gyrus [5]. Researches on OCD have reported the corticostriatalthalamiccortical (CSTC) circuit as playing an important role in OCD classification [1].

In this paper, we propose a Hierarchical Dynamic GCN (HD-GCN) for functional MRI classification and interpretation. The objective is to address the above-mentioned two problems, as the hierarchical and dynamic nature of fMRI networks as well as the GCN interpretability. The proposed network identifies and processes high-order functional connectivity graph patterns from end to end. In HD-GCN, we used new node clustering and edge clustering layers to learn a group-wise graph pooling. These layers could help extract the hierarchical graph information and form high-order brain circuits. In addition, the dynamic graph convolutional layers are used on both the original functional connectivity graph and the high-order brain graph. Such a hierarchical design also improves the interpretability of graph convolutional networks for visualization of disease related connections and subnetworks.

2   Method

An overview of the proposed HD-GCN framework is shown in Fig. 1. Overall, dynamic graphs are first extracted from fMRI sequences using sliding windows, where nodes represent brain regions of interest (ROIs), and edges are pairwise correlations between nodes. Then, graphs are fed into a module of graph convolutional LSTM (GCLSTM) for low-order graph processing. Next, nodes and edges are clustered together, where brain circuits are embedded as nodes in the newly generated high order graphs. After that, the node representations and edge connections are refined through a module of edge learning. At last, graphs are used for diagnosis using a module of GCLSTM with global average pooling (GAP) and fully connected (FC) layers.

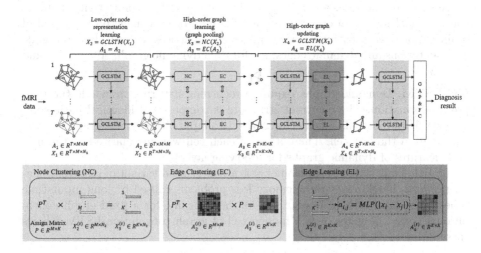

Fig. 1. Overview of the framework of the proposed HD-GCN algorithm. A denotes the adjacency matrix, and X represents the node feature matrix of a graph. (A_1, X_1) and (A_2, X_2) are the low-order graphs at the original functional connectivity space. (A_3, X_3) and (A_4, X_4) are the high-order graphs representing the connections and features of brain circuits. "$\Longleftrightarrow$" implies parameter sharing. Node Clustering (NC) and Edge Clustering (EC) generate clustered graphs by an assignment matrix P. The edge learning layer learns a refined connectivity structure between each pair of clusters by multi-layer perceptron (MLP).

2.1 Proposed HD-GCN for Classification

Graph Construction. A graph $\mathcal{G}(\mathcal{V}, \mathcal{E})$ is formed by a set of nodes and connections between these nodes, named as edges. Mathematically, a graph can be defined by two matrices: the node representation matrix X, describing the features of each node, and the edge matrix A, containing the topological structure of the graph. Conventionally, the nodes of functional brain graph are brain ROIs, and the edge between each pair of brain ROIs is computed by Pearson's correlation.

In our method, we proposed to use dynamic graph to model brain functions. Dynamic functional graph is defined by time-varying node representations and dynamic functional connectivity matrices. The respective node representation matrix $X^{(t)} \in R^{M \times N}$ describes the N-D features for each of the M nodes. T, M and N represent the number of time-points, the number of nodes and the dimension of features, respectively.

Each entry of the dynamic edge matrix at time-point t, $A^{(t)} \in R^{M \times M}$, represents the dynamic functional connectivity between two brain ROIs. Dynamic connectivity is calculated by sliding-window method. A window with fixed length slides over the entire fMRI time series, and only data points inside the window are used to calculate the functional connectivity.

Node representations are aggregated by the strength of connectivity in graph convolutional layers. In order to obtain the high order connectivity pattern of brain regions, we used functional connectivity matrices as both dynamic node representations and dynamic edges, i.e. for each dynamic graph, $A^{(t)} = X^{(t)}$ and $M = N$.

GC-LSTM. Dynamic graphs require a recurrent structure to handle the temporal information. The recurrent structure is composed of identical basic components, known as cells. Each cell receives two inputs: the current graph and the output from the last cell. The output of each cell was summarized as the new node features of dynamic graphs for following layers.

LSTM (Long-Short Term Memory) is a widely used variant of recurrent neural network. It addresses the memory loss problems caused by long input time series by recording the cell state C_t. Mathematically, for a fixed graph convolutional layer, the gates of t-th hidden cell of graph convolution LSTM follows these formula:

$$ForgetGate: f_t = \sigma(\omega_{xf} * X^{(t)} + \omega_{hf} * h_{t-1} + \omega_{Cf} \odot C_{t-1} + b_f)$$

$$InputGate: i_t = \sigma(\omega_{xi} * X^{(t)} + \omega_{hi} * h_{t-1} + \omega_{Ci} \odot C_{t-1} + b_i)$$

$$MemoryCell: C_t = f_t \odot C_t + i_t \odot tanh(w_{xc} * X^{(t)} + w_{hc} * h_{t-1} + b_c)$$

$$OutputGate: o_t = \sigma(\omega_{xo} * X^{(t)} + \omega_{ho} * h_{t-1} + \omega_{Co} \odot C_t + b_o)$$

$$OutputHiddenState: h_t = o \odot tanh(C_t),$$

$$(1)$$

where $X^{(t)}$ is the t-th feature representation matrix. σ represents the activate function, and w-s are graph convolutional kernels and b-s are biases. $*$ denotes the graph convolution operator using message passing model. Information flows from one cell to following cells along C_t, and inside each cell, information is selected to be discarded (by forget gate) or memorized (by input gate) from the cell state C_t. Cell state is then updated after forget gate and input gate. The final output is computed from the new cell state.

The simplified message passing model for graph convolutional operation can be mathematically written as,

$$X^{(t,l+1)} = \Phi(A^{(t,l)} X^{(t,l)} \Theta^{(t,l)}). \tag{2}$$

Here, $A^{(t,l)}$ and $X^{(t,l)}$ indicates the correlation matrix and feature matrix at layer l corresponding to time-point t respectively, $\Theta^{(t,l)}$ is the network parameter, and Φ is the activation function. The message passing model updates the features on every node according to its correlations with other nodes, which maintains the graph structure but lacks high-order representation learning.

Node Clustering and Edge Clustering. The graph clustering can be achieved by using an assignment matrix P to pool M nodes into K clusters as,

$$\begin{aligned} X^{(t,l+1)} &= P^T X^{(t,l)}, \\ A^{(t,l+1)} &= P^T A^{(t,l)} P. \end{aligned} \tag{3}$$

Here, each element of $P \in R^{M \times K}$ represents the contribution from one original node to a new cluster. In DIFFPOOL [12], the assignment matrix was learned from the output of graph convolutional layers, which means that each graph has its distinctive graph pooling rule according to their graph topology. However, for the purpose of disease classification and etiology investigation, a time-consistent and group-wise graph pooling rule is required. Therefore, we proposed to parameterize the assignment matrix P as a learnable parameter and updated its values during training of all time-points on batches.

Edge Learning. The Edge Clustering layer initialized the connections between brain circuit pair by averaging the original node connections. In order to combine connection information in the cascaded graph convolutional structure, the network was also generalized to learn edge features from the node representations. An Edge learning layer stacked behind a GC-LSTM layer on high order graphs learns refined high-order graph structures from the hidden representations of every cluster, as follows,

$$a_{i,j} = MLP(|x_i - x_j|), \tag{4}$$

where $a_{i,j}$ is the (i,j)-th element of matrix A and is learned by a nonlinear projection (MLP) of the absolute difference between the hidden representations of every clusters. According to Eq. 4, the symmetry and identity of adjacency matrices could be acquired by $a_{i,j} = a_{j,i}$ and $a_{i,i} = 0$.

2.2 Visualization of Affected Neurological Circuits

Integration and segregation features are often identified as major brain functional connectivity patterns. Although many algorithms [9,13] have tried to explain the

mechanism behind deep learning networks, they only focus on one or two independent regions. Our proposed method generates high-order graphs based on
brain region clusters, and therefore can highlight the most important subnetworks contribute to the classifier.

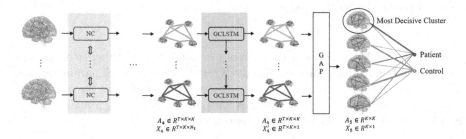

Fig. 2. The process of decisive brain circuit generation. The GAP layer reduces the
dimension of feature maps X_4'. The fully connected layer generates diagnosis result by
combining the contribution of each brain cluster. We identified the cluster, which corresponds to the largest weight for class Patient, as the most decisive cluster. According
to the node clustering parameter matrix P, major brain regions in the decisive cluster
could also be identified.

Figure 2 illustrates how such decisive subnetworks are determined. One global
average pooling (GAP) layer was stacked behind the final dynamic graph convolutional layer to reduce the temporal dimension of the feature maps. After batch
normalization, one fully connected (FC) layer was used to make a prediction.
The weight in FC layer could be used as the importance score of each cluster.
Moreover, based on the node clustering assignment matrix P, we can determine
the brain regions that were clustered to this decisive cluster. Herein, the top 5
brain regions which contribute the most to the decisive cluster are selected. In
this way, the brain subnetwork that contributes the most to the group differences
according to the HD-GCN framework can be identified and visualized.

3 Experiments

3.1 Data

We used fMRI images from two datasets to demonstrate the generalizability
of the proposed method. A total of 292 subjects were employed from ADNI II
dataset, of which 177 subjects are AD patients and 115 subjects are healthy controls. Functional images from ADNI II dataset were acquired with $TR = 3000\,ms$,
$TE = 30\,ms$, flip angle $= 80°$, resolution $= 3.3 \times 3.3 \times 3.3\,mm^3$, 48 axial slices with
137 dynamic time-points. Our in-house OCD dataset contains 128 subjects, of
which 60 subjects are OCD patients and 68 subjects are healthy controls. Functional images from OCD dataset were acquired with $TR = 2000\,ms$, $TE = 60\,ms$,

flip angle $= 90°$, resolution $= 3.0 \times 3.0 \times 4.0 \, \text{mm}^3$, 33 sagittal slices with 170 time-points.

To avoid over-fitting, we performed a five-fold validation on both dataset. All subjects are randomly partitioned into five equal size subsamples. Each subsample was used as validation dataset with other four subsamples as training dataset. All resting state fMRI data were pre-processed under a standard pipeline, including slice time correction, motion correction, spatial and temporal filtering and covariates regression. To obtain dynamic functional connectivity, a sliding window with a length of 60 time points and a stride of 7 time points were used.

Methods for ablation studies include Support Vector Machine (SVM) with linear kernel, Static Graph Convolutional Networks (Static GCN), and GC-LSTM [11]. For SVM, static functional correlation matrices computed from the entire fMRI sequences are reshaped as vectors of input features. Static GCN contains two conventional graph convolutional layers [7] followed by batch normalization layer and fully connected layers. GC-LSTM receives dynamic graphs as input.

3.2 Experimental Results

Table 1. Classification results on two datasets. The classification results were achieved after five-fold validation.

Dataset	Model	Accuracy	Sensitivity	Specificity
ADNI II	SVM	72.6%	64.9%	84.3%
	Static GCN	82.8%	84.7%	80.0%
	GC-LSTM	83.9%	84.2%	83.5%
	HD-GCN	**89.4%**	**90.4%**	**87.8%**
OCD	SVM	68.0%	68.3%	67.6%
	Static GCN	77.3%	80.0%	75.0%
	GC-LSTM	80.5%	78.3%	82.3%
	HD-GCN	**89.1%**	**91.7%**	**86.8%**

Classification Performance. The classification results on both datasets are shown in Table 1, and we also plotted the ROC curve in Fig. 3. For both datasets, we set the cluster number $K = 10$, and the number of features for each layer as $N_1 = 116, N_2 = 64$ and $N_3 = 16$. Since we are looking for the high order connectivity pattern of brain regions, we used functional connectivity matrices as low order adjacency matrices and initial node representations in our experiment, i.e. $A_1 = X_1$. In this case, the initial features on each brain region became the functional connectivity with all other nodes.

Decisive Clusters. Using BrainNetViewer [10], we plotted the most decisive clusters for both AD patients and OCD patients. The result is shown in Fig. 4.

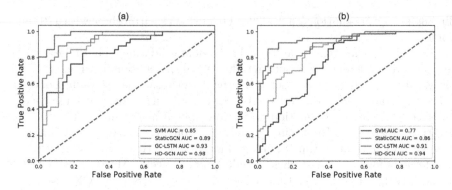

Fig. 3. The classification ROC curves on (a) ADNI dataset and (b) OCD dataset.

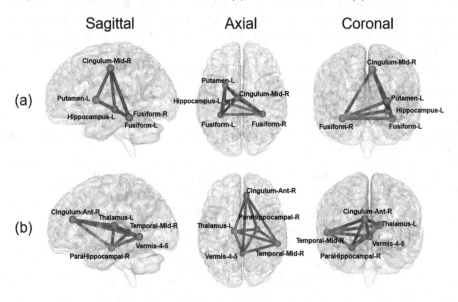

Fig. 4. The identified most decisive cluster for (a) AD patients and (b) OCD patients.

The top 5 regions composing the most decisive cluster for AD classification are left hippocampus, left and right fusiform, left putamen and right heschl. Hippocampus and temporal lobe have been widely identified as the affected region during the progression of AD [3]. The proposed method further investigates the neurological relevance among these regions. For OCD classification, the top 5 regions composing the most decisive cluster are right cingulum, right amygdala, right pallidum, right middle temporal lobe and vermis. As is shown in Fig. 4(b), the functional connectivity pattern affecting OCD reported from our method resembles with the CSTC circuits.

High Order Graph. Our algorithms partitioned original functional connectivity graph into ten clusters (i.e. $K = 10$), while the proposed Edge Clustering and Edge Learning layers compute the functional connectivity between brain region clusters and output the topology of high order functional graph. We visualized the averaged high order graph topology after Edge Learning layer from patients group in Fig. 5. We discovered that the most decisive cluster (cluster 3 for AD classification and cluster 7 for OCD classification) has the most degree centrality, which indicates that most links arise from the most decisive cluster.

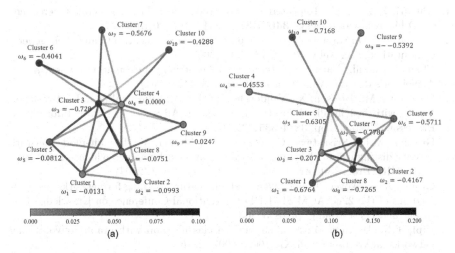

Fig. 5. Averaged high-order graph topology learned from Edge Learning Layer. The color of each node depends on its weight ω in the last fully connected layer. The length of edges (blue lines) are reciprocals of the results from the Edge Learning layer, and longer edges represent weaker correlations. Only edges with magnitude under 0.19 (the average edge magnitude for AD patients) or 0.35 (the average for OCD patients) are shown. Besides, we also visualize the betweenness centrality [2] of all edges shown. Betweenness centrality of an edge is the sum of the fraction of all pairs of shortest paths that pass through this edge, which indicates the graphical importance of this edge. (Color figure online)

4   Conclusion

We proposed a hierarchical dynamic graph convolutional network for fMRI classification. Our algorithm processes connectivity graphs hierarchically at different levels: low-order graphs based on anatomical regions and high-order graph based on brain circuits or subnetworks. A group-wise graph pooling is designed to connect low-order graphs to high-order graphs over the dynamic time range based on node clustering and edge clustering layers. An edge learning layer was also inserted to refine the relationship between each brain region cluster. Experiments demonstrated that our method not only performs better in terms of classification but also helps identify the affected brain circuits for neurological diseases and better understand the hidden mechanism behind graph convolutional networks and the pathology of brain diseases. However, there are still some limitations in this study. For example, we only used functional connectivity as node features, while features on each node could be the volume, image intensity and shape of every brain region.

References

1. Ahmari, S.E., et al.: Repeated cortico-striatal stimulation generates persistent OCD-like behavior. Science **340**(6137), 1234–1239 (2013)
2. Brandes, U.: On variants of shortest-path betweenness centrality and their generic computation. Soc. Netw. **30**(2), 136–145 (2008)
3. Chan, D., et al.: Patterns of temporal lobe atrophy in semantic dementia and Alzheimer's disease. Ann. Neurol. **49**(4), 433–442 (2001)
4. Defferrard, M., Bresson, X., Vandergheynst, P.: Convolutional neural networks on graphs with fast localized spectral filtering. In: Advances in Neural Information Processing Systems, pp. 3844–3852 (2016)
5. Greicius, M.D., Srivastava, G., Reiss, A.L., Menon, V.: Default-mode network activity distinguishes Alzheimer's disease from healthy aging: evidence from functional MRI. Proc. Nat. Acad. Sci. **101**(13), 4637–4642 (2004)
6. Grover, A., Leskovec, J.: node2vec: scalable feature learning for networks. In: Proceedings of the 22nd ACM SIGKDD International Conference on Knowledge Discovery and Data Mining, pp. 855–864 (2016)
7. Kipf, T.N., Welling, M.: Semi-supervised classification with graph convolutional networks. arXiv preprint arXiv:1609.02907 (2016)
8. Perozzi, B., Al-Rfou, R., Skiena, S.: Deepwalk: online learning of social representations. In: Proceedings of the 20th ACM SIGKDD International Conference on Knowledge Discovery and Data Mining, pp. 701–710 (2014)
9. Selvaraju, R.R., Cogswell, M., Das, A., Vedantam, R., Parikh, D., Batra, D.: Grad-CAM: visual explanations from deep networks via gradient-based localization. In: Proceedings of the IEEE International Conference on Computer Vision, pp. 618–626 (2017)
10. Xia, M., Wang, J., He, Y.: BrainNet Viewer: a network visualization tool for human brain connectomics. PLoS ONE **8**(7), e68910 (2013)
11. Xing, X., et al.: Dynamic spectral graph convolution networks with assistant task training for early MCI diagnosis. In: Shen, D., et al. (eds.) MICCAI 2019. LNCS, vol. 11767, pp. 639–646. Springer, Cham (2019). https://doi.org/10.1007/978-3-030-32251-9_70
12. Ying, Z., You, J., Morris, C., Ren, X., Hamilton, W., Leskovec, J.: Hierarchical graph representation learning with differentiable pooling. In: Advances in Neural Information Processing Systems, pp. 4800–4810 (2018)
13. Zhou, B., Khosla, A., Lapedriza, A., Oliva, A., Torralba, A.: Learning deep features for discriminative localization. In: Proceedings of the IEEE Conference on Computer Vision and Pattern Recognition, pp. 2921–2929 (2016)

Graph Matching Based Connectomic Biomarker with Learning for Brain Disorders

Rui Sherry Shen[1]($\boxtimes$), Jacob A. Alappatt[1], Drew Parker[1], Junghoon Kim[2], Ragini Verma[1], and Yusuf Osmanlıoğlu[1]

[1] Diffusion and Connectomics in Precision Healthcare Research Lab, Perelman School of Medicine, University of Pennsylvania, Philadelphia, USA
ruishen@seas.upenn.edu
[2] Department of Molecular, Cellular, and Biomedical Sciences, CUNY School of Medicine, City College of New York, New York City, USA

Abstract. Advances in neuroimaging techniques such as diffusion MRI and functional MRI enabled evaluation of the brain as an information processing network that is called connectome. Connectomic analysis has led to numerous findings on the organization of the brain its pathological changes with diseases, providing imaging-based biomarkers that help in diagnosis and prognosis. A large majority of connectomic biomarkers benefit either from graph-theoretical measures that evaluate brain's network structure, or use standard metrics such as Euclidean distance or Pearson's correlation to show between-connectomes relations. However, such methods are limited in diagnostic evaluation of diseases, because they do not simultaneously measure the difference between individual connectomes, incorporate disease-specific patterns, and utilize network structure information. To address these limitations, we propose a graph matching based method to quantify connectomic similarity, which can be trained for diseases at functional systems level to provide a subject-specific biomarker assessing the disease. We validate our measure on a dataset of patients with traumatic brain injury and demonstrate that our measure achieves better separation between patients and controls compared to commonly used connectomic similarity measures. We further evaluate the vulnerability of the functional systems to the disease by utilizing the parameter tuning aspect of our method. We finally show that our similarity score correlates with clinical scores, highlighting its potential as a subject-specific biomarker for the disease.

Keywords: Graph edit distance · Learning edit costs · Graph matching · MCMC · Connectome · Imaging biomarker

1 Introduction

Connectomics, the study of connectivity in the brain, has become an indispensable tool in the analysis of brain network organization. With the advent of

The original version of this chapter was revised: Figure 2 was updated with the correct numbers. The correction to this chapter is available at https://doi.org/10.1007/978-3-030-60365-6_21

C. H. Sudre et al. (Eds.): UNSURE 2020/GRAIL 2020, LNCS 12443, pp. 131–141, 2020.
https://doi.org/10.1007/978-3-030-60365-6_13

imaging techniques such as diffusion MRI or functional MRI, structural or functional connectivity of the brain regions can be modeled efficiently with connectomes, which are annotated graphs with nodes representing brain regions and edges denoting the relationship between region pairs. Graph theoretical analysis of connectomes has provided novel insights into the network organization of the healthy brain, widening our understanding of the relationship between brain and behavior. Additionally, it also introduced imaging biomarkers for neurological diseases and disorders in the brain along with useful information about their recovery patterns [8,25].

Connectomic analysis studies that utilize graph-theoretical tools generally focus on summary metrics that quantify network properties such as centrality, local efficiency, small-worldness, or participation coefficient [22]. While making statistical analysis with these measures is useful for characterizing neurological patterns at the population level, such an approach is limited in two main aspects which become more crucial in the assessment of brain disorders. First, these standalone measures describing network structure do not reveal information on how much an individual connectome differ from the healthy controls, which is essential for quantifying the subject-specific brain condition. Second, such standard measures evaluate generic properties of networks and do not leverage disorder-specific information that can enhance diagnostic evaluation. On the other hand, standard measures such as Euclidean distance [18] or Pearson's correlation [5] are commonly used to quantify similarity of a connectome (of possibly a patient) relative to a population (of controls) mainly by considering the edges independently. However, such standard measures are limited in not leveraging the connectivity information embedded into the network topology as well as not being specific to the disease.

Graph matching is a powerful technique for quantifying similarity between graphs by considering overall network topology in an optimization problem setup, which is well-studied and widely used in pattern recognition and computer vision over several decades [4]. Despite its strong potential, graph matching is seldom applied to connectomics [17], with matching-based measures recently starting to emerge to assess connectomic similarity [14] in healthy subjects [15] as well as in patients [13,16]. Although graph matching methods presented in such studies provide subject-specific connectomic similarity scores, they are still generic measures that do not incorporate disease-specific information. Although learning over graphs was proposed using Graph Neural Networks in determining proper distance metrics for connectomes [12], such methods are prone to overfitting and lack interpretability, especially for diseases that are generally examined using datasets of limited sample size. Consequently, connectomic biomarkers that i) quantifying differences among connectomes, ii) that utilize network topology information while iii) allowing to be tuned for specific diseases with limited sample size are desirable.

In this work, we propose a graph matching based method to quantify connectomic similarity, which can be trained for diseases to provide a subject-specific score that offers better separation between patients and controls. We use graph edit distance (GED) to attain graph matching, where we train edit cost parameters using Markov Chain Monte Carlo (MCMC) to make our method disease-specific. We consider the average GED between an individual's brain graph and the healthy control population as the measure assessing the state of the disease for that individual. We demonstrate the utility of our method over a moderate-to-severe traumatic brain injury (TBI) dataset to provide a connectomic measure for TBI. The contribution of our study is threefold. First, our score is subject-specific and it incorporates network topology information in the presence of pathology. Second, training of GED parameters provides us insights about which functional systems are affected more by the disease at the population level. Third, the proposed score can be used as a potential connectomic biomarker of the disease as it correlates well with clinical scores.

2   Methods

2.1   Graph Edit Distance

Human brain constitutes a network structure that can be represented as connectomes, which are simply graphs encoding structural or functional connectivity information of brain regions. The presence of neurological disorders commonly results in changes in the network topology of the brain, such as increased or decreased connectivity relative to a healthy subject. Consequently, measuring the connectomic dissimilarity of patients relative to healthy controls is of great importance in evaluating the effect of pathology.

Graph edit distance is a powerful graph matching technique that quantifies dissimilarity between two graphs G_p, G_q by calculating the minimum edit cost to transform G_p into G_q [7]. Edit cost in GED is accounted for by node insertion, deletion, and substitution operations, which is characterized by the amount of distortion that each operation introduces. These edit operations, also referred to as edit paths, reveal a correspondence between nodes of the two graphs. Since connectomes are special graphs where nodes correspond to brain regions that are based on the same anatomical atlas for all subjects, nodes in one graph are likely to get matched to their counterparts in another graph due to anatomical similarity across people. Structural differences due to subject-specific variations and alterations induced by pathology of neurological disorders, on the other hand, would lead to node mismatches, resulting in a larger graph edit distance.

Calculating edit cost requires defining proper cost functions for edit operations. Since neurological disorders can cause certain cognitive deficits that involve functional systems of the brain in varying degrees, the manifestation of structural alterations may be localized or widely distributed, and can be expected to differ by functional subnetworks rather than having a uniform effect over all nodes of the graph [8]. To capture such subnetwork dependent patterns at the population level, we define node substitution cost as the Manhattan distance between the node attributes weighted by a system-level dysfunction coefficient.

$$C(\mathbf{v}_i^p \rightarrow \mathbf{v}_j^q; \boldsymbol{\alpha}) = \alpha_{s_i} \times \alpha_{s_j} \times d_{Manhattan}(\mathbf{v}_i^p, \mathbf{v}_j^q) = \alpha_{s_i} \times \alpha_{s_j} \times ||\mathbf{v}_i^p - \mathbf{v}_j^q||_1 \quad (1)$$

where $\mathbf{v}_i^p$ and $\mathbf{v}_j^q$ represent ith and jth nodes in G_p and G_q, respectively. Each node $\mathbf{v}$ is annotated with an N_{node}-dimensional feature vector that represents its connectivity to the rest of the graph, where N_{node} is the number of nodes in the parcellation. The dysfunction coefficient $\alpha_{s_i} > 0$ characterizes the population-level effect of an edit operation for the system that node i belongs to. The GED parameter $\boldsymbol{\alpha} = \{\alpha_0, ..., \alpha_{N_{sys}}\}$ is an N_{sys}-dimensional vector representing the dysfunction coefficient for N_{sys} functional systems pre-defined by the atlas.

We define node insertion and deletion costs similarly, as the weighted Manhattan distance between the feature vector of the node and a zero vector.

$$C(\varnothing \rightarrow \mathbf{v}_j^q; \boldsymbol{\alpha}) = \alpha_{s_j}^2 \times d_{Manhattan}(\mathbf{0}, \mathbf{v}_j^q) = \alpha_{s_j}^2 \times ||\mathbf{v}_j^q||_1 \qquad (2)$$

$$C(\mathbf{v}_i^p \rightarrow \varnothing; \boldsymbol{\alpha}) = \alpha_{s_i}^2 \times d_{Manhattan}(\mathbf{v}_i^p, \mathbf{0}) = \alpha_{s_i}^2 \times ||\mathbf{v}_i^p||_1 \qquad (3)$$

Given the edit cost parameter $\boldsymbol{\alpha}$, GED aims to find optimum edit path $\mathcal{P}(G_p, G_q; \boldsymbol{\alpha})$ that transforms graph G_p into G_q with minimum edit cost.

$$d_{GED}(G_p, G_q; \boldsymbol{\alpha}) = \min_{(e_1, ... e_K) \in \mathcal{P}(G_p, G_q; \boldsymbol{\alpha})} \sum_{k=1}^{K} C(e_k; \boldsymbol{\alpha}) \qquad (4)$$

where e_k indicates an edit operation.

Utilizing the one-to-one mapping between nodes that ensues GED calculation, we calculate matching accuracy as the rate of correct matches of nodes between the two graphs [17].

$$A_{GED}|_{\mathcal{P}(G_p, G_q; \boldsymbol{\alpha})} = \frac{\sum_{k=1}^{N_{node}} \delta(e_k = \mathbf{v}_k^p \rightarrow \mathbf{v}_k^q)}{N_{node}} \qquad (5)$$

where $\delta(\cdot) = 1$ if the edit path matches a node to its counterpart and 0 otherwise.

We calculate the GED for each subject relative to the healthy population and consider the average of these distances as the disease biomarker for each subject. Since the exact computation of GED is intractable, we use the Kuhn-Munkres algorithm to calculate an approximate solution to the problem [20].

2.2 Edit Cost Parameter Estimation

In order to tailor the similarity measure specifically for one brain disorder, we train our algorithm to learn the system-level dysfunction coefficient $\boldsymbol{\alpha}$ by using the Metropolis-Hastings algorithm, a Markov chain Monte Carlo (MCMC) method. Our objective in training is based on our hypothesis that matching accuracy between a patient and a healthy control should be low due to distortions induced by disease while matching accuracy between healthy controls should be high due to a lack of pathology. This objective can be achieved by minimizing the following energy function:

$$E_d[\tilde{\boldsymbol{\alpha}}, \mathbf{G}] = \frac{1}{N_p} \sum_{i=1}^{N_p} \max\{0, -(\overline{A_{GED}}|_{\mathcal{P}(\mathbf{G}_c; \tilde{\alpha})} - A_{GED}|_{\mathcal{P}(G_{p_i}, \mathbf{G}_c; \tilde{\alpha})}) + \gamma\} \qquad (6)$$

where $\mathbf{G}$ denotes the dataset of graphs, $\overline{A_{GED}}|_{\mathcal{P}(\mathbf{G_c};\tilde{\alpha})}$ is the mean of average matching accuracy of healthy controls while $A_{GED}|_{\mathcal{P}(G_{p_i},\mathbf{G_c};\tilde{\alpha})}$ is the average matching accuracy of patient p_i relative to healthy controls. Maximizing $E_d[\tilde{\alpha}, \mathbf{G}]$ encourages matching accuracy among controls to become higher than matching accuracy between patients and controls at least by a margin γ. The estimated dysfunction coefficient $\tilde{\alpha}$ is therefore tuned to capture disease-related distortion in the brain.

We further impose the following prior term to ensure that all dysfunction coefficients would be positive:

$$E_p[\tilde{\alpha}] = \begin{cases} 0 & \text{if } \tilde{\alpha}_i > 0, \ \forall i \in \{0, .., N_{sys}\} \\ +\infty & \text{otherwise} \end{cases} \tag{7}$$

Thus, final objective function is defined as follows:

$$E[\tilde{\alpha}, \mathbf{G}] = E_d[\tilde{\alpha}, \mathbf{G}] + E_p[\tilde{\alpha}] \tag{8}$$

We apply simulated annealing for the optimization with the temperature T controlling the annealing schedule. Current parameter $\tilde{\alpha}^t$ will be updated by a new parameter $\tilde{\alpha}^{t+1}$ with the acceptance rate:

$$a = \min\{1, \exp\{-\frac{E[\tilde{\alpha}^{t+1}, \mathbf{G}] - E[\tilde{\alpha}^t, \mathbf{G}]}{T}\}\} \tag{9}$$

2.3   Interpretation of Dysfunction Coefficients

To interpret the estimated dysfunction coefficients, we highlight that the nodal structural alterations captured by the Manhattan distance between a subject and a healthy control would have two components: difference due to disease-induced pathology and non-disease-related difference due to subject-specific variations. Tuning GED for dysfunction coefficients could give us information about the vulnerability of systems to the disease. Intuitively, a larger dysfunction coefficient will discourage a node in a patient from matching to its counterpart in a healthy control. Likewise, a small dysfunction coefficient will encourage correct matching of nodes even with a large difference between two nodal features. Since our objective function maximizes matching accuracy within controls while minimizing matching accuracy between patients and controls, functional systems that are affected by the disease will have a larger dysfunction coefficient to encourage mismatches for patients. On the other hand, a region where non-disease-related difference is dominant will have a small dysfunction coefficient to improve matching accuracy for controls. Therefore, learning of dysfunction coefficients in MCMC is equivalent to estimating the distribution of pathology in connectomes at the systems level.

3   Experiments

3.1   Dataset and Preprocessing

We validate our method over a traumatic brain injury dataset consisting of 34 moderate-to-severe patients (12 female) and 35 healthy controls (9 female) that pass quality assurance, with the age of patients ranging from 18 to 65 years (mean $= 33.9$ years, std $= 14.9$ years), and the age of healthy controls ranging from 19 to 56 years (mean $= 34.9$ years, std $= 10.3$ years), respectively. Imaging scans are taken at 3 months post-injury. The Glasgow Outcome Scale-Extended (GOSE) is used to assess global functional outcome of the TBI patients at the time of imaging (range $= [2, 8]$, mean $= 5.1$, std $= 1.5$).

Diffusion weighted imaging scans are acquired on a Siemens 3T TrioTim whole-body scanner with an 8-channel array head coil (single-shot, spin-echo sequence, TR/TE $= 6500/84$ ms, b $= 1000$ s/mm^2, 30 directions, flip angle $= 90°$, resolution $= 2.2 \times 2.2 \times 2.2$ mm). High-resolution T1-weighted anatomic images are also obtained using a 3D MPRAGE imaging sequence with TR $= 1620$ ms, TI $= 950$ ms, TE $= 3$ ms, flip angle $= 15°$, 160 contiguous slices of 1.0 mm thickness, FOV $= 192 \times 256$ mm^2, 1NEX, resolution $= 1 \times 1 \times 1$ mm. 100 regions of interests from Schaefer atlas [21] and additional 16 subcortical regions are extracted to represent the nodes of the structural network (116 nodes in total). A mask is defined using voxels with an FA of at least 0.15 for each subject. We perform deterministic tractography to generate and select 10 million streamlines, which is seeded randomly within the mask. Angle curvature threshold of $60°$, and a minimum and maximum length threshold of 5 mm and 400 mm are applied, resulting in a 116×116 adjacency matrix of weighted connectivity values, where each element represents the number of streamlines between regions. Eight functional systems are identified including 7 subnetworks as described in [24] and another for representing subcortical regions.

3.2   Experimental Setup

We conduct fivefold cross-validation to evaluate our method. Each testing set consists of 14 subjects and each training set consists of 55 subjects. In the training, 8 dysfunction coefficients are initialized with equal weights $\tilde{\alpha}^0 = [1, ..., 1]$. We use Multivariate Gaussian distribution $\alpha^{t+1} \sim \mathcal{N}(\tilde{\alpha}^t | \Sigma)$ with $\sigma^2 = 0.001$ as the transition probability for iteration $t + 1$ to generate new parameters. We set the margin as $\gamma = 0.5$. The temperature for simulated annealing is initially set as $T_0 = 0.01$ and scheduled to decrease as number of iteration $t \geq 0$ increases, following the equation $T = \frac{T_0}{\ln(t+1)}$. We set the maximum iterations of MCMC to be 100 for each fold.

In evaluating test subjects in each fold, we compare our proposed measure of GED with training of parameters (denoted GED-tr) with two commonly used connectomic similarity measures: Euclidean distance and Pearson's distance (defined as $1 - r_{Pearson}$). We evaluate the effect of training dysfunction coefficients in GED-tr by contrasting it with the standard GED without parameter tuning (denoted GED-st). We normalized all four measure s by calculating z-score to make them comparable. All measures were validated at both population and subject-specific level. For the population analysis, we use Welch's t-test to examine the group difference of the dissimilarity score between patients and healthy controls for each fold and use Hedges' g method to estimate effect size. As each testing set is independent, p-values and effect sizes in the 5-fold study can be combined using Fisher's method [6] and inverse variance-weighted average method [10]. For the subject-specific analysis, we use linear regression to examine the relationship between each measure and the GOSE score.

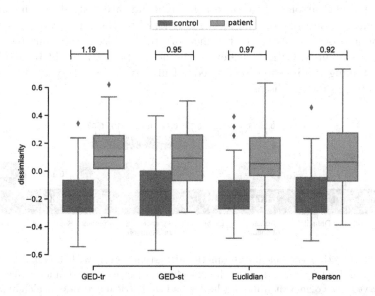

Fig. 1. Dissimilarity scores of subjects in each group (healthy controls and patients) with respect to healthy control population (values are normalized using z-score for comparison). Our proposed method GED-tr achieves the best separation by reducing variation of scores in controls and increasing the separation between patients and controls. Note that, effect sizes for significant group differences between patients and controls are shown above boxes, with significance level after Bonferroni correction being $p \leq 0.0125$.

3.3   Results and Discussions

Population Analysis

Dissimilarity at Connectome Level. Dissimilarity of subjects relative to healthy controls is shown in Fig. 1 along with effect sizes of group differences between patients and controls. We observed that although all four dissimilarity measures show significant group differences between patients and controls (with $p < 0.0125$, after Bonferroni multiple comparison correction), our proposed method GED-tr with parameter tuning demonstrates the largest group difference with an effect size of 1.19, achieving the best separation between patients and healthy controls on the TBI dataset. It is followed by Euclidean, GED-st, and Pearson distance with effect sizes of 0.97, 0.95, and 0.92, respectively. Comparing group differences between patients and controls for GED with and without training of parameters, we observe that GED-tr shows improvements in reducing the score range and variation in controls while preserving the score range for patients, highlighting the importance of training parameters for the disease. It is interesting to note that effect size of GED-st is similar to those of Euclidean and Pearson's distance, which might indicate that, although standard GED considers network topology that is ignored by the other two measures, it does not improve sensitivity of the measure to the disease without parameter tuning. In summary, GED-tr achieving the best separation might be attributed to it combining the information embedded in network topology with tuning of the parameters for the disease.

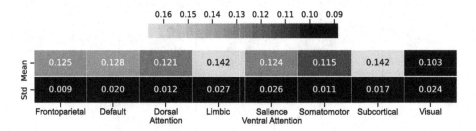

Fig. 2. Dysfunction coefficients at functional systems level, with larger dysfunction coefficients indicating a dominant pathology effect at the associated functional systems. We observe large coefficient values for limbic and subcortical networks, which highlights their vulnerability to injury. Note that, dysfunction coefficients are normalized by the total sum of coefficients to show the relative vulnerability of the systems.

System-Level Dysfunction Coefficients. We present the system-level dysfunction coefficients estimated by our algorithm for each functional system in Fig. 2. The limbic system and the subnetwork consisting of subcortical regions are shown to have the largest values among eight functional systems. These results indicate that network topology of the nodes comprising these systems is affected by TBI the most. This finding is supported by the significant decline in fractional anisotropy and the volume reduction in these two subnetworks in the presence of TBI [3,23,26]. Limbic system and subcortical regions, which are generally associated with memory and regulating emotions [11,19], also overlaps with the cognitive deficits such as memory loss and emotional disorders that are commonly observed after the brain injury [1]. Our results suggest that default mode, frontoparietal, salience ventral attention, and dorsal attention network show TBI specific patterns that can help discriminate TBI patients from healthy controls. Structural alteration of these regions might be correlated with impairment of sustained attention and executive function in TBI [2,9]. We note that, since these results indicate the level of dysfunction at 3 months post-injury, we could expect to see more immediate or long-term outcomes of the disease by evaluating a longitudinal TBI dataset that spans acute phase of the disease up to a year post-injury.

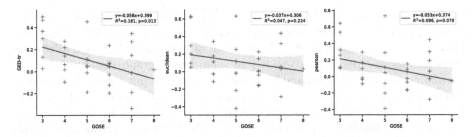

Fig. 3. Linear regression with GOSE in the patient population. The proposed measure GED-tr ($p = 0.013, R^2 = 0.181$) has significant linear relationship with GOSE. Euclidean distance ($p = 0.224, R^2 = 0.047$) and Pearson distance ($p = 0.079, R^2 = 0.096$) are not significant in terms of linear regression with GOSE. Note that, significance level after Bonferroni correction is $p \leq 0.016$.

Subject-Specific Analysis. Lastly, we report the linear regression analysis results between each measure and the GOSE score for the patient population in Fig. 3. We observe that the proposed measure GED-tr shows a significant negative correlation with GOSE and demonstrates the highest relationship with $R^2 = 0.181$, while neither Euclidean nor Pearson distance shows significant correlation. The results demonstrate that our measure quantifying dissimilarity of patients relative to controls correlates well with the clinical score, which shows its potential as a subject-specific biomarker for the disease. It is interesting to note that, although we observed in Fig. 1 that our method achieves the smallest variation among the patient group, it shows a higher correlation with the clinical score relative to Euclidean and Pearson distance as shown in Fig. 3. This might suggest that our proposed score discards non-disease-related variations while preserving information about the pathology.

4   Conclusion

In this study, we present a novel subject-specific measure that utilizes a learning-based graph edit distance to quantify dissimilarity of patients relative to healthy controls. Our measure provides better separation between patients and controls for the specific disease as it learns the pattern of the pathology at functional systems level. With the optimal parameters obtained via MCMC, we demonstrate on a TBI dataset that our method shows superiority over alternative connectomic dissimilarity measures in terms of increased group differences between patients and healthy controls. Our method enables a multi-resolution analysis of brain dysfunction, with the GED capturing subject-specific structural alterations due to the disease at the level of the whole brain, and the parameter tuning capturing the vulnerability of functional systems to pathology. Moreover, our measure is clinically meaningful, since it correlates well with a commonly used clinical measure of functional outcome in TBI, highlighting its potential to be used as a connectomic biomarker for neurological diseases.

We note that factors external to the disease such as age, gender, and volume of brain, as well as inaccuracies arising from data acquisition and tractographic biases, could have affected clinical outcomes of our study. Although effects of these factors are partially alleviated by minimizing graph distance between healthy controls, we will expand our analysis to regress out these effects in our future work. In this work, we only demonstrate the utility of our method with a case study on structural connectomes of TBI patients, the proposed method can easily be customized as a biomarker for other diseases and disorders, and be extended to capture the patterns of change over both functional and structural connectomes. The proposed measure can further be applied in domains other than disease quantification, such as clustering brain states, participant identification using connectomic fingerprinting, as well as longitudinal analysis of connectomes.

References

1. Blennow, K., et al.: Traumatic brain injuries. Nat. Rev. Dis. Primers **2**(1), 1–19 (2016)
2. Bonnelle, V., et al.: Default mode network connectivity predicts sustained attention deficits after traumatic brain injury. J. Neurosci. **31**(38), 13442–13451 (2011)
3. Caeyenberghs, K., et al.: Brain connectivity and postural control in young traumatic brain injury patients: a diffusion MRI based network analysis. NeuroImage Clin. **1**(1), 106–115 (2012)
4. Conte, D., Foggia, P., Sansone, C., Vento, M.: Thirty years of graph matching in pattern recognition. Int. J. Pattern Recogn. Artif. Intell. **18**(03), 265–298 (2004)
5. Finn, E.S., et al.: Functional connectome fingerprinting: identifying individuals using patterns of brain connectivity. Nat. Neurosci. **18**(11), 1664–1671 (2015)
6. Fisher, R.A.: Statistical methods for research workers. In: Kotz, S., Johnson, N.L. (eds.) Breakthroughs in Statistics, pp. 66–70. Springer, New York (1992). https://doi.org/10.1007/978-1-4612-4380-9_6
7. Gao, X., Xiao, B., Tao, D., Li, X.: A survey of graph edit distance. Pattern Anal. Appl. **13**(1), 113–129 (2010)
8. Griffa, A., Baumann, P.S., Thiran, J.P., Hagmann, P.: Structural connectomics in brain diseases. Neuroimage **80**, 515–526 (2013)
9. Han, K., Chapman, S.B., Krawczyk, D.C.: Disrupted intrinsic connectivity among default, dorsal attention, and frontoparietal control networks in individuals with chronic traumatic brain injury. J. Int. Neuropsychological Soc. **22**(2), 263–279 (2016)
10. Hartung, J., Knapp, G., Sinha, B.K.: Statistical Meta-Analysis with Applications, vol. 738. Wiley, Hoboken (2011)
11. Kandel, E.R., Schwartz, J.H., Jessell, T.M., Siegelbaum, S., Hudspeth, A.: Principles of Neural Science, vol. 4. McGraw-Hill, New York (2000)
12. Ktena, S.I., et al.: Distance metric learning using graph convolutional networks: application to functional brain networks. In: Descoteaux, M., Maier-Hein, L., Franz, A., Jannin, P., Collins, D.L., Duchesne, S. (eds.) MICCAI 2017. LNCS, vol. 10433, pp. 469–477. Springer, Cham (2017). https://doi.org/10.1007/978-3-319-66182-7_54

13. Ktena, S.I., Parisot, S., Passerat-Palmbach, J., Rueckert, D.: Comparison of brain networks with unknown correspondences. arXiv preprint arXiv:1611.04783 (2016)
14. Mheich, A., Wendling, F., Hassan, M.: Brain network similarity: methods and applications. Netw. Neurosci. **4**(3), 507–527 (2020)
15. Osmanlıoğlu, Y., Alappatt, J.A., Parker, D., Verma, R.: Connectomic consistency: a systematic stability analysis of structural and functional connectivity. J. Neural Eng. **17**(4), 045004 (2020). https://doi.org/10.1088/1741-2552/ab947b
16. Osmanlıoğlu, Y., et al.: A graph representation and similarity measure for brain networks with nodal features. In: Stoyanov, D., et al. (eds.) GRAIL/Beyond MIC -2018. LNCS, vol. 11044, pp. 14–23. Springer, Cham (2018). https://doi.org/10.1007/978-3-030-00689-1_2
17. Osmanlıoğlu, Y., et al.: System-level matching of structural and functional connectomes in the human brain. NeuroImage **199**, 93–104 (2019)
18. Ponsoda, V., et al.: Structural brain connectivity and cognitive ability differences: a multivariate distance matrix regression analysis. Hum. Brain Mapp. **38**(2), 803–816 (2017)
19. Preston, A.R., Eichenbaum, H.: Interplay of hippocampus and prefrontal cortex in memory. Curr. Biol. **23**(17), R764–R773 (2013)
20. Riesen, K., Bunke, H.: Approximate graph edit distance computation by means of bipartite graph matching. Image Vis. Comput. **27**(7), 950–959 (2009)
21. Schaefer, A., et al.: Local-global parcellation of the human cerebral cortex from intrinsic functional connectivity MRI. Cereb. Cortex **28**(9), 3095–3114 (2018)
22. Sporns, O.: Graph theory methods: applications in brain networks. Dialogues Clin. Neurosci. **20**(2), 111 (2018)
23. Stevens, M.C., Lovejoy, D., Kim, J., Oakes, H., Kureshi, I., Witt, S.T.: Multiple resting state network functional connectivity abnormalities in mild traumatic brain injury. Brain Imaging Behav. **6**(2), 293–318 (2012)
24. Yeo, B.T., et al.: The organization of the human cerebral cortex estimated by intrinsic functional connectivity. J. Neurophysiol. **106**, 1125–1165 (2011)
25. Zhang, D., Raichle, M.E.: Disease and the brain's dark energy. Nat. Rev. Neurol. **6**(1), 15–28 (2010)
26. Zhu, Y., et al.: Loss of microstructural integrity in the limbic-subcortical networks for acute symptomatic traumatic brain injury. BioMed Res. Int. **2014**, 548392 (2014). https://doi.org/10.1155/2014/548392

Multi-scale Profiling of Brain Multigraphs by Eigen-Based Cross-diffusion and Heat Tracing for Brain State Profiling

Mustafa Sağlam and Islem Rekik[✉] [iD]

BASIRA Lab, Faculty of Computer and Informatics,
Istanbul Technical University, Istanbul, Turkey
irekik@itu.edu.tr
http://basira-lab.com

Abstract. The individual brain can be viewed as a highly-complex *multigraph* (i.e. a set of graphs also called connectomes), where each graph represents a unique connectional view of pairwise brain region (node) relationships such as function or morphology. Due to its multi-fold complexity, understanding how brain disorders alter not only a single view of the brain graph, but its *multigraph representation* at the individual and population scales, remains one of the most challenging obstacles to profiling brain connectivity for ultimately disentangling a wide spectrum of brain states (e.g.., healthy vs. disordered). Existing graph theory based works on comparing brain graphs in different states have major drawbacks. *First*, these techniques are conventionally designed to operate on single brain graphs, while brain multigraph representations remain widely untapped. *Second*, the bulk of such works lies in using graph comparison techniques such as kernel-based or graph distance editing methods, which fail to simultaneously satisfy graph scalability, node- and permutation-invariance criteria. To address these limitations and while cross-pollinating the fields of spectral graph theory and diffusion models, we unprecedentedly propose an eigen-based cross-diffusion strategy for multigraph brain integration, comparison, and profiling. Specifically, we first devise a brain multigraph fusion model guided by eigenvector centrality to rely on most central nodes in the cross-diffusion process. Next, since the graph spectrum encodes its shape (or geometry) as if one can hear the shape of the graph, for the first time, we profile the *fused multigraphs* at several diffusion timescales by extracting the compact heat-trace signatures of their corresponding Laplacian matrices. Such brain multigraph heat-trace profiles nicely satisfy the three graph comparison criteria. More importantly, we reveal for the first time autistic and healthy profiles of morphological brain multigraphs, derived from T1-w magnetic resonance imaging (MRI), and demonstrate their discriminability in boosting the classification of unseen samples in comparison with state-of-the-art methods. This study presents the first step towards hearing the shape of the brain multigraph that can be leveraged

GitHub: http://github.com/basiralab.

© Springer Nature Switzerland AG 2020
C. H. Sudre et al. (Eds.): UNSURE 2020/GRAIL 2020, LNCS 12443, pp. 142–151, 2020.
https://doi.org/10.1007/978-3-030-60365-6_14

for profiling and disentangling comorbid neurological disorders, thereby advancing precision medicine.

Keywords: Brain multigraph profiling · Eigen-based graph cross-diffusion · The shape of a graph · Neurological disorders · Graph heat-tracing

1   Introduction

The development of network neuroscience [1] aims to present a holistic picture of the brain graph (also called network or connectome), a universal representation of heterogeneous pairwise brain region relationships (e.g.., correlation in neural activity or dissimilarity in morphology). Due to its multi-fold complexity, the underlying causes of neurological and psychiatric disorders, such as Alzheimer's disease, autism, and depression remain largely unknown and difficult to pin down [2,3]. How these brain disorders unfold at the individual and population scales remains one of the most challenging obstacles to understanding how the *brain graph* gets altered by disorders, let alone a *brain multigraph*. Indeed, using different measurements, one can build a brain multigraph, composed of a set of graphs, each capturing a unique view of the brain construct (such as morphology or function) [1,4,5]. Profiling brain multigraphs remains a formidable challenge to identify the most representative and shared brain alterations caused by a specific disorder, namely *'disorder profile'*, in a population of brain multi-graphs. Such integral profile can be revealed by what we name as *multigraph brain profile*, which would constitute an unprecedented contribution to network neuroscience and brain mapping literature as it would chart the connectional geography of the brain.

Estimating such profiles highly depends on using reliable graph comparison techniques. However, existing graph theory based works on comparing brain graphs in different states have major drawbacks. *First*, these techniques are conventionally designed to operate on single brain graphs, while brain multigraph representations remain widely untapped. *Second*, the bulk of such works lies in using graph comparison techniques such as kernel-based or graph distance editing methods, which fail to simultaneously satisfy graph scalability, node- and permutation-invariance criteria. For instance, one can use graph edit distance (GED) technique [6] that estimates the minimal number of edit operations needed to transform a graph into another. However, this is an NP hard problem that becomes intractable when scaling up graph sizes. Graph multiple kernel-based comparison methods, on the other hand, are more natural when desiring scale-adaptivity since each kernel can capture a particular graph scale such as the multi-scale Laplacian graph kernel method proposed in [7]. However, such techniques raise a computational overhead cubic in deriving Laplacian matrix eigenvalues and when the size of the graph exponentially grows. Traditional statistical methods including the family of spectral distances (FGSD) [8] produces a high-dimensional sparse representation as a histogram on the dense biharmonic graph kernel; however, such methods are not scale-adaptive and are also inapplicable to reasonably large graphs due to their quadratic time complexity.

Adding to the difficulty of profiling the state of a single brain graph, profiling a population of brain *multigraphs*, to eventually discover disorder-specific profiles, presents a big jump in the field of network neuroscience, which we set out to take in this paper. Specifically, while addressing the aforementioned limitations and while cross-pollinating the fields of spectral graph theory and diffusion models, we unprecedentedly propose an eigen-based cross-diffusion strategy for brain multigraph *integration, comparison, and profiling*. In the first step, we aim to learn how to fuse a population of brain multigraphs into a single graph by capitalizing on unsupervised graph diffusion and fusion technique presented in [9]. However, while cross-diffusing a set of graphs for eventually estimating a representative integral graph representation of each individual brain multigraph, [9] overlooks the topological properties of graph nodes such as node centrality, which better capture local and global structure of the brain connectivity providing a more holistic measurement of the brain graph. To address this limitation, we propose a novel multigraph cross-diffusion based on a graph Laplacian derived from eigen-centrality measures. In the second step, since a graph spectrum encodes its shape (or geometry) as if one can hear the shape of the graph [10], for the first time, we profile the *fused multigraphs* at several diffusion timescales by extracting the compact heat-trace signatures of their corresponding Laplacian matrices. To this aim, we adopt network Laplacian spectral descriptor (NetLSD) introduced in [11] to produce brain multigraph heat-trace profiles, which nicely satisfy permutation- and size-invariance, and scale-adaptivity. As one can "hear" the connectivity of the drum if we were to represent its shape as a graph [10], in this paper, we hear the connectivity of autistic and healthy morphological brain multigraphs, derived from T1-w magnetic resonance imaging (MRI). To further evaluate the discriminability of the discovered population-specific profiles, we use the heat-traces of fused brain multigraphs to train and test a linear support vector machine (SVM) classifier using 5-fold cross-validation. This work presents the first step towards 'hearing' the shape of the brain multigraph that can be leveraged for profiling and disentangling comorbid neurological disorders, thereby advancing precision medicine.

2   Proposed Eigen-Based Cross-diffusion and Heat Tracing of Brain Multigraphs

Problem Statement. Given a population $\mathbb{G}^s = \{\mathcal{G}^1, \ldots, \mathcal{G}^S\}$ of S brain multigraphs of state s, we aim to profile the brain state of the given population $\mathbb{G}^s$ by graph cross-diffusion and Laplacian-based heat tracing. To this aim, we first propose an eigen-based cross-diffusion to integrate each individual brain multigraph into a single graph. Second, we heat the fused graph by Laplacian spectral decomposition and discover the profile of a given population $\mathbb{G}^s$ by averaging all subject-specific heat tracing profiles. In this section, we detail the steps of our

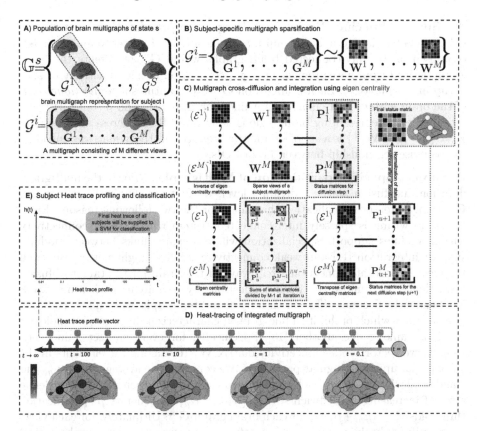

Fig. 1. *Proposed eigen-based multigraph cross-diffusion for profiling and comparing brain multigraphs.* **A)** Dataset $\mathbb{G}^s$ of S brain multigraphs of state s (e.g.., disordered or healthy), each represented as a tensor $\mathcal{G}$ with M frontal views encoded in symmetric connectivity matrices $\{\mathbf{W}^1, \ldots, \mathbf{W}^M\}$. **B)** To remove noisy connectivities and for a more effective graph cross-diffusion, we sparsify each brain graph in $\mathcal{G}$. **C)** Proposed brain multigraph cross-diffusion and fusion using eigen centrality to produce the integrated multigraph (i.e., status matrix). **D)** For each node v in the fused multigraph, we heat the final status matrix using its Laplacian matrix at different timescales t. The red arrow points at the active node v. **E)** Heat-trace based profiling and classification. For a given subject i, we average the heat traces across all nodes, producing a *time-dependent* heat trace $h(t)$ stored in a heat trace profile vector. By extracting the final heat-traces of all training profiles and supplying them to a support vector machine (SVM), we evaluate the discriminative power of our approach in disentangling different brain states (Color figure online).

eigen-based cross-diffusion for multigraph integration, profiling and comparison framework. In Fig. 1, we present a flowchart of the five proposed steps including: A) representation of an individual brain multigraph, B) subject-specific sparsification of brain multigraphs, C) cross-diffusion and integration of a multigraph using eigen centrality, D) heat-tracing the integrated multigraph, and E) heat-trace profiling and classification of brain multigraphs.

A- Subject-Specific Brain Multigraph Representation. Let $\mathcal{G}^i = \{\mathbf{G}^1, \ldots, \mathbf{G}^M\}$ denote a brain multigraph of subject i in the population $\mathbb{G}^s$, composed of M fully-connected brain graphs where $\mathbf{G}^m$ represents the brain graph derived from measurement m (e.g.., correlation in neural activity or similarity in morphology). Each brain graph $\mathbf{G}^m \in \mathcal{G}^i$ captures a *connectional view* of the brain wiring. Particularly, we define a brain multigraph $\mathcal{G}^i = (V, \mathcal{W})$ as a set of nodes V representing brain regions of interest (ROIs) across all views and $\mathcal{W} = \{\mathbf{W}^1, \ldots, \mathbf{W}^M\}$ is a set of symmetric brain connectivity matrices encoding the pairwise relationship between brain ROIs.

B- Subject-Specific Sparsification of Multigraphs. Prior to the multigraph diffusion and fusion at the individual level, we first sparsify each brain graph $\mathbf{G}^m$ using different sparsification thresholds for the two following reasons. First, the brain wiring is sparsely inter-connected system where strong connectivity within modules supports specialization whereas sparse links between modules support integration [12] and weak connectivity weights might not capture well the most important connectional pathways in the brain for the target diffusion task. Hence, we remove the weak connections by sparsifying each brain graph independently. Second, diffusion on fully-connected graphs will rapidly converge to a constant which prohibits a fine-grained characterization of graph topologies to diffuse among one another [13]. Specifically, for every subject i and each view m, we vectorize its connectivity matrix $\mathbf{W}^m$ by taking the elements in the off-diagonal upper triangular part. Next, we compute the average mean μ_m and standard deviation σ_m for each view m across all S subjects in $\mathbb{G}^s$. We also define a set of increasing α coefficients, $\alpha = \{\alpha_1, \ldots, \alpha_p\}$ to generate p sparsification thresholds $\rho_m^p = \mu_m + \alpha_p \sigma_m$ for each brain graph $\mathbf{G}^m$. Ultimately, for each view, we sparsify all brain graphs. For easy reference, we keep the same mathematical notation $\{\mathbf{W}^1, \ldots, \mathbf{W}^M\}$ for the sparsified multigraph adjacency matrices at fixed thresholds $\{\rho_m^p\}_{m=1}^M$, respectively (Fig. 1–B).

C- Cross-Diffusion and Integration of a Multigraph Using Eigen Centrality. Given a *sparsified* brain multigraph $\mathcal{G}^i$ of subject i, one can leverage the conventional graph cross-diffusion method introduced in [9] to diffuse each brain graph across the average of the remaining brain graphs –progressively altering the individual brain topology in such a way that it resembles more the 'average' brain topology. Following the iterative cross-diffusion step, one can integrate all *diffused* graphs by simply linearly averaging them as they lie locally near to one other in the diffused graph manifold. Although compelling, such a technique only relies on the node degree to define the normalized diffusion kernel, which is a limited measure of graph topology that can only capture the local neighborhood of a node in terms of quantify (i.e., number of its neighboring nodes). To better preserve the graph topology during the diffusion process, we unprecedentedly introduce a graph diffusion strategy rotted in eigen centrality, a measure of the influence of a node in a graph based on its eigen centrality. An eigen central node is directly related to nodes which are central themselves [14]. Hence, it presents a stronger definition of graph centrality taking into account the entire pattern in a graph, which is also an intrinsic property of brain networks [15].

Eigen centrality is a function of the connections of the nodes in one's neighborhood [16]. For a single view m, let $\{\lambda_1, \ldots, \lambda_{|V|}\}$ denote the set of eigenvalues of the graph adjacency matrix $\mathbf{W}^m$ and $\psi = max_i|\lambda_i|$ its spectral radius, the eigen centrality of the kth node in $\mathbf{G}^m$ is defined as the lth entry component of the principal eigen vector $\mathbf{x}$, that is $\mathbf{x}_l = \frac{1}{\psi} \sum_{k=1}^{|V|} \mathbf{W}^m(l, k)\mathbf{x}_k$ [16], where $|V|$ denotes the number of nodes in the graph. Next, for each graph in $\mathcal{G}^i$, we define a diagonal matrix $\mathcal{E}^m$ for its mth view storing graph node eigen centralities. This will be used to define an *eigen centrality-normalized* connectivity matrix $\mathbf{P}^m$ as follows (Fig. 1–C): $\mathbf{P}^m = \mathcal{E}^{m^{-1}} \mathbf{W}^m$.

Next, for each view m, we iteratively update the status matrix $\mathbf{P}^m$ through diffusing the average global structure of other $(M - 1)$ views of the brain multigraph $\mathcal{G}^i$ along the eigen centrality diagonal matrix $\mathcal{E}^m$, thereby forcing the connectivity diffusion to go through the most central ROIs in the brain. As such, we cast a new formalization of *edge-based* diffusion on graphs guided by most central nodes, which may overlook noise that distributes randomly and sparsely in $\mathbf{G}^m$ as well as irrelevant connections. At iteration $u + 1$, we use the following update rule to compute the status matrix of $\mathbf{G}^m$:

$$\mathbf{P}_{u+1}^m = \mathcal{E}^m \times \left(\frac{1}{M - 1} \sum_{k \neq m} \mathbf{P}_u^k\right) \times (\mathcal{E}^m)^T \tag{1}$$

Following u^* iterations of graph cross-diffusion, we then produce the fused brain multigraph $\mathbf{P}_{u^*}^i$ for subject i by linearly averaging the view-specific status matrices as follows: $\mathbf{P}_{u^*}^i = \frac{1}{M} \sum_{m=1}^M \mathbf{P}_{u^*}^m$.

D- Subject-Specific Heat-Tracing of the Fused Multigraph. In this stage, given the fused status matrix $\mathbf{P}_{u^*}^i$, we set out to define a continuous time-dependent profile (i.e., curve) of the fused brain multigraph of subject i using a *node-based* diffusion process. Inspired from the work of [10], we leverage the graph spectrum encoding its shape (or geometry) to profile $\mathbf{P}_{u^*}^i$. To this aim, we first define the normalized Laplacian matrix $\mathcal{L}^i$ of the final status matrix $\mathbf{P}_{u^*}^i$ as $\mathcal{L}^i = \mathbf{I} - \mathbf{S}^{\frac{-1}{2}} \mathbf{P}_{u^*}^i \mathbf{S}^{\frac{-1}{2}}$, where $\mathbf{S}$ is the diagonal strength matrix and $\mathbf{I}$ is the identity matrix. Second, we estimate the spectrum of the normalized Laplacian $\mathcal{L}^i$ with eigenvalues $\{\lambda_1^i, \ldots, \lambda_{|V|}^i\}$ (Fig. 1–D). Next, we use the heat equation to heat a node v in the fused multigraph at timescale t as follows: $h_t(v) = \sum_{k=1}^{|V|} e^{-t\lambda_k}(v)$, which is also referred to as the *heat trace* of node v [11]. By averaging the *heat traces* of all nodes in the fused brain multigraph, we can estimate its heat trace at time t. Ultimately, we create a logarithmic sample space spanning from 10^{-2} to 10^3 to better inspect the descend of heat-traces by acceleratingly increasing timescales. For n_t different timescales in the logarithmic space, we compute n_t different averaged heat-traces to create a heat trace vector $[h_{t_1}^i, h_{t_2}^i, \ldots, h_{t_{n_t}}^i]$ and profile the fused multigraph of a subject i. The steps of our method are detailed in Algorithm 1.

E- Heat-Trace Profiling and Discriminability of Brain Profiles. Given a population $\mathbb{G}^{s_1}$ of brain multigraphs of state s_1 (e.g.., healthy) and a population $\mathbb{G}^{s_2}$ of state s_2 (e.g.., disordered), we compute the heat trace profile for each

Algorithm 1. Eigen-based cross-diffusion for multigraph integration and profiling

---

1: **INPUTS:**
      $\mathcal{G}^i = \{\mathbf{G}^1, \ldots, \mathbf{G}^M\}$: multigraph of the ith subject in dataset $\mathbb{G}^s$ of state s
2: **for** $m := 1$ **to** M **do**
3:    $\mathbf{W}^m \leftarrow$ matrix representation of graph $\mathbf{G}^m$ (m^{th} view of $\mathcal{G}^i$)
4:    $\mathcal{E}^m \leftarrow$ diagonal matrix built from eigen centralities of $\mathbf{W}^m$
5:    $\mathbf{P}_1^m \leftarrow \mathcal{E}^{m^{-1}} \mathbf{W}^m$ (eigen centrality normalization)   ▷ first status matrix
6: **end for**
7: **for** each diffusion iteration $u \in \{1, 2, \ldots, u^*\}$ **do**
8:    **for** $m := 1$ **to** M **do**
9:        Update the status matrix of the mth view via cross-diffusion using
$$\mathbf{P}_{u+1}^m \leftarrow \mathcal{E}^m \times (\tfrac{1}{M-1} \sum_{k \neq m} \mathbf{P}_u^k) \times (\mathcal{E}^m)^T$$
10:    **end for**
11: **end for**
12: Compute the final status matrix for subject i using $\mathbf{P}_{u*}^i \leftarrow \frac{1}{M} \sum_{m=1}^M \mathbf{P}_{u*}^m$
13: $\mathcal{L}^i \leftarrow$ normalized Laplacian matrix of $\mathbf{P}_{u*}^i$ of subject i
14: $\{\lambda_1^i, \ldots, \lambda_k^i\} \leftarrow$ eigenvalues of Laplacian $\mathcal{L}^i$ of subject i
15: **for** each logarithmic timescale $t \in \{t^1, t^2, \ldots, t^{n_t}\}$ **do**
16:    **for** each node v of the normalized Laplacian $\mathcal{L}^i$ of subject i **do**
17:        Compute heat-trace $h_t(v) = \sum_{k=1}^{|V|} e^{-t\lambda_k^i}(v)$
18:    **end for**
19:    Compute time-dependent heat-trace h_t^i for subject i averaged across subject nodes at timescales t
20: **end for**
21: **OUTPUTS:** heat-trace vector of subject i, $[h_{t^1}^i, h_{t^2}^i, \ldots, h_{t^{n_t}}^i]$

---

brain multigraph in each population. Next, we report the average population heat trace profile by averaging the profiles of all individual multigraphs in the population. To evaluate the discriminability of the estimated fused multigraph heat tracing profiles, we train a support vector machine (SVM) with a sigmoid kernel classifier to classify brain multigraphs in state s_1 or s_2 using the stable heat trace value at the tail of the profile curve (Fig. 1–E). Specifically, we use 5-fold cross-validation to train an SVM classifier using the single-valued heat trace of each subject i. We also define a margin $\delta(s_1, s_2)$ between the two brain states by computing the absolute difference between the heat trace value at the tail of both heating profiles.

3   Results and Discussion

Brain Multigraph Dataset and Parameter Setting. We evaluated our framework on 200 subjects (100 ASD and 100 NC) from Autism Brain Imaging Data Exchange (ABIDE). For each cortical hemisphere, each subject is represented by 4 cortical morphological brain networks derived from maximum principal curvature, the mean cortical thickness, the mean sulcal depth, and the average curvature. These networks were derived from T1-weighted magnetic resonance imaging (MRI). Each hemisphere was parcelled into 35 anatomical regions defining the nodes of each brain graph and encoded in a symmetric matrix that quantifies morphological dissimilarity between pairs of cortical regions using a particular measurement (e.g.., cortical thickness) [17–19]. Hence, each cortical hemisphere is represented by a multigraph consisting of 4 different graphs.

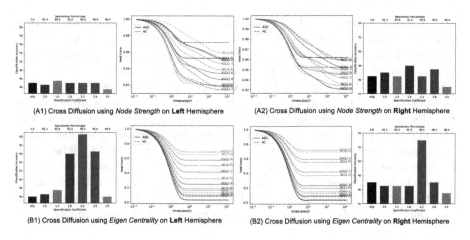

Fig. 2. *Heat-trace profiles of morphological brain multigraphs with healthy and autistic states and SVM classification results using both proposed eigen-based cross-diffusion and conventional strength based cross-diffusion method* [9]. NC: normal controls. ASD: autism spectrum disorders. Clearly, our method produces orderly and smooth heat-trace profiles with larger gaps between brain states, whereas the conventional method produces fluctuating and wavy profiles. This nicely results in our method achieving higher classification accuracy at different sparsification thresholds, thereby demonstrating the discriminativeness of the estimated profiles.

Brain Multigraph Sparsification. For each hemisphere, we set the sparsification coefficients α to $\{1.0, 1.4, 1.8, 2.2, 2.6, 3.0\}$ to sparsify the 4 brain graphs in each multigraph. Next, we plot the average heat-trace profile across subjects in the same population (i.e., sharing the same state) and report SVM classification results using 5-fold cross-validation in Fig. 2.

Evaluation and Comparison Methods. We compare the performance of our eigen-based cross-diffusion framework with conventional strength based cross-diffusion method [9]. As conventional cross-diffusion method uses a diagonal matrix storing node strengths on the diagonal, it cannot capture the quality of the local neighborhoods (e.g.., presence of hub neighbors); whereas our method is based on eigen centrality measures which assesses the quality of local neighbors to a given node. Figure 2 shows that [9] produces unstable and highly fluctuating heat-trace plots, whereas our eigen-based cross-diffusion method generates ordered and smooth heat-trace plots for ASD and NC brain populations $\mathbb{G}^{ASD}$ and $\mathbb{G}^{NC}$. This can be explained by the fact that [9] diffuses a sparse similarity matrix encoding node similarity to nearby data points, whereas we diffuse the eigen diagonal matrix which enhances the role of hub nodes as reliable mediators of information diffusion which cannot be captured by only considering nearest neighbors. Besides, central nodes are generally more resistant to noise which can permeate local neighborhoods, thereby privileging their use for stable and robust diffusion. The orderliness of our method shows its true power in brain state classification by SVM. Our proposed method of eigen-based cross-diffusion boosts the classification results by 2–12% in comparison with baseline method.

In Fig. 3, we display the margin $\delta(ASD, NC)$ between two brain populations for right and left hemispheres at different sparsification thresholds. Clearly, our method produces larger gaps between autistic and healthy brain state profiles (blue bars), which demonstrates its discriminative potential for neurological disorder diagnosis and classifying brain states. As we increase the sparsification level of brain multigraphs, the gap first increases then decreases fitting a smooth polynomial curve. We also note that the margin is very low $\delta(ASD, NC)$ when using the original non-sparsified brain multigraphs, implying lower state discriminativeness. In fact, the sparsification threshold is a hyper-parameter that requires a deeper investigation. Ideally, one would learn how to identify the best threshold that allows to identify what individualizes a population of brain multigraphs.

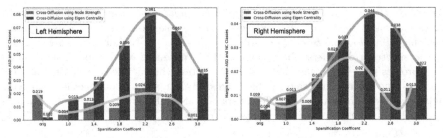

(C1) Comparing Conventional and Proposed Methods on **Left** Hemisphere   (C2) Comparing Conventional and Proposed Methods on **Right** Hemisphere

Fig. 3. *Comparison the margin $\delta(ASD, NC)$ between ASD and NC classes shown in Fig. 2 at different sparsification levels by our method and* [9]. *We fitted 5th degree polynomials to the bar plots.*

4   Conclusion

In this work, we introduced a multigraph cross-diffusion, integration and profiling technique based on eigen centrality. The discovered brain multigraph profiles were smooth and highly discriminative in comparison with baseline method, which have utility in diagnosing neurological disorders. Indeed, the wide spectrum of the disordered brain connectome [2] demands not only advanced graph analysis techniques and scalable graph comparison strategies, but it also calls for new multigraph analysis tools that can unify the multiple graph representations of the brain including structure and function. In our future work, our goal is to profile a wide spectrum of brain disorders using functional, structural and morphological brain graphs in future population comparative connectomics [20,21].

Acknowledgments. I. Rekik is supported by the European Union's Horizon 2020 research and innovation programme under the Marie Sklodowska-Curie Individual Fellowship grant agreement No 101003403 (http://basira-lab.com/normnets/).

References

1. Bassett, D.S., Sporns, O.: Network neuroscience. Nat. Neurosci. **20**, 353 (2017)
2. Fornito, A., Zalesky, A., Breakspear, M.: The connectomics of brain disorders. Nat. Rev. Neurosci. **16**, 159–172 (2015)
3. Van den Heuvel, M.P., Sporns, O.: A cross-disorder connectome landscape of brain dysconnectivity. Nat. Rev. Neurosci. **20**, 435–446 (2019)
4. Corps, J., Rekik, I.: Morphological brain age prediction using multi-view brain networks derived from cortical morphology in healthy and disordered participants. Sci. Rep. **9**, 1–10 (2019)
5. Bilgen, I., Guvercin, G., Rekik, I.: Machine learning methods for brain network classification: application to autism diagnosis using cortical morphological networks. arXiv preprint arXiv:2004.13321 (2020)
6. Sanfeliu, A., Fu, K.: A distance measure between attributed relational graphs for pattern recognition. IEEE Trans. Syst. Man Cybern. SMC **13**, 353–362 (1983)
7. Kondor, R., Pan, H.: The multiscale Laplacian graph kernel. Adv. Neural Inf. Process. Syst. **29**, 2990–2998 (2016)
8. Verma, S., Zhang, Z.L.: Hunt for the unique, stable, sparse and fast feature learning on graphs. Adv. Neural Inf. Process. Syst. **30**, 88–98 (2017)
9. Wang, B., Jiang, J., Wang, W., Zhou, Z.H., Tu, Z.: Unsupervised metric fusion by cross diffusion. In: Proceedings/CVPR, IEEE Computer Society Conference on Computer Vision and Pattern Recognition. IEEE Computer Society Conference on Computer Vision and Pattern Recognition, pp. 2997–3004 (2012)
10. Kac, M.: Can one hear the shape of a drum? Am. Math. Mon. **73**, 1–23 (1966)
11. Tsitsulin, A., Mottin, D., Karras, P., Bronstein, A., Müller, E.: Netlsd: hearing the shape of a graph. In: Proceedings of the 24th ACM SIGKDD International Conference on Knowledge Discovery & Data Mining, pp. 2347–2356 (2018)
12. Rubinov, M., Sporns, O.: Weight-conserving characterization of complex functional brain networks. Neuroimage **56**, 2068–2079 (2011)
13. Hammond, D.K., Gur, Y., Johnson, C.R.: Graph diffusion distance: a difference measure for weighted graphs based on the graph Laplacian exponential kernel, pp. 419–422 (2013)
14. Grassi, R., Stefani, S., Torriero, A.: Some new results on the eigenvector centrality. Math. Sociol. **31**, 237–248 (2007)
15. Joyce, K.E., Laurienti, P.J., Burdette, J.H., Hayasaka, S.: A new measure of centrality for brain networks. PloS One **5**, e12200 (2010)
16. Bonacich, P.: Technique for analyzing overlapping memberships. Sociol. Methodol. **4**, 176–185 (1972)
17. Mahjoub, I., Mahjoub, M.A., Rekik, I.: Brain multiplexes reveal morphological connectional biomarkers fingerprinting late brain dementia states. Sci. Rep. **8**, 4103 (2018)
18. Soussia, M., Rekik, I.: Unsupervised manifold learning using high-order morphological brain networks derived from T1-w MRI for autism diagnosis. Front. Neuroinform. **12**, 70 (2018)
19. Nebli, A., Rekik, I.: Gender differences in cortical morphological networks. Brain Imaging Behav. 1–9 (2019)
20. Van den Heuvel, M.P., Bullmore, E.T., Sporns, O.: Comparative connectomics. Trends Cogn. Sci. **20**, 345–361 (2016)
21. Arbabshirani, M.R., Havlicek, M., Kiehl, K.A., Pearlson, G.D., Calhoun, V.D.: Functional network connectivity during rest and task conditions: a comparative study. Hum. Brain Mapp. **34**, 2959–2971 (2013)

Graph Domain Adaptation for Alignment-Invariant Brain Surface Segmentation

Karthik Gopinath$^{(\boxtimes)}$, Christian Desrosiers, and Herve Lombaert

ETS Montreal, Montreal, Canada
`karthik.gopinath.1@etsmtl.net`

Abstract. The varying cortical geometry of the brain creates numerous challenges for its analysis. Recent developments have enabled learning cortical data directly across multiple brain surfaces via graph convolutions. However, current graph learning algorithms fail when brain surface data are misaligned across subjects, thereby requiring to apply a costly alignment procedure in pre-processing. Adversarial training is widely used for unsupervised domain adaptation to improve segmentation performance on target data whose distribution differs from the training source data. In this paper, we exploit this technique to learn surface data across inconsistent graph alignments. This novel approach comprises a segmentator that uses graph convolution layers to enable parcellation across brain surfaces of varying geometry, and a discriminator that predicts the alignment-domain of surfaces from their segmentation. By trying to fool the discriminator, the adversarial training learns an alignment-invariant representation which yields consistent parcellations for differently-aligned surfaces. Using manually-labeled brain surface from MindBoggle, the largest publicly available dataset of this kind, we demonstrate a 2%–13% improvement in mean Dice over a non-adversarial training strategy, for test brain surfaces with no alignment or aligned on a different reference than source examples.

1 Introduction

The cerebral cortex is essential to a wide range of cognitive functions. Automated algorithms for brain surface analysis thus play an important role in understanding the structure and working of this complex organ. Nowadays, deep learning models such as convolutional neural networks (CNNs) provide state-of-the-art performance for most image analysis tasks, including image classification, registration, and segmentation [1]. However, these models typically require large annotated datasets for training, which are often expensive to obtain in medical applications. This limitation is especially true for the task of cortical segmentation, also known as *parcellation*, where generating ground truth data requires labeling possibly thousands of nodes on a highly-convoluted surface. This burden also explains why datasets for such tasks are relatively small. For instance, the

© Springer Nature Switzerland AG 2020
C. H. Sudre et al. (Eds.): UNSURE 2020/GRAIL 2020, LNCS 12443, pp. 152–163, 2020.
https://doi.org/10.1007/978-3-030-60365-6_15

largest publicly-available dataset for cortical parcellation, MindBoggle [2], contains only 101 manually-annotated brain surfaces. Moreover, another common problem of deep learning models is their lack of robustness to differences in the distribution of training and test data. Hence, a CNN model trained on the data from a source domain usually fails to generalize to samples from other domains, i.e., the *target* domains.

Unsupervised domain adaptation (UDA) [3] has proven to be a powerful approach for making algorithms trained on source data generalize to examples from a target domain, without having explicit labels for these examples. Generative adversarial networks (GANs) [4] leverage adversarial training to produce realistic images. In this type of approach, a discriminator network classifies images produced by a generator network as real or fake, and the generator improves by learning to fool the discriminator. Following the success of GANs, adversarial techniques have later been proposed to improve the learning capability of CNNs across different domains. Adversarial domain adaptation methods for segmentation [5–10] involve the concurrent training of two networks: a segmentator that learns to produce accurate segmentation outputs for labeled source examples, and a discriminator which forces the segmentator to have a similar prediction for examples of both source and target domains. These adversarial techniques usually rely on either feature space adaptation or output space adaptation. Initial works [11,12] focused on matching the distributions of features from source and target domain examples for classification tasks. As the output of CNNs for segmentation contains rich semantic information, [13] proposed a method that instead leverages output space adaptation. Various pixel-wise domain adaptation approaches have been developed for natural color images [12,14]. In medical image analysis, [15] proposed an adversarial neural network for MRI image segmentation which does not require additional labels on test examples from the target domain. Likewise, [10] presented a vessel segmentation approach for fundus images, which uses a gradient reversal layer for adversarial training. Recent work [16] also addressed the problem of domain adaptation by adding a differentiable penalty on the target domain. However, these domain adaptation techniques focus on data lying in the Euclidean space (natural or medical images) and, therefore, are not suitable for graph structures such as surface meshes.

The image space is inadequate to capture the varying geometry of the cerebral cortex. Differences in brain surface geometry hinder statistical frameworks from exploiting spatial information in Euclidean space. The extension of standard convolutions to non-Euclidean spaces like manifolds and graphs has led to the development of various geometric deep learning frameworks [17,18]. A recent work [19] proposed to use geometric deep learning for segmenting three cortical regions by relying on the spatial representation of the brain surface mesh. Later, based on the spectral representation of such meshes, [20] developed a graph convolution network (GCN) to parcellate the cerebral cortex. Despite offering more flexibility than Euclidean-based approaches, these methods are domain-dependent and would fail to generalize to new datasets (domains) without explicit re-training. Moreover, obtaining annotations for these new datasets

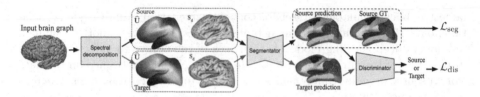

Fig. 1. Overview of our architecture: The input brain graph is mapped to a spectral domain by decomposition of the graph Laplacian. The source and target domain are obtained by aligning the eigenbases to source reference and targets reference respectively. A segmentator GCN learns to predict a generic cortical parcel label for each domain. The discriminator aims at classifying the segmentator predictions, thereby assisting the segmentator GCN in adapting to both source and target domains.

is also challenging and time-consuming, due to the complexity of visualizing and labeling intricate surfaces.

In this paper, we address the limitations of existing techniques for cortical parcellation by proposing an adversarial domain adaptation method on surface graphs. Specifically, we focus on a problem shared by most GCN-based approaches, which is the need for a common basis to represent and operate on graphs. For approaches operating in Euclidean space, bringing surface graphs to this common basis usually involves transforming and possibly sub-sampling meshes to match a given reference, which is particularly difficult for convoluted surfaces like the cortex. As described in [20], this process can be greatly simplified by instead operating in the spectral domain, for instance using spectral GCNs [21,22]. Nevertheless, spectral GNCs also need to perform some alignment to work. Hence, these models require computing the eigendecomposition of the graph Laplacian matrix to embed graphs in a space defined by a fixed eigenbasis. However, separate graphs may have different eigenbases, and the eigenvectors obtained for a given graph are only defined up to a sign and a rotation (if different eigenvectors share close eigenvalues). Due to these ambiguities, spectral GCNs cannot be used to compare multiple graphs directly and need an explicit alignment of graph eigenbases as an additional pre-processing step. Here, we focus on generalizing parcellation across multiple brain surface domains by removing the dependency on these domain-specific alignments.

The contributions of our work are multifold:

- We present, to the best of our knowledge, the first adversarial graph domain adaptation method for surface segmentation. Our novel method trains two networks in an adversarial manner, a fully-convolutional GCN segmentator and a GCN domain discriminator, both of which operate on the spectral components of surface graphs.
- Compared to existing approaches, our surface segmentation method offers greater robustness to differences in domain-specific alignment. Hence, our method yields a higher accuracy for non-aligned brain surfaces compared to a strategy without adversarial learning. Moreover, it also provides a better

generalization for surfaces aligned to a different reference, without requiring an explicit re-alignment or manual annotations of these surfaces.
- We demonstrate the potential of our method for alignment-invariant parcellation of brain surfaces, using data from MindBoggle, the largest publicly-available manually-labeled surface dataset. Our results show significant mean Dice improvements compared to the same segmentation network without adversarial training and over a strong baseline approach based on Spectral Random Forest.

In the next section, we detail the fundamentals of our graph domain adaptation method for surface segmentation, followed by experiments validating the advantages of our method and a discussion of results.

2 Method

An overview of our proposed method is shown in Fig. 1. In the initial step, the cortical brain graph is embedded into the spectral domain using the graph Laplacian operator. Next, samples from the source domain only are aligned to a reference template using the Iterative Closest Point (ICP) algorithm. This algorithm works by repeating the following two steps until convergence: 1) mapping each node of the graph to align to its nearest reference node in the embedding space; 2) computing the orthogonal transformation (i.e., rotation and flip) which brings nodes nearest to their corresponding reference node. Since this process is iterative and external to the network architecture, it can be computationally expensive to run. However, we only need to apply it during training and, as shown in experiments, the proposed method can achieve good performance on non-aligned test examples by learning an alignment-invariant representation. Finally, a graph domain adaptation network is trained to perform alignment-independent parcellation. The segmentator network learns a generic mapping from input surface features, e.g. the spectral coordinates and sulcal depth of cortical points, to cortical parcel labels.

2.1 Spectral Embedding of Brain Graphs

We start by describing the spectral graph convolution model used in this work. Denote as $\mathcal{G} = \{\mathcal{V}, \mathcal{E}\}$ a brain surface graph with node set $\mathcal{V}$, such that $|\mathcal{V}| = N$, and edge set $\mathcal{E}$. Each node i has a feature vector $\mathbf{x}_i \in \mathbb{R}^3$ representing its 3D coordinates. We map $\mathcal{G}$ to a low-dimension manifold using the normalized graph Laplacian operator $\mathbf{L} = \mathbf{I} - \mathbf{D}^{-\frac{1}{2}} \mathbf{A} \mathbf{D}^{-\frac{1}{2}}$, where $\mathbf{A}$ is the weighted adjacency matrix and $\mathbf{D}$ the diagonal degree matrix. Here, we consider weighted edges and measure the weight between two adjacent nodes as the inverse of their Euclidean distance, i.e. $a_{ij} = (\|\mathbf{x}_i - \mathbf{x}_j\| + \epsilon)^{-1}$ where ϵ is a small positive constant. Letting $\mathbf{L} = \mathbf{U} \mathbf{\Lambda} \mathbf{U}^\top$ be the eigendecomposition of $\mathbf{L}$, the normalized spectral coordinates of nodes are given by $\widehat{\mathbf{U}} = \mathbf{\Lambda}^{-\frac{1}{2}} \mathbf{U}$. The normalization with $\mathbf{\Lambda}^{-\frac{1}{2}}$ is used so that coordinates corresponding to smaller eigenvalues are given more importance in the embedding.

Denote the neighbors of node $i \in V$ as $\mathcal{N}_i = \{j \mid (i,j) \in \mathcal{E}\}$. The convolution operation used in our spectral GCN is defined as

$$z_{ip}^{(l)} = \sum_{j \in \mathcal{N}_i} \sum_{q=1}^{M_l} \sum_{k=1}^{K_l} w_{pqk}^{(l)} y_{jq}^{(l)} \varphi(\widehat{\mathbf{u}}_i, \widehat{\mathbf{u}}_j; \Theta_k^{(l)}) + b_p^{(l)},$$

$$y_{ip}^{(l+1)} = \sigma(z_{ip}^{(l)})$$

(1)

where $y_{jq}^{(l)}$ is the feature of node j in the q-th feature map of layer l, $w_{pqk}^{(l)}$ is the weight in the k-th convolution filter between feature maps q and p of subsequent layers, $b_p^{(l)}$ is the bias of feature map p at layer l, and σ is a non-linear activation function. The information of the spectral embedding relating nodes i and j is included via a symmetric kernel $\varphi(\widehat{\mathbf{u}}_i, \widehat{\mathbf{u}}_j; \Theta_k)$ parameterized by Θ_k. In this work, we follow [20] and use a Gaussian kernel: $\varphi(\widehat{\mathbf{u}}_i, \widehat{\mathbf{u}}_j; \boldsymbol{\mu}_k, \sigma_k) = \exp(-\sigma_k \|(\widehat{\mathbf{u}}_j - \widehat{\mathbf{u}}_i) - \boldsymbol{\mu}_k\|^2)$.

2.2   Graph Domain Adaptation

Our graph domain adaptation architecture contains two blocks: a segmentator GCN S performing cortical parcellation and a discriminator GCN D, which predicts if a given parcellation comes from a source or target graph. Let $\mathcal{X}_{\text{src}}$ be the set of source graphs and $\mathcal{X}_{\text{tgt}}$ the set of unlabeled domain graphs, with $\mathcal{X} = \mathcal{X}_{\text{src}} \cup \mathcal{X}_{\text{tgt}}$ the entire set of graphs available in training. In the first step, we optimize the segmentator GCN using labeled source graphs $\mathcal{G} \in \mathcal{X}_{\text{src}}$. We feed the segmentation network's prediction $S(\mathcal{G})$ to the discriminator D whose role is to identify the input's domain (i.e., source or target). The gradients computed from an adversarial loss on target domain graphs are back-propagated from D to S, forcing the segmentation to be similar for both the source and target domain graphs.

As in other adversarial approaches, we define the learning task as a minimax problem between the segmentator and discriminator networks,

$$\max_D \min_S \mathcal{L}(D, S) = \frac{1}{|\mathcal{X}_{\text{src}}|} \sum_{\mathcal{G} \in \mathcal{X}_{\text{src}}} \mathcal{L}_{\text{seg}}(S(\mathcal{G}), \mathbf{y}_{\mathcal{G}}) - \frac{\lambda}{|\mathcal{X}|} \sum_{\mathcal{G} \in \mathcal{X}} \mathcal{L}_{\text{dis}}(D(S(\mathcal{G})), z_{\mathcal{G}}),$$

(2)

where $\mathcal{L}_{\text{seg}}$ is the supervised segmentation loss on labeled source graphs, and $\mathcal{L}_{\text{dis}}$ is the discriminator loss on both source and target graphs, which is optimized in an adversarial manner for S and D.

Segmentator Loss. For each input graph, the segmentator network outputs a parcellation prediction $\widehat{\mathbf{y}}$ where $\widehat{y}_{ic}$ is the probability that node i belongs to parcel c. In this work, we define the supervised segmentation loss as a combination of weighted Dice loss and weighted cross-entropy (CE),

$$\mathcal{L}_{\text{seg}}(\widehat{\mathbf{y}}, \mathbf{y}) = \left[1 - \frac{\epsilon + 2\sum_{i=1}^{N}\sum_{c=1}^{C} \omega_c\, y_{ic}\, \widehat{y}_{ic}}{\epsilon + \sum_{i=1}^{N}\sum_{c=1}^{C} \omega_c(y_{ic} + \widehat{y}_{ic})} \right] - \sum_{i=1}^{N}\sum_{c=1}^{C} \omega_c\, y_{ic}\, \widehat{y}_{ic}, \quad (3)$$

with y_{ic} being a one-hot encoding of the reference segmentation and ϵ a small constant to avoid zero-division. The weights ω_c balances the loss for parcels by increasing the importance given to smaller-sized regions. We follow [20] and set class weights ω_c as the total number of nodes divided by the number of nodes with label c. In the loss of Eq. (3), CE improves overall accuracy of node classification while Dice helps to have structured output for each parcel.

Discriminator Loss. Since the discriminator D is a domain classifier, we define its loss as the binary cross-entropy between its domain prediction (i.e., $\widehat{z} = 1$ for source or $\widehat{z} = 0$ for target):

$$\mathcal{L}_{\text{dis}}(\widehat{z}, z) = -(1 - z)\log(1 - \widehat{z}) - z\log\widehat{z}. \qquad (4)$$

As mentioned before, this loss is maximized while updating the segmentator's parameters and minimized when updating the discriminator. Thus, the segmentator learns to produce surface parcellations that are alignment-invariant.

2.3 Network Architecture

Segmentator: The segmentator is a fully-convolutional GCN comprised of 3 graph convolution layers with respective feature map sizes of 256, 128, and 32. At the input of the network, each node has 4 features: 3D spectral coordinates and an additional scalar measuring sulcal depth. All layers have $K_l = 6$ Gaussian kernels, similar to [20]. Since the output has 32 parcels, our last layer size is set to 32. In the last layer, softmax operation is applied for parcellation prediction, and the remaining layers employ Leaky ReLU as an activation function to obtain filter responses in Eq. (1).

Discriminator: Similar to the segmentator network, we use 2 graph convolution layers, an average pooling layer, and 3 fully connected (linear) layers for classifying the segmentation domain. The first graph convolution layer takes segmentation predictions with 32 feature maps as input. Moreover, the output sizes of the first two layers output are 128 and 64, respectively. Average pooling is used to reduce the input graph to a 1-D vector for the classification task. Three fully-connected layers are placed at the end of the network, with respective sizes of 32, 16, and 1. Each graph convolution layer has $K_l = 6$ Gaussian kernels. Sigmoid activation is applied to the last linear layer to predict the input domain of the graph sample and the remaining layers use Leaky ReLU.

3 Results

We evaluate the performance of our method using MindBoggle [2], the largest manually-labeled brain surface dataset. This dataset contains the cortical mesh data of 101 subjects aggregated from multiple sites. Each brain surface includes 32 manually labeled parcels. We split this dataset into 70-10-20 training, validation and test sets. The training set has only 35 samples for the source and

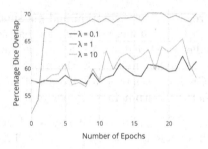 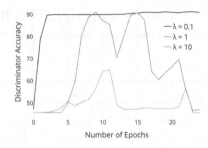

Fig. 2. Effect of hyper-parameter λ: Segmentation performance in mean Dice (**left**) and Discriminator classification accuracy (**right**) on test examples, obtained for $\lambda \in \{0.1, 1, 10\}$.

target domains each. To have more training samples and thus reduce overfitting, we sub-sample the node embeddings of each mesh to generate 25 examples of 10K nodes. This data augmentation technique, which is not possible in regular CNNs, is enabled by the spectral embedding of our approach.

Let P_c be the nodes predicted as having label $c \in \{1, \ldots, 32\}$, and G_c be the actual set of nodes with this label in the ground-truth parcellation. We evaluate performance using the mean Dice overlap:

$$\text{MeanDice}(\mathbf{P}, \mathbf{G}) \;=\; \frac{1}{32} \sum_{c=1}^{32} \frac{2\,|P_c \cap G_c|}{|P_c| + |G_c|}. \tag{5}$$

All experiments were carried out on an i7 desktop computer with 16 GB of RAM and an Nvidia Titan X 12 GB GPU. The code for our work is available at the following URL: https://tinyurl.com/yawdw7hh.

3.1 Effect of λ on Parcellation

The loss function for adversarial training involves hyper-parameter λ, which controls the trade-off between parcellation accuracy on labeled source data and fooling the discriminator (i.e., alignment invariance). To assess the impact of this important hyper-parameter on performance, we show in Fig. 2 the segmentator mean Dice and discriminator classification accuracy on test examples at different training epochs, for $\lambda \in \{0.1, 1, 10\}$. As expected, when using a large $\lambda = 10$, the model focuses mostly on fooling the discriminator. This results in a low segmentation Dice, and a discriminator accuracy near 50% since the discriminator cannot distinguish between source and target parcellation outputs. Conversely, for a small $\lambda = 0.1$, the adversarial training gives less importance to fooling the discriminator, which translates in a high discriminator accuracy. However, this also leads to a poor performance on target examples, since the parcellation output for these examples differs greatly from those of source examples. This illustrates that a stronger adversarial learning is required to align the source and target domains. For the rest of our experiments, we selected $\lambda = 1$ based on the parcellation accuracy for *validation* examples.

Table 1. Comparison with surface segmentation approaches: Mean Dice and standard deviation on test data. The first result column corresponds to the default setting where test (i.e., target domain) graphs are not aligned. For the second column, test graphs were aligned on the same reference as training (i.e., source domain) graphs. Result columns 3–7 correspond to the setting where all test graphs are aligned to four randomly-selected target graphs (a different graph for each column). Bold font highlights a performance statistically higher than all other methods (t-test $p < 0.01$).

Method	No alignment	Alignment to reference graph				
		Source	Rand. target 1	Rand. target 2	Rand. target 3	Rand. target 4
Spectral RF [23]	65.4 ± 9.0	81.9 ± 3.4	60.0 ± 1.8	55.3 ± 2.1	60.2 ± 4.0	55.2 ± 3.0
Seg-GCN [20]	71.4 ± 7.9	86.5 ± 2.8	67.8 ± 2.0	58.8 ± 2.8	63.5 ± 3.2	60.1 ± 3.6
Adv-GCN (ours)	$\mathbf{73.8 \pm 6.0}$	85.7 ± 3.5	$\mathbf{73.5 \pm 2.0}$	$\mathbf{72.5 \pm 2.6}$	$\mathbf{72.4 \pm 2.4}$	$\mathbf{71.7 \pm 3.3}$

3.2 Comparison with the State-of-the-art

We next compare our method, called Adv-GCN in the following results, against two other graph-based approaches for surface parcellation. This first one is the Spectral Random Forest (RF) algorithm proposed in [23], which performs the same spectral graph embedding as our method, and then uses the spectral coordinates and sulcal depth at individual nodes to train a RF classifier. As done in [23], we employed 50 trees to build the RF model. This comparison baseline was included to show the limitation of point-based approaches which ignore the relationship between nodes when predicting labels. The second approach, called Seg-GCN, is the same segmentation GCN as in our method, but trained without the adversarial loss. For this baseline, which is similar to the method presented in [20], our goal is to show the benefit of learning an alignment-invariant representation with adversarial domain adaptation.

The surface parcellation approaches are compared in three different test settings. In the first one, the approaches are applied on target examples without any alignment. This corresponds to the normal application setting of our alignment-invariant method. For the second one, we align all target examples on the same reference surface as the one used for source examples. This setting requires to retain the reference surface and apply ICP alignment in pre-processing for each test surface. Finally, in the third setting, target examples are aligned to a reference surface chosen randomly in the test set. This last setting corresponds to the case where we want to parcel surfaces from a dataset which was processed differently than the source dataset.

Results of this experiment are summarized in Table 1. When test examples are aligned to the same source reference (i.e., no domain shift), our segmentation GCN architecture, with or without adversarial learning, outperforms Spectral RF by a large margin. This illustrates the importance of considering the relationship between different nodes in the graph, as in our graph convolution model. However, when applied to non-aligned test surface, our Adv-GCN method achieves a 2.4% improvement in mean Dice over Seg-GCN, and 8.4%

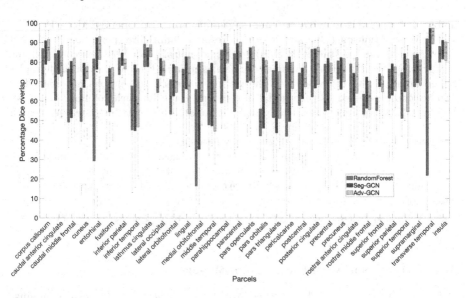

Fig. 3. Segmentation Dice for individual parcels: Box-plot of mean Dice overlap achieved by three different methods for all 32 cortical parcels when *test subjects are not aligned.*

over Spectral RF. This demonstrates the benefit of learning an alignment-invariant representation via adversarial domain adaptation. Furthermore, the improvement provided by our Adv-GCN method is even more significant for surfaces aligned to a random target reference (last four columns of Table 1). Thus, across the four random target references, Adv-GCN yields an average improvement of 14.9% compared to Spectral RF and 10.0% compared to Seg-GCN. This shows the strength of adversarial learning to match the output distribution for two fixed domains.

The average Dice overlap for individual parcels is shown in Fig. 3. As can be seen, Adv-GCN provides a higher mean and smaller variance for most of the 32 parcels. By inspecting results, we find that accuracy is correlated with parcel size, with larger parcels generally better segmented than smaller ones. Figure 4 shows qualitative results for different graph segmentation methods. As highlighted by the red circle, our Adv-CGN gives a more accurate segmentation compared to Seg-GCN and Spectral RF, with an improvement over 13% in parcel-averaged Dice.

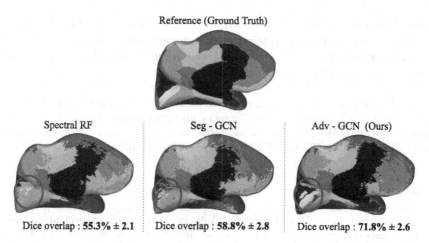

Fig. 4. Qualitative comparison: Parcellation outputs of the three surface segmentation approaches for a single non-aligned test surface. For better visualization, segmented parcels are drawn on an inflated surface. For each approach, we report the average Dice and standard deviation computed over the 32 parcels. As highlighted by the red circle, our adversarial GCN (Adv-CGN) gives a more accurate segmentation compared to the same model without adversarial training (Seg-GCN) and Spectral Random Forest (RF).

4   Conclusion

In this paper, we presented a novel adversarial domain adaptation framework for brain surface parcellation. The proposed algorithm leverages an adversarial training mechanism to obtain an alignment-invariant surface segmentation, and overcomes the limitations of spectral GCNs [21, 22] that require finding an explicit alignment of graph eigenbases. Table 1 shows a clear improvement in performance over the same spectral GCN without adversarial training (Seg-GCN) and the Spectral Random Forest (RF) algorithm [23]. Specifically, our method yields a 2.4% mean Dice improvement over Seg-GCN and 8.4% over Spectral RF, for non-aligned test surfaces. This improvement reaches over 10% for test surface aligned to a random target reference. Qualitative results in Fig. 4 illustrate the better parcellation of our method for non-aligned surfaces.

In some experiments, we observed a tendency of the discriminator to overfit the training set, which impeded domain adaptation in the learning process. In a future study, two strategies could be explored to overcome this problem: using other types of discriminator, for instance the Least Squares GAN [24] or Wasserstein GAN [25], and applying data augmentation on labeled brain surface meshes. While our adversarial graph domain adaptation technique was demonstrated on cortical parcellation, it also has potential for other surface segmentation problems where a domain shift is present. Likewise, our method could be useful for semi-supervised surface segmentation, thereby mitigating the need for large amounts of labeled surfaces. In this setting, the same architecture could be used, however the discriminator would predict if the segmentation output is for a labeled or unlabeled example from the same domain. We plan to evaluate the impact of higher frequency input representations with performance measures such as Hausdorff distance in future work.

Acknowledgments. This research work was partly funded by the Fonds de Recherche du Quebec (FQRNT) and Natural Sciences and Engineering Research Council of Canada (NSERC). We gratefully acknowledge the support of NVIDIA Corporation for the donation of the Titan X Pascal GPU used for this research.

References

1. Arbabshirani, M.R., Plis, S., Sui, J., Calhoun, V.D.: Single subject prediction of brain disorders in neuroimaging: promises and pitfalls. Neuroimage **145**, 137–165 (2017)
2. Klein, A., et al.: Mindboggling morphometry of human brains. PLOS Comput. Biol. **13**, e1005350 (2017)
3. Tajbakhsh, N., Jeyaseelan, L., Li, Q., Chiang, J., Wu, Z., Ding, X.: Embracing imperfect datasets: a review of deep learning solutions for medical image segmentation. Med. Image Anal. **63**, 101693 (2019)
4. Goodfellow, I., et al.: Generative adversarial nets. In: Advances in Neural Information Processing Systems (2014)
5. Zhang, Y., David, P., Gong, B.: Curriculum domain adaptation for semantic segmentation of urban scenes. In: Proceedings of the IEEE International Conference on Computer Vision (2017)
6. Zou, Y., Yu, Z., Vijaya Kumar, B.V.K., Wang, J.: Unsupervised domain adaptation for semantic segmentation via class-balanced self-training. In: Ferrari, V., Hebert, M., Sminchisescu, C., Weiss, Y. (eds.) ECCV 2018. LNCS, vol. 11207, pp. 297–313. Springer, Cham (2018). https://doi.org/10.1007/978-3-030-01219-9_18
7. Ghafoorian, M., et al.: Transfer learning for domain adaptation in MRI: application in brain lesion segmentation. In: Descoteaux, M., Maier-Hein, L., Franz, A., Jannin, P., Collins, D.L., Duchesne, S. (eds.) MICCAI 2017. LNCS, vol. 10435, pp. 516–524. Springer, Cham (2017). https://doi.org/10.1007/978-3-319-66179-7_59
8. Vu, T.H., Jain, H., Bucher, M., Cord, M., Pérez, P.: Advent: adversarial entropy minimization for domain adaptation in semantic segmentation. In: Proceedings of the IEEE Conference on Computer Vision and Pattern Recognition (2019)
9. Zhang, Y., Miao, S., Mansi, T., Liao, R.: Task driven generative modeling for unsupervised domain adaptation: application to x-ray image segmentation. In: Frangi, A.F., Schnabel, J.A., Davatzikos, C., Alberola-López, C., Fichtinger, G. (eds.) MICCAI 2018. LNCS, vol. 11071, pp. 599–607. Springer, Cham (2018). https://doi.org/10.1007/978-3-030-00934-2_67
10. Javanmardi, M., Tasdizen, T.: Domain adaptation for biomedical image segmentation using adversarial training. In: 2018 IEEE 15th International Symposium on Biomedical Imaging (ISBI 2018). IEEE (2018)
11. Long, M., Cao, Y., Wang, J., Jordan, M.: Learning transferable features with deep adaptation networks. In: International Conference on Machine Learning (2015)
12. Ganin, Y., Lempitsky, V.: Unsupervised domain adaptation by backpropagation. In: International Conference on Machine Learning (2015)

13. Tsai, Y.H., Hung, W.C., Schulter, S., Sohn, K., Yang, M.H., Chandraker, M.: Learning to adapt structured output space for semantic segmentation. In: Proceedings of the IEEE Conference on Computer Vision and Pattern Recognition (2018)
14. Hoffman, J., Wang, D., Yu, F., Darrell, T.: Fcns in the wild: pixel-level adversarial and constraint-based adaptation. arXiv preprint arXiv:1612.02649 (2016)
15. Kamnitsas, K., et al.: Unsupervised domain adaptation in brain lesion segmentation with adversarial networks. In: International Conference on Information Processing in Medical Imaging (2017)
16. Bateson, M., Kervadec, H., Dolz, J., Lombaert, H., Ayed, I.B.: Constrained domain adaptation for segmentation. In: International Conference on Medical Image Computing and Computer-Assisted Intervention (2019)
17. Bronstein, M.M., Bruna, J., LeCun, Y., Szlam, A., Vandergheynst, P.: Geometric deep learning: going beyond Euclidean data. IEEE Signal Process. **34**, 18–42 (2017)
18. Monti, F., Boscaini, D., Masci, J., Rodolà, E., Svoboda, J., Bronstein, M.: Geometric deep learning on graphs using mixture model CNNs. In: CVPR (2017)
19. Cucurull, G., et al.: Convolutional neural networks for mesh-based parcellation of the cerebral cortex. In: MIDL (2018)
20. Gopinath, K., Desrosiers, C., Lombaert, H.: Graph convolutions on spectral embeddings for cortical surface parcellation. Med. Image Anal. **54**, 297–305 (2019)
21. Bruna, J., Zaremba, W., Szlam, A., Lecun, Y.: Spectral networks and locally connected networks on graphs. In: ICLR (2014)
22. Defferrard, M., Bresson, X., Vandergheynst, P.: Convolutional neural networks on graphs with fast localized spectral filtering. In: NIPS (2016)
23. Lombaert, H., Criminisi, A., Ayache, N.: Spectral forests: learning of surface data, application to cortical parcellation. In: Navab, N., Hornegger, J., Wells, W.M., Frangi, A.F. (eds.) MICCAI 2015. LNCS, vol. 9349, pp. 547–555. Springer, Cham (2015). https://doi.org/10.1007/978-3-319-24553-9_67
24. Mao, X., Li, Q., Xie, H., Lau, R.Y., Wang, Z., Paul Smolley, S.: Least squares generative adversarial networks. In: Proceedings of the IEEE International Conference on Computer Vision, pp. 2794–2802 (2017)
25. Arjovsky, M., Chintala, S., Bottou, L.: Wasserstein GAN. arXiv preprint arXiv:1701.07875 (2017)

Min-Cut Max-Flow for Network Abnormality Detection: Application to Preterm Birth

Hassna Irzan[1,2($\boxtimes$)], Lucas Fidon[2], Tom Vercauteren[2], Sebastien Ourselin[2], Neil Marlow[3], and Andrew Melbourne[1,2]

[1] Department of Medical Physics and Biomedical Engineering, University College London, London, UK
hassna.irzan.17@ucl.ac.uk
[2] School of Biomedical Engineering and Imaging Sciences, Kings College London, London, UK
[3] Institute for Women's Health, University College London, London, UK

Abstract. Neuroimaging studies of structural connectomes typically average the data from many subjects and analyse the average properties of the resulting network. We propose a new framework for individual brain-network structural abnormality detection. The framework uses a graph-based anomaly detection algorithm that allows to detect abnormal structural connectivity on a subject level. The proposed method is generic and can be adapted for a broad range of network abnormality detection problems. In this study, we apply our method to investigate the integrity of white matter tracts of 19-year-old extremely preterm born individuals. We show the feasibility to cast the network abnormality detection problem into a min-cut max-flow problem, and identify consistent abnormal white matter tracts in extremely preterm subjects, including a common network involving the bilateral thalamus and frontal gyri.

1 Introduction

The neuropsychological outcome and neuroimaging phenotype of preterm-born children and infants is greatly influenced by premature exposure to the extrauterine environment [2,3,9]. Studies have shown anatomical [2], micro-structural [3] and a range of neuropsychological differences [9] linked to prematurity. The majority of neuroimaging studies on preterm populations analyse the average properties of the preterm group compared to that of the controls. Such population-level studies usually register all images of a population into a common space. Due to the anatomical abnormalities associated with the preterm

---

Electronic supplementary material The online version of this chapter (https://doi.org/10.1007/978-3-030-60365-6_16) contains supplementary material, which is available to authorized users.

C. H. Sudre et al. (Eds.): UNSURE 2020/GRAIL 2020, LNCS 12443, pp. 164–173, 2020.
https://doi.org/10.1007/978-3-030-60365-6_16

brain, such as ventriculomegaly, this step can lead to misleading results. Generally, analysis that contrast two populations inherently ignore considerable inter-subject heterogeneity in each group. In the present work, we acknowledge that besides the normal individual variability, preterm birth has a broad range of effects on the brain. The most-reported impairments in the preterm born population are negative neuropsychological outcome [9] and white matter (WM) differences [5] with a varied pattern of severity.

Researchers' efforts in investigating WM led to developing brain structural connectomes (or networks) as a promising tool to investigate major brain pathways and examine essential circuits [12].

The connectome can be studied as a graph where the nodes are the brain regions, and the edges quantify inter-connectivity between those areas. The main aim of the present paper is to detect abnormal WM connectivity. Labels for WM abnormalities are difficult to obtain. However, we hypothesise that abnormalities in edge connectivity are unlikely to be isolated and that conversely, anomalies are likely to be contiguous. Graph-based methods allow us to model this anatomical hypothesis and to detect abnormalities even in the absence of ground-truth labels.

The min-cut max-flow framework is applied to investigate the integrity of WM tracts of 19-year-old extremely preterm individuals (born before 27 weeks completed gestation). We analyse WM connectivity in the individual subject space by mapping the tracts into structural connectomes; then we separate aberrant connectivity from the aged-matched control-group connectivity using the min-cut max-flow framework. The framework takes into account the anatomical information of the WM tracts and brain regions to which they are connected. We use a graph similarity measure based on a Laplacian matrix to measure the global differences in structural connectivity between a reference connectivity matrix and the connectivity matrix under investigation. While the distance matrix estimates a global measure of divergence, the min-cut max-flow framework localises the abnormality. We experimentally show that the proposed framework can detect consistent abnormal WM tracts across the subjects, and the abnormal WM tracts identified for each subject correlate with the changes in structural connectivity as measured by the graph similarity measure.

2   Methods

We describe the data in Sect. 2.1 and the steps to perform tractography and network extraction in Sect. 2.2. Section 2.3 describes the measure we use to quantify the distance between two brain-networks, while Sect. 2.4 describes the min-cut max-flow formulation to detect brain-network abnormalities. Figure 1 illustrates the main steps of the pipeline.

2.1   Data

Diffusion weighted MRI and T1-weighted MRI acquisitions were performed on a 3T Philips Achieva system for $N_p = 80$ (49/31 females/males) extremely

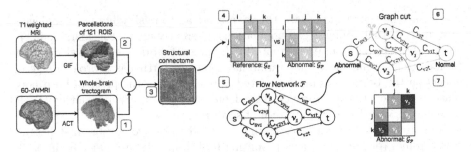

Fig. 1. Outline of the methodology to estimate structural networks and find abnormal structural connections. We performed Anatomically Constrained Tractography (ACT) (1) [10] to estimate the white matter streamlines. We estimate the structural connectome (3) by quantifying the connectivity between brain regions obtained from Geodesic Information Flow (GIF) [4] parcellations (2). We compare the structural connectivity matrix of each extremely preterm born subject $\mathcal{G}_P$ to the average structural connectivity matrix of the full-term born subjects $\mathcal{G}_C$ (4); similar edges have the same colour, the colour of the abnormal edge in $\mathcal{G}_P$ is different to the corresponding edges in $\mathcal{G}_C$ (4). We cast the problem into a min-cut max-flow framework (5). The detection of structural brain abnormality (7) results from the graph cut after solving the min-cut max-flow problem (6).

preterm born 19-year-old individuals and $N_c = 36$ (19/17 females/males) full-term born age-matched peers. T1-weighted MRI images were acquired at $TR = 6.93\,ms$, $TE = 3.14\,ms$ and $1\,mm$ isotropic resolution. EPI-SE volumes of dWMRI were acquired at $(2.5 \times 2.5 \times 3)\,mm$ resolution across b-values of $(0, 300, 700, 2000)\,s/mm^2$, n: 4, 8, 16, 32 directions, TE: 70 ms, TR: 3500 ms, FOV: $(240 \times 240 \times 150)\,mm$, flip angle: 90°, and SENSE factor of 1.

T1-weighted images were bias-corrected using N4ITK algorithm [14]. Diffusion-weighted MRI volumes were corrected for thermal noise [15], Gibbs-ringing artefacts [7], eddy current-induced distortion and subject movements artefacts [1].

The median gestational age at birth for extremely preterm born individuals is 25.14 (CI 95% 22.14–25.86) weeks of gestation. The full term born subjects were born after 37 weeks of gestation. All the subjects had MRI assessment at 19 years of age.

2.2 Tractography and Networks Extraction

As shown in step 1 of Fig. 1, we generate a whole-brain tractogram for each subject. A multi-shell multi-tissue approach [6] was used to estimate the response function for each tissue type. The fibre orientation distribution (FOD) was first calculated in each voxel using constrained spherical deconvolution (CSD) [13] and then normalised for inter-subject comparisons. Anatomically Constrained Tractography (ACT) was performed using dynamic seeding and backtrack re-tracking algorithms [10]. To account for the fact that the density of the estimated fibres is not representative of the density of the underlying white matter fibres, the ten million streamlines generated per subject were filtered using the spherical-deconvolution informed filtering of tracks (SIFT2) procedure [11]. SIFT2 determines an adequate cross-sectional area for each estimated streamline, such that the estimated streamlines densities throughout the white matter are reflective of the fibre densities computed using the spherical deconvolution model [11]. As illustrated in Fig. 1, in step 2, tissue parcellations of the corrected T1-weighted volumes were obtained using Geodesic Information Flow (GIF) [4]. Brain regions of interest (ROI) were defined based on the GIF labelling protocol [4]. The grey matter areas (121 brain regions) formed the nodes for the brain network derivation. For each subject $n \in N$, a network $\mathcal{G}_n = (Q, Z)$ is defined, in which each node corresponds to an ROI, and Z is the set of edges connecting the ROIs. In the network $\mathcal{G}_n$, for all of edges (i, j), we denote g_{ij} the strength of the connectivity between i and j defined by the weighted (SIFT2) [11] contribution of each streamline connecting i and j. This is illustrated in step 3 of Fig. 1.

2.3   Graph Similarity Measure

We aim to evaluate the divergence of the connectivity matrix of each extremely preterm born subject from the normality. The graph similarity is quantified using the spectral distance (SD) [16] of the normalised Laplacian. The eigenvalues of the normalised Laplacian describe aspects of the global network structure. The difference between the spectra of normalised Laplacians can be used to quantify the similarity between networks. The normalised Laplacian $\mathcal{L}$ of a graph $\mathcal{G}$ with edge weights g_{ij} is defined as $\mathcal{L} = \mathcal{I} - \mathcal{D}^{-\frac{1}{2}} \mathcal{G} \mathcal{D}^{-\frac{1}{2}}$ [16], where $\mathcal{I}$ is the identity matrix and $\mathcal{D}$ is a diagonal matrix such that $\mathcal{D} = \text{diag}(d_i)$ with $\forall i$ $d_i = \sum_{j \in Q} g_{ij}$. To avoid the use of arbitrary control connectivity matrices, we consider the mean connectivity matrix $\mathcal{G}_C$ of the full-term born subjects and the corresponding normalised Laplacian $\mathcal{L}_C$. Let $\mathcal{L}_P$ be the Laplacian of the connectivity matrix $\mathcal{G}_P$ of the extremely preterm born subject, the spectral distance $SD(\mathcal{L}_C, \mathcal{L}_P)$ is defined as the Euclidean distance between the eigenvalues of $\mathcal{L}_C$ and $\mathcal{L}_P$ [16]

$$SD(\mathcal{L}_C, \mathcal{L}_P) = \sum_u \sqrt{(\lambda_u^C - \lambda_u^P)^2} \tag{1}$$

Therefore we aim to measure the normality of $\mathcal{G}_P$ using $SD(\mathcal{L}_C, \mathcal{L}_P)$.

2.4   Graph Cut Optimisation for the Detection of Abnormal Connectivity

This section shows how the problem of detecting anomalies in subject's connectivity network can be cast as a min-cut max-flow problem.

Min-Cut Max-Flow Framework: Given the group-level reference connectivity matrix $\mathcal{G}_C$ and the subject-level abnormal connectivity matrix $\mathcal{G}_P$ (as illustrated in step 4 of Fig. 1), we aim to identify the abnormal connectivity in $\mathcal{G_P}$ with respect to $\mathcal{G_C}$. As each edge (i, j) connects brain regions i and j with strength of connectivity g_{ij}, by comparing the strength of connectivity g_{ij} in the reference connectivity matrix $\mathcal{G_C}$ and the abnormal connectivity matrix $\mathcal{G_P}$, we aim to separate abnormal edges from normal edges.

We cast this problem into a min-cut max-flow framework [8]. A max-flow framework involves a fully connected bi-directed graph $\mathcal{F} = (\mathcal{V}, \mathcal{E})$ with $|\mathcal{V}|$ nodes and $|\mathcal{E}|$ directed edges connecting them. An edge $(i, j) \in Z$ in the connectivity matrix $\mathcal{G}_n$ is a node $v \in \mathcal{V}$ in the graph $\mathcal{F}$ as illustrated in step 5 of Fig. 1. The graph $\mathcal{F}$ has two additional nodes: the source node $s \in \mathcal{V}$ and the sink node $t \in \mathcal{V}$. Each edge of $\mathcal{F}$ has a fixed and non-negative capacity C which is the maximum flow that edge can handle. The graph $\mathcal{F}$ has three types of edges. Namely: 1) the edges that connect the source node $s \in \mathcal{V}$ to the nodes $v \in \mathcal{V}$ with capacity $C_{s,v}$, the edges that link the sink node $t \in \mathcal{V}$ to the nodes $v \in \mathcal{V}$ with capacity $C_{t,v}$ and the edges that connect the nodes $v \in \mathcal{V}$ between each other with capacity $C_{v1,v2}$. The source node s and the sink node t are not directly connected. According to the max-flow min-cut theorem, the maximum flow from the source node $s \in \mathcal{V}$ to the sink node $t \in \mathcal{V}$ corresponds to the minimum total capacities of the edges, which, if removed, would partition the graph $\mathcal{F}$ into two subsets: the abnormal nodes set $\mathcal{S}$ and the normal nodes set $\mathcal{T}$.

In order to reflect the similarity between the edge $(i, j) \in \mathcal{G_C}$ and the corresponding edge $(i, j) \in \mathcal{G_P}$, we define the capacity $C_{t,v}$ as the Gaussian similarity function between the edge weights $g_{ij}^{\mathcal{G_C}}$ and $g_{ij}^{\mathcal{G_P}}$

$$C_{t,v}(g_{ij}^{\mathcal{G_C}}, g_{ij}^{\mathcal{G_P}}) = K \cdot \exp\left(\frac{-\left(g_{ij}^{\mathcal{G_C}} - g_{ij}^{\mathcal{G_P}}\right)^2}{2\sigma^2}\right) \tag{2}$$

where K is an arbitrary multiplicative constant. The capacity $C_{s,v}$ of the edges connecting the source node $s \in \mathcal{V}$ with the nodes $v \in \mathcal{V}$ is set to $K - C_{t,v}(g_{ij}^{\mathcal{G_C}}, g_{ij}^{\mathcal{G_P}})$. The capacity $C_{s,v}$ reflects the extent to which the strength of connectivity associated with the edge $(i, j) \in \mathcal{G_P}$ is abnormal while the capacity $C_{t,v}$ reflects the degree to which the strength of connectivity associated with the edge $(i, j) \in \mathcal{G_P}$ is normal.

In addition, if one brain region has an abnormal edge connection (i, j), then the likelihood it has other abnormal edge connections is high. Sporadic abnormal connections are more likely to be due to noise or error in the streamline reconstruction. Pair of edges of the form (i, j) and (i, y) that are connected to the same brain region i are considered as neighbours in $\mathcal{G}_n$. To account for that in the graph $\mathcal{F}$, the capacity of the edges $C_{v1,v2}$ is set to a positive constant value M if the two nodes represent two neighbouring edges in the connectivity matrices $\mathcal{G}_n$ and zero otherwise. Therefore, partitioning the graph into sets $\mathcal{S}$ and $\mathcal{T}$ maximises

$$E = \sum_{v \in \mathcal{S}} K - C_{t,v}(g_{ij}^{\mathcal{G_C}}, g_{ij}^{\mathcal{G_P}}) + \sum_{v \in \mathcal{T}} C_{t,v}(g_{ij}^{\mathcal{G_C}}, g_{ij}^{\mathcal{G_P}}) - \sum_{v1 \in \mathcal{S}, v2 \in \mathcal{T}} C_{v1,v2} \tag{3}$$

which is solved using highest-label preflow-push algorithm.

Parameter Tuning: The average full-term connectivity matrix is the reference connectivity matrix $\mathcal{G}_C$. The parameters of the graph $\mathcal{F}$ are K, σ and M. As K and M are dependent, we fix $K = 10^4$ and determine σ and M using a grid search such that when the reference connectivity matrix $\mathcal{G}_C$ is compared to the connectivity matrix of each full-term born subject, the graph-cut framework identifies minimal abnormal edges E_c; when the reference connectivity matrix $\mathcal{G}_C$ is compared to the connectivity matrix of each extremely preterm subjects, the graph-cut identifies the maximum number of abnormal edges E_p. Therefore, the best σ and M maximise the quantity $E_p - E_c$.

Framework Evaluation: To assess the performance of the min-cut max-flow framework, we evaluate two aspects: 1) the consistency of the identified abnormal edges across the subjects and 2) the consistency of the number of the identified edges E_p with respect to the graph similarity measure $SD(\mathcal{L}_C, \mathcal{L}_P)$. We expect the number of the identified abnormal edges to correlate with the similarity measure $SD(\mathcal{L}_C, \mathcal{L}_P)$, as higher $SD(\mathcal{L}_C, \mathcal{L}_P)$ indicates stronger structural deviation from the reference matrix $\mathcal{G}_C$. The identified edges constitute a sub-network for each subject. It is expected that the identified sub-networks show two characteristics: 1) a general pattern that is shared between the extremely preterm subjects as being born extremely preterm might induce similar brain abnormalities, and 2) a distinctive one that is characteristic to individual subjects as result of individual variability. To investigate how the identified sub-networks cluster across the extremely preterm subjects, we use principal component analysis (PCA) to derive a low-dimensional set of features X_{red} that represent the original abnormal sub-networks X. We apply PCA to the set of edges $X \in R^{N_p \times |Z|}$ in which for each extremely preterm subject, we set the edges that have been identified as abnormal to 1 and 0 otherwise.

Simulation: The weight of each edge is proportional to the WM connecting the corresponding brain regions. A WM abnormality is a reduction or increase in the weight of the edges with respect to the reference group (full term born subjects). Since reduction in WM connectivity is a characteristic of the preterm brain phenotype [5], we simulate abnormalities of WM connectivity by reducing weights in $\mathcal{G}_P$ with respect to $\mathcal{G}_C$. To show the ground-truth link between SD and the percentage of edges identified abnormal edges. We consider $\mathcal{G}_C$ as a 15×15 zero-diagonal symmetric matrix of ones, and consider $\mathcal{G}_P$ as a 15×15 matrix with synthetic abnormalities. In the beginning, $\mathcal{G}_P$ is identical to $\mathcal{G}_C$, then the abnormalities are induced by randomly reducing the weights associated with the edges connected to the same node in $\mathcal{G}_P$. In each iteration an additional node is reduced at random by 90% to 100% until 99% of all the edges are reduced. This simulation has been carried out on 6 pairs of $\mathcal{G}_C$ and $\mathcal{G}_P$. We used the same K, σ and M parameters as in real data.

3   Results

The grid search over the parameters σ and M that minimise the number of abnormal edges E_c detected in the full-term born subjects and maximise the number of abnormal edges E_p identified in the extremely preterm born group shows that the best values are $\sigma = 0.01$ and $M = 51$.

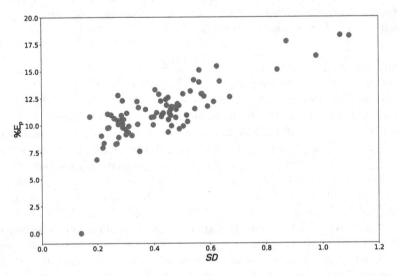

Fig. 2. Visualisation of the relationship between the spectral distance $SD(\mathcal{L}_C, \mathcal{L}_P)$ and proportion of abnormal edges $\%E_P$ identified for each extremely preterm subject. The correlation between $SD(\mathcal{L}_C, \mathcal{L}_P)$ and the proportion of abnormal edges is $\rho = 0.71$ with p-value $= 10^{-14}$.

Figure 2 shows the relationship between SD and the ratio of abnormal to normal edges in each extremely preterm subject. The correlation between SD and the total number of abnormal edges E_p is statistically significant (p-value $= 10^{-14}$) with a correlation coefficient of $\rho = 0.71$. On average $11.3\% \pm 2.5\%$ of the total edges in extremely preterm subjects have been identified as abnormal. Figure 3 shows the most identified edges (in 98% of the extremely preterm subject). These edges form a sub-network related to WM connecting mainly frontal cortex and deep grey matter regions such as bilateral thalamus and bilateral frontal gyrus. Moreover, the pattern of the identified sub-network shows hemispheric symmetry. Figure 4 shows a plot of the identified abnormal sub-networks with respect to the first and second principal components. In addition, the subjects have been colour-coded with respect to the percentage of abnormal edges that were identified for that subject. Figure 4 shows that the subjects with higher percentage of abnormal edges form different clusters.

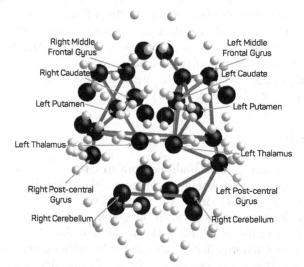

Fig. 3. Visualisation of the most common identified edges in the extremely preterm subjects. The connections in green are the abnormal edges, the brain regions in black are connected by abnormal edges while brain regions in white do not have abnormal edges.

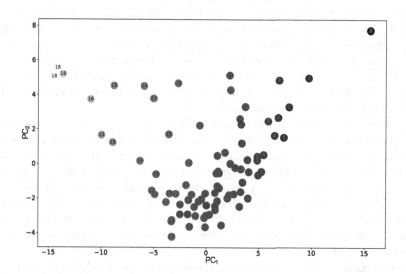

Fig. 4. Visualisation of the PCA results. The reduced sub-network data is plotted with respect to the first and second principal component. To visualise the data, an annotated colour scale is used to represent the percentages of abnormal edges found in each subject, with black being the least and white being the most.

Simulation: The figure in the Supplementary Material shows the results for the relationship between SD and the proportion of abnormal edges that have been detected in the connectivity matrix with synthetic abnormalities. The figure displays the results for 6 pairs of $\mathcal{G}_P$ and $\mathcal{G}_C$. The mean correlation coefficient between the SD and the proportion of abnormal edges is $\rho = 0.98$ (p-value $= 4 \times 10^{-9}$). This suggests that the SD metric summarised the amount of local abnormalities present in the connectivity matrix.

4   Discussion

We propose a new framework for brain-network structural abnormality detection. The framework is based on a min-cut max-flow algorithm and aims to detect abnormal structural connectivity at the subject level.

The results show agreement between the graph similarity measure (SD) and the number of abnormal edges E_p both on the real data (Fig. 2) and on the data with simulated abnormalities (figure in the Supplementary Material). This indicates that the framework can detect the number of abnormal edges that is proportional to how different is the individual connectivity matrix with respect to the reference connectivity matrix. In the case of real data, the most identified sub-network across the extremely preterm born subjects (Fig. 3) demonstrates that there is consistency across the subjects as the abnormal WM connectivity is distributed between the deep grey matter regions and the frontal cortex. These results are consistent with previous findings in extremely preterm neonatal population [3] and in extremely preterm adolescents [5]. The agreement between these findings suggests that WM connectivity in these brain areas is vulnerable to extreme preterm exposure to the extra-uterine environment. Moreover, it appears that the extremely preterm brain at adolescence does not recover from early-life WM injury. However, it is still unclear whether the WM alteration represents a developmental delay or permanent damage. Further analysis of older preterm samples needs to be performed.

Figure 4 shows clusters of identified sub-networks suggesting that the identified sub-networks have a variable pattern. The subjects with similar abnormal sub-networks form clusters. The clustering along the first principal component might be driven by the number of abnormal edges, while the clustering along the second principal component is more subtle. In general, it seems that the degree to which each extremely preterm born subject has been affected by extremely preterm exposure to the extrauterine environment is variable. In the future, it would be interesting to analyse how this translates to the varied cognitive outcome of these subjects [9].

In this study, we demonstrated for the first time the feasibility of casting the network abnormality detection problem into a min-cut max-flow problem. This method is able to detect abnormal connectivity at an individual level, compared to conventional group-wise comparisons. Although the method was employed to analyse abnormal structural connectivity in extremely preterm subjects, it can be extended to detect abnormal functional connectivity. This could be of great relevance to other conditions such as dementia or autism. Moreover, the proposed framework could be applied to a broad range of network abnormality detection beyond the proposed medical application.

Acknowledgements. This work is supported by the EPSRC-funded UCL Centre for Doctoral Training in Medical Imaging (EP/L016478/1). We would like to acknowledge the MRC (MR/J01107X/1) and the National Institute for Health Research (NIHR).

References

1. Andersson, J.L.R., Sotiropoulos, S.N.: An integrated approach to correction for off-resonance effects and subject movement in diffusion MR imaging. NeuroImage **125**, 1063–1078 (2016)
2. Ball, G., et al.: The effect of preterm birth on thalamic and cortical development. Cereb. Cortex **22**(5), 1016–1024 (2012). (New York, N.Y.: 1991)
3. Ball, G., et al.: Thalamocortical connectivity predicts cognition in children born preterm. Cereb. Cortex **25**(11), 4310–4318 (2015). (New York, N.Y.: 1991)
4. Cardoso, M.J., et al.: Geodesic information flows: spatially-variant graphs and their application to segmentation and fusion. IEEE Trans. Med. Imaging **34**(9), 1976–1988 (2015)
5. Irzan, H., et al.: A network-based analysis of the preterm adolescent brain using PCA and graph theory. In: 2019 MICCAI International Workshop on Computational Diffusion MRI (CDMRI). Springer, Cham (2019). https://doi.org/10.1007/978-3-030-52893-5
6. Jeurissen, B., et al.: Multi-tissue constrained spherical deconvolution for improved analysis of multi-shell diffusion MRI data. NeuroImage **103**, 411–426 (2014)
7. Kellner, E., et al.: Gibbs-ringing artifact removal based on local subvoxel-shifts. Magn. Reson. Med. **76**(5), 1574–1581 (2019)
8. Fulkerson, D.R., Ford, L.R.: Flows in Networks. Rand Corporation Research Studies Series. PUP (1962)
9. O'Reilly, H., et al.: Neuropsychological outcomes at 19 years of age following extremely preterm birth. Pediatrics **145**(2), e20192087 (2020)
10. Smith, R.E., et al.: Anatomically-constrained tractography: improved diffusion MRI streamlines tractography through effective use of anatomical information. NeuroImage **62**(3), 1924–1938 (2012)
11. Smith, R.E., et al.: Sift2: enabling dense quantitative assessment of brain white matter connectivity using streamlines tractography. NeuroImage **119**, 338–351 (2015)
12. Sporns, O., Tononi, G., Kötter, R.: The human connectome: a structural description of the human brain. PLOS Comput. Biol. **1**(4), e42 (2005)
13. Tournier, J.D., et al.: Robust determination of the fibre orientation distribution in diffusion MRI: non-negativity constrained super-resolved spherical deconvolution. NeuroImage **35**(4), 1459–1472 (2007)
14. Tustison, N.J., et al.: N4ITK: improved N3 bias correction. IEEE Trans. Med. Imaging **29**(6), 1310–1320 (2010)
15. Veraart, J., et al.: Denoising of diffusion MRI using random matrix theory. NeuroImage **142**, 394–406 (2016)
16. von Luxburg, U.: A tutorial on spectral clustering. Stat. Comput. **17**(4), 395–416 (2007)

Geometric Deep Learning for Post-Menstrual Age Prediction Based on the Neonatal White Matter Cortical Surface

Vitalis Vosylius, Andy Wang, Cemlyn Waters, Alexey Zakharov,
Francis Ward, Loic Le Folgoc, John Cupitt, Antonios Makropoulos,
Andreas Schuh, Daniel Rueckert, and Amir Alansary[✉]

Imperial College London, London, UK
a.alansary14@imperial.ac.uk

Abstract. Accurate estimation of the age in neonates is useful for measuring neurodevelopmental, medical, and growth outcomes. In this paper, we propose a novel approach to predict the post-menstrual age (PA) at scan, using techniques from geometric deep learning, based on the neonatal white matter cortical surface. We utilize and compare multiple specialized neural network architectures that predict the age using different geometric representations of the cortical surface; we compare MeshCNN, Pointnet++, GraphCNN, and a volumetric benchmark. The dataset is part of the Developing Human Connectome Project (dHCP), and is a cohort of healthy and premature neonates. We evaluate our approach on 650 subjects (727 scans) with PA ranging from 27 to 45 weeks. Our results show accurate prediction of the estimated PA, with mean error less than one week.

Keywords: Brain age · Cortical surface · Developing brain ·
Geometric deep learning · MeshCNN · PointNet · Graph neural
networks

1 Introduction

Precise age estimation in neonates helps measure the risk of neonatal pathology and organ maturity. Given that prematurity complications are the leading cause of all neonatal deaths, according to the world health organization (WHO)[1], precise age estimation may help to reduce the number of neonatal deaths significantly.

There are different age terminologies during the prenatal period such as gestational age (GA), post-menstrual age (PA), and chronological age (CA) [10]. PA measures the time from the first day of the last menstrual period and the

---

V. Vosylius, A. Wang, C. Waters, A. Zakharov and F. Ward—Equal contribution.

[1] https://www.who.int/news-room/fact-sheets/detail/preterm-birth.

C. H. Sudre et al. (Eds.): UNSURE 2020/GRAIL 2020, LNCS 12443, pp. 174–186, 2020.
https://doi.org/10.1007/978-3-030-60365-6_17

birth time (GA) added to the time elapsed after birth (CA). PA usually represents the age at scan taken during the neonatal period after the day of birth, and is normally measured in weeks.

The accuracy of the estimated PA is dependent on GA calculations; however, traditional methods of calculating the GA use the first day of the last menstrual period (LMP) as a reference point. As a result, the accuracy of these measurements is error-prone and relies on the patient's memory. Another method is to measure the diameter and circumference of the head, cranium, abdomen, and femur from 2D fetal ultrasound (US) images [26]. However, this method also relies on operator expertise as well as the biological variations and inconsistencies in skull size approximation, which may lead to age approximation errors [2]. Therefore, developing automatic models that accurately predict the age can help with the diagnosis of several neurodevelopmental and psychiatric illnesses that are rooted in the early neonatal period [29]. In this work, we propose a deep learning model that can accurately predict the PA using the white matter (WM) cortical brain surface.

Related Work: A number of machine learning and statistical methods have been presented for perinatal brain age prediction based on brain image data or measurements. For example, Towes et al. [31] proposed a feature-based model for infant age prediction using scale-invariant image features extracted from T1-weighted MRI scans. Brown et al. [6] presented a method to predict the brain network age using random forests (RF) classification [3] from diffusion magnetic resonance imaging (dMRI) data. The output of their model was used to detect delayed maturation in structural connectomes for preterm infants. Deprez et al. [9] used logistic growth models to estimate the age of preterm infants based on segmented myelin-like signals in the thalami and brainstem. Ouyang et al. [25] predicted the PA of preterm infants by measuring the temporal changes of cortical mean kurtosis (MK) and fractional anisotropy (FA) from non-Gaussian diffusion kurtosis imaging (DKI) and conventional diffusion tensor imaging (DTI). Hu et al. [18] predicted the infant age using a two-stage hierarchical regression model based on cortical features. Recently, Galdi et al. [12] combined features from structural and diffusion MRI to model morphometric similarity networks (MSNs) that identify the inter-regional similarities between the features. The calculated MSNs were later used for predicting neonatal brain age. However, neonatal brain age prediction using deep learning methods has not yet been explored in the literature.

At the same time, other works have leveraged recent advances in deep learning for adult brain age prediction. For instance, Jiang et al. [20] presented a 3D convolutional neural network (CNN) to predict the brain age of healthy adults using structural network images as an input. Gutiérrez-Becker and Wachinger [14] proposed a PointNet-based [27] architecture for predicting Alzheimer's disease and brain age using multiple brain structures as an input for their model. Recently, Besson et al. [1] utilize graph CNNs on a surface representation of the cortical ribbon for sex and age prediction on a data set of 6,410 healthy subjects with ages ranging 6–89 years. Compared to the previous methods, this work explores a number of directions for predicting the PA from the neonatal brain surface using geometric deep learning (GDL) approaches.

Contributions: To the best of our knowledge, this is the first work that evaluates age prediction from neonatal cortical surface representations. We evaluate a number of GDL architectures, namely PointNet++ [28], MeshCNN [15], and Graph CNN (GCN) [22]. Each architecture utilizes a different representation of the cortical surface: PointNet++ performs operations on a point cloud, MeshCNN operates on the edges of a mesh, and GCN operates directly on the adjacency, degree, and feature matrices of a graph. Our experiments show that these GDL techniques can accurately predict the PA from the neonatal cortical surface and outperform a 3D CNN benchmark that utilizes volumetric MRI data. We use a large dataset of 650 unique subjects (727 scans) with PA ranging from 26 to 45 weeks.

Outline: The rest of this paper is structured as follows: Sect. 2 provides a brief background to geometric deep learning (GDL). In Sect. 3 we then describe the structural details of each GDL architecture that we use. Section 4 outlines the details of our experiments. We finish by presenting our results followed by the conclusions and future directions.

2 Background

The majority of work in deep learning for medical imaging typically focuses on the application of CNNs to Euclidean data, e.g. MRI and ultrasound images [11,21]. However, CNN-based methods are usually restricted to exploit 2D or 3D volumetric images in Euclidean domains. This limits their application to complex geometric data defining embedded manifolds, e.g. brain cortical surfaces. In this case, convolutions are not well-defined, and the notion of CNN must be generalized to approximate functions in non-Euclidean domains. GDL methods aim to apply the power of CNNs to such non-Euclidean characterizations [5,24]. GDL methods in the literature can be categorized based on the representation of their input data as:

- **Voxel based:** The nodes on a surface are projected to their corresponding (or nearest) locations in the 3D image [4,32], where typical CNNs can be applied naturally. The main drawback is losing the surface representation, where two points far apart on the surface, in terms of its intrinsic geometry, can be very close in the volumetric or ambient Euclidean space. Furthermore, the projection to the 3D volume can introduce sampling accuracy errors.
- **Point set based:** Models encode a set of points or nodes into 3D feature maps that can be processed by a typical neural network architecture. The best known models utilizing this approach are PointNet [27] and PointNet++ [28]. They are agnostic to the origin of the point clouds they process and

have an ability to leverage geometric features of non-Euclidean data. These
models have been shown to achieve good performance efficiently; however,
they cannot preserve relational information between the nodes on the surface.

- **Graph based:** Models operate on graphs, which additionally encode connectivity information (edges) between the nodes on the surface. Variants of
  graph-based methods utilize GCNs to process the Laplacian of the graph in
  the spectral domain [7,17]. There are also special graph-based models that
  exploit meshes as their input graph. They are designed to operate on mesh
  edges and learn generalized convolution and pooling layers [15]. The main
  drawback of these models is the difficulty to increase the model capacity or
  scale up for large input data.

3   Methods

As mentioned previously, the attempt to generalize the power of CNNs to non-
Euclidean data leads to a set of techniques known as geometric deep learning
(GDL) [5]. In this section, we present a number of GDL techniques for age-
regression on brain surface representations: PointNet++ [28], MeshCNN [15],
and GCN [22]. The cortical surface meshes are extracted from MRI data as
described in [30]. The point-cloud representation is extracted directly from the
nodes (with node features), the graph from the same nodes together with the
connectivity information, and the mesh representation is defined with geometric
edge features described below. We also implement a volumetric 3D CNN as a
baseline. As noted in Sect. 1, each architecture operates on a different representation of the brain surface, with each representation capturing subtly different
geometric information. The architectures we present here also vary functionally,
i.e., they perform different functions on the surface and therefore learn different
abstractions of the brain surface. By proving that this range of GDL techniques
performs brain-age regression with high accuracy, we show the utility of GDL
to tasks related to the brain surface in general. We now describe the details of
each architecture's structure and functional operation.

Voxel Based: Similar to [8], we leverage a 3D CNN on spatially-normalized
gray-matter (GM) maps as a baseline model. This baseline ensures the integrity
of our experimentation and allows for a more in-depth analysis of the results
using typical 3D volumetric images instead of surface representation. For this
approach, we consider a set of voxels, $V = (v^{(111)}, v^{(112)}, \ldots, v^{(XYZ)})$, where
(X, Y, Z) are the dimensions of the volumetric MRI image, and $v^{(xyz)} \in \mathbb{R}$
denotes voxel intensity at position (x, y, z). The output of the l-th 3D convolutional layer for the j-th feature map at (x, y, z) position is given by:

$$v_{(l+1)j}^{(xyz)} = \text{ReLU}\left(b_{(l)j} + \sum_{m}\sum_{a}^{A-1}\sum_{b}^{B-1}\sum_{c}^{C-1} W_{(l)jm}^{(abc)}\, v_{(l)m}^{(x+a)(y+b)(z+c)}\right), \qquad (1)$$

where $b_{(l)j}$ is the feature map bias term. A, B and C are kernel dimensions. m indexes the set of feature maps in the l-th layer. $W_{(l)jm}^{(abc)}$ denotes weight value at kernel's position (a, b, c) in m-th feature map. $v_{(l)m}^{(x+a)(y+b)(z+c)}$ is input value at $(x + a, y + b, z + c)$ in the m-th feature map. Combining several such layers with ReLU activation, dropout, 3D batch normalization, and the final linear layer, we are able to learn the weight matrices (kernels) optimizing for L1 loss function. Figure 1 displays our proposed 3D CNN architecture.

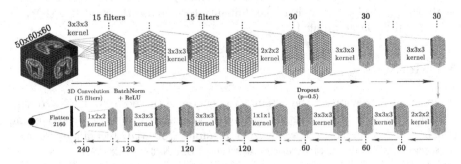

Fig. 1. 3D CNN architecture for age prediction using volumetric spatially-normalized gray-matter (GM) maps as an input.

Point Based: We consider only the nodes on the brain surface, defined as a set of points (or point-cloud), $V = \{v_1, v_2, \ldots, v_n\}$ with $v_i \in \mathbb{R}^d$ ($d = 3$ in our case) and n is number of nodes. A separate vector containing information about local features, $x_i \in \mathbb{R}^l$, is assigned to each point v_i, where l is the number of local features considered. The original PointNet architecture [27], is able to learn a function f with the use of neural networks γ and h such that,

$$f(v_1, v_2, \ldots, v_n) = \gamma\big(\max_i\{h(v_i)\}\big). \tag{2}$$

This technique can approximate functions invariant to input permutation and linear transformations by using symmetric functions and alignment networks, respectively. PointNet++ [28] extends this idea to hierarchical learning and includes sampling and grouping layers together with mini-PointNet layers. Sampling is performed using the farthest-point sampling (FPS), which provides better coverage than a completely random selection. Given the sampled centroids, the grouping layer then creates local point-sets around the centroids using a distance metric. PointNet++'s hierarchical structure allows for a progressive abstraction of the input yielding richer encoding of the global and local information described by the point-cloud. Figure 2 shows a representation of the PointNet++ network architecture.

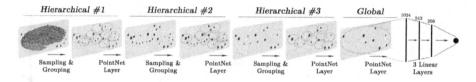

Fig. 2. PointNet++ architecture for age prediction using the nodes on the brain surface as an input.

Mesh Based: A mesh is defined as a pair of sets consisting of vertices (V) and connectivity information (F), with edges (E) defined as a set of connected pairs of vertices. In contrast to point-cloud techniques, mesh representation provides non-uniform, geodesic neighborhood information. Here, we use triangulated meshes as commonly used in the brain surface literature. The MeshCNN architecture [15] consists of two main components for geometric learning: mesh convolution and pooling, see Fig. 3. Both are operations defined over the input edges. Mesh convolution can be defined as:

$$e \cdot k_0 + \sum_{i=1}^{4} k_i \cdot e^i, \tag{3}$$

where k is a kernel and e is an edge feature. e^i denotes an edge feature of the i-th neighboring edge, while total number of neighboring edges equal to 4. The input edge feature is a 5-dimensional vector containing geometric features: the dihedral angle, two inner angles, and two edge-length ratios for each face. Importantly, symmetric functions are applied to ambiguous edge pairs to ensure invariance with respect to the permutation of the convolutional neighbors. The pooling component of MeshCNN uses the topology of the mesh to identify adjacency, and learn to non-uniformly collapse edges that contain the weakest features for the task at hand. Hence, it forms a process where the network exposes the important features while discarding the redundant ones. MeshCNN, to our knowledge, is the only architecture which exhibits such convolution and pooling properties specialized for triangulated meshes.

Graph Based: A graph, $\mathcal{G} = (V, E)$, is defined by a set of nodes (V) and a set of edges (E). Each node, v_i, represents a point on the brain surface and has an associated local feature vector, X_i. A graph convolution operation [22] takes feature matrix $X^{(l)}$ in the l-th layer and outputs:

$$X^{(l+1)} = \sigma(\hat{D}^{-\frac{1}{2}} \hat{A} \hat{D}^{-\frac{1}{2}} X^{(l)} W^{(l)}), \tag{4}$$

where $\hat{A} = A + I_N$ is the adjacency matrix of the graph modified by adding self-connections using identity matrix I_N. N denotes the number of nodes on the graph. $\hat{D} = \sum_j \hat{A}_{ij}$ is the modified degree matrix. $X^{(l+1)}$ is the feature matrix

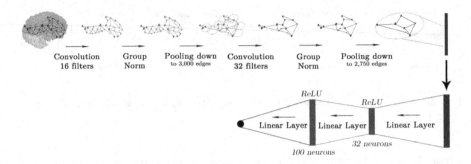

Fig. 3. MeshCNN architecture for age prediction using the input brain mesh surface.

in the $(l+1)$-th layer. Note, that the extracted local features of the surface are defined by a feature matrix at $l = 0$ as $X^{(0)}$. Figure 4 demonstrates our proposed GCN architecture for age prediction. The graph convolutional layers allow the network to learn meaningful feature vectors at each node using neighboring node information. Local features across the whole brain are aggregated by averaging feature vectors across all the nodes, which creates a global feature vector representing global geometric information of the graph. This global feature vector is used as input to a linear layer that outputs the predicted scan age.

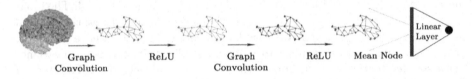

Fig. 4. GCN architecture for age prediction using the input brain surface graph.

Note the key similarities and differences between the previous architectures: The graph and mesh based methods operate on the connections between vertices, and local features are encoded as edge features, in contrast to point-wise features and operations on points. The graph methods therefore capture more information about the local geometric relations between points, which may require more computational resources to increase the capacity of the model (e.g. GPU memory). However, point-clouds are simple and unified structures that avoid the combinatorial irregularities and complexities of meshes, and thus it is easier to implement more efficient and larger PointNet-based models.

Furthermore, the specialized graph and mesh convolutional operations leverage the intrinsic geodesic connections to learn hidden layer representations that encode both local graph structure and features of nodes. This is especially powerful when combined with MeshCNN's edge-pooling operations which expose and expand important features, whilst discarding irrelevant ones, allowing even richer encodings of the surface to be learned. This is comparable to PointNet++, in which the point sampling and grouping layers allow the hierarchical learning of informative points and encodes these into a rich high-level representation.

4   Experiments

4.1   Data

The neonatal data used in this work are publicly available from the developing human connectome project (dHCP)[2]. We excluded files with bad surface quality. Selected data consists of a cohort of 727 total term and preterm neonatal MRI scans (650 unique subjects) with PA ranging from 27 to 45 weeks. These data are split into 477 (65.7%) train, 125 (17.15%) test, and 125 (17.15%) validation sets. To avoid any bias between these subsets, the data split is stratified on multiple features: PA (scan age), birth age, and sex. The split is also done on the unique subjects to avoid data leakage from multiple scans between the subsets. We validate our approach with experiments on the left and right hemispheres, as well as on both hemispheres merged. Surface files are decimated to 10,000 vertices to ensure comparable results between all proposed architectures. The surfaces are extracted from the segmented T2-weighted images in their native coordinates [30]. Furthermore, we compare the performance of the GDL models using only geometric features, and with a range of other local point features, such as cortical thickness (CT), sulcal depth (SD), curvature (C), and the myelin map (MM). All cortical features are extracted using the dHCP structural MRI processing pipeline [23].

4.2   Implementation

3D CNN: Similar to [8], we first segment the cortical gray matter from the 3D MRI scans. Our 3D CNN consists of 12 convolutional layers with ReLU activation and 3D batch normalization. Three dropout layers with 0.5 probability are also added after every third convolutional layer. Setting the initial learning rate to $6.88e-3$, we train the model for 1000 epochs and batch size 32, with Adam optimizer and a scheduler, which decays the learning rate by a factor of $\gamma = 0.9795$ after every epoch. The input images are down-sampled and smoothed using a discrete Gaussian kernel of size 8.

PointNet: For the implementation of PointNet++, we employ the PyTorch Geometric[3] python library. We use three hierarchical levels containing a sampling layer, a grouping layer and a PointNet layer. We also use ReLU activation functions and batch normalization [19]. After hierarchical levels, another Point-Net layer and global max pooling produce the final vector of size 1024 which is input to 3 fully connected layers producing the final age prediction. Mean square

---

[2] http://www.developingconnectome.org/second-data-release.
[3] https://github.com/rusty1s/pytorch_geometric.

error (MSE) loss criterion, Adam optimizer, and a learning rate scheduler are employed to train the model, with an initial learning rate of 1e−3 and a lower bound of 5e−5.

MeshCNN: We adapt the original MeshCNN code[4] for the task of age regression. We use group normalization with two groups, an MSE loss criterion, Adam optimizer, and a ReduceOnPlateau learning rate scheduler, with an initial learning rate of 3e−4 and a lower bound of 3e−5. Because of the expensive GPU memory requirements of the MeshCNN implementation we use a mini-batch of size one. Weights are initialized using Kaiming normal initialization [16].

GCN: Our GCN implementation is based on the DGL[5] library using the graph convolutions (GCs) defined in [22]. The network architecture consists of two GC layers, each using ReLU activation, finally the mean feature vector is calculated across all nodes in the graph before being fed to the linear layer. The weights of the graph convolutional layers are initialized using Glorot uniform [13] and the biases were set to zero. We use Adam optimizer with a cosine annealing learning rate, starting at 8e−4 and decreasing down to 1e−6 with $T_{\max}$ set to 10. Our implementation of all previous architectures is publicly available on GitHub: https://github.com/andwang1/BrainSurfaceTK.

5 Results

Table 1 shows the results of PA prediction using the proposed architectures. With each of our GDL models, we report mean absolute error (MAE) less than one week on both the validation and test sets. The best performance ($\text{MAE}_{val} = 0.701$, $\text{MAE}_{test} = 0.6211$ weeks) is attained by PointNet++ with added (local) cortical features (cortical thickness, curvature, and sulcal depth). This is competitive with the 3D CNN benchmark and indeed, performs better on the test set (0.62 against 0.82 weeks). The variation in performance between the validation and test sets is due to slight differences in feature distributions between these sets, since the number of samples is relatively small and there are many constraints to satisfy in the splits (sex and age distribution etc.). Due to containing local connections between points, the data in mesh form is expected to carry more information than the point cloud representation. Despite this, the results show that PointNet++ outperforms MeshCNN in both validation and test MAE. However, an important observation to note is that the MeshCNN implementation used to generate these results uses only 8k parameters compared to PointNet's 1.5M. This suggests that the data representation and the features used by MeshCNN are very informative and suitable for the regression tasks. On the other hand, our GCN implementation had only 68k trainable parameters.

---

[4] https://github.com/ranahanocka/MeshCNN.
[5] https://www.dgl.ai.

Table 1. The detailed results from the proposed architectures using: left or right hemispheres, or the whole brain.

Model	Hemisphere	Input size	Validation error (wks)	Test error (wks)	Cortical features
3D CNN	GM Maps	50 × 60 × 60	0.6765 ± 0.5821	0.8221 ± 0.6858	-
PointNet++	Right	10k	0.8980 ± 0.6651	1.0417 ± 0.9201	-
	Left	10k	0.9380 ± 0.7012	0.9810 ± 0.9043	-
	Whole	10k	0.8128 ± 0.7513	0.8100 ± 0.6918	-
PointNet++ (with cortical features)	Right	10k	0.7217 ± 0.6138	0.7084 ± 0.5982	CT, C, SD
	Left	10k	0.8140 ± 0.5813	0.6915 ± 0.6647	CT, C, SD
	Whole	10k	**0.7010 ± 0.6209**	**0.6211 ± 0.4784**	CT, C, SD
MeshCNN	Right	10k	0.8273 ± 0.6692	0.8797 ± 0.6691	-
	Left	10k	0.8986 ± 0.6590	0.8811 ± 0.7056	-
	Whole	10k	0.8810 ± 0.6746	0.9555 ± 0.6513	-
GCN	Right	10k	1.3029 ± 1.0266	1.3391 ± 1.0307	-
	Left	10k	1.2455 ± 0.9432	1.2455 ± 0.9804	-
	Whole	10k	1.1208 ± 1.1208	1.1617 ± 0.9348	-
GCN (with cortical features)	Right	10k	0.7956 ± 0.9819	0.7793 ± 0.6818	CT, C, SD
	Left	10k	0.7589 ± 0.6395	0.7273 ± 0.6403	CT, C, SD
	Whole	10k	0.7511 ± 0.6205	0.7182 ± 0.5741	CT, C, SD

Table 2 shows a summary of previous reported results for age prediction in the literature. Although our results are not directly comparable with the reported works in the table, because of the differences in the employed input data modalities, validation techniques and variations in age ranges, our prediction error is the lowest. We also use the biggest dataset size for our experiments compared to the other published works.

6   Conclusion and Discussions

To the best of our knowledge, this work presents the first study to assess a number of geometric deep learning (GDL) architectures on the task of PA regression based on the neonatal white matter surface. We compare several GDL architectures from the literature that utilize different representations of the brain surface, either point-clouds, meshes, or graphs. We compare our models against a 3D CNN baseline architecture for age prediction using the 3D volumetric gray matter maps. Models are evaluated on a large cohort of 727 term and preterm scans (650 subjects) with a wide PA range of 27–45 weeks. Our results show accurate prediction of the estimated PA, with the best model's average error around 0.62 weeks. It is the lowest error compared to previously published works for predicting PA.

Limitation and Future Direction: We note that there is a trade-off between graph and point based methods such that graph representations capture more

Table 2. Results from previous works for age prediction. Our experiments utilize the biggest dataset for evaluation, showing the lowest error.

Method	Input	Size of the data	Age range (wks)	Error (wks)
Toews et al. [31]	Scale-invariant T1w features	92 subjects (230 infant structural MRIs)	1.1–84.2 CA	10.28
Brown et al. [6]	FA-weighted structural connectivity	168 DTIs	27–45 PA	1.6
Ouyang et al. [25]	Cortical FA and MK (mean kurtosis)	89 preterm infants	31.5–41.7 PA	1.41
Deprez et al. [9]	Signals in the thalami and brainstem	114 preterm infants	29–44 PA	2.56
Hu et al. [18]	Cortical measures	50 healthy subjects (251 longitudinal MRIs)	2–6.9 CA	1.58 ± 0.04
Galdi et al. [12]	Structural and diffusion MRI	105 neonates (59 preterm and 46 term)	38–44.56 PA	0.70 ± 0.56
PointNet++ (proposed)	WM surface nodes	650 subjects (727 MRIs)	27–45 PA	**0.6211 ± 0.4784**
MeshCNN (proposed)	WM surface mesh	650 subjects (727 MRIs)	27–45 PA	0.9555 ± 0.6513
GCN (proposed)	WM surface graph	650 subjects (727 MRIs)	27–45 PA	0.7182 ± 0.5741

geometric information and the networks are more efficient (in that they attain similar performance with much fewer parameters). However, graph based techniques are also computationally expensive which may limit the model size. On the other hand, PointNet methods are computationally efficient but the points do not capture as much information, so much larger models are needed. Similar to typical CNNs, the proposed GDL architectures can be sensitive to the input data, e.g. errors on the extracted surface. Hence, as well as suggesting developmental abnormalities, surfaces for which our models predict anomalously inaccurate PA may have been extracted incorrectly. A future direction of our work will be to investigate the application of GDL to the association of brain regions with accurate age prediction. GDL could also be applied to the classification of preterm neonates from the brain surface, and may provide insights into the development of the neonatal cortical surface.

References

1. Besson, P., Parrish, T., Katsaggelos, A.K., Bandt, S.K.: Geometric deep learning on brain shape predicts sex and age. BioRxiv (2020)
2. Bottomley, C., Bourne, T.: Dating and growth in the first trimester. Best Pract. Res. Clin. Obstet. Gynaecol. **23**(4), 439–452 (2009)
3. Breiman, L.: Random forests. Mach. Learn. **45**(1), 5–32 (2001)

4. Brock, A., Lim, T., Ritchie, J.M., Weston, N.: Generative and discriminative voxel modeling with convolutional neural networks. arXiv preprint arXiv:1608.04236 (2016)
5. Bronstein, M.M., Bruna, J., LeCun, Y., Szlam, A., Vandergheynst, P.: Geometric deep learning: going beyond Euclidean data. IEEE Sig. Process. Mag. **34**(4), 18–42 (2017)
6. Brown, C.J., et al.: Prediction of brain network age and factors of delayed maturation in very preterm infants. In: Descoteaux, M., Maier-Hein, L., Franz, A., Jannin, P., Collins, D.L., Duchesne, S. (eds.) MICCAI 2017. LNCS, vol. 10433, pp. 84–91. Springer, Cham (2017). https://doi.org/10.1007/978-3-319-66182-7_10
7. Bruna, J., Zaremba, W., Szlam, A., LeCun, Y.: Spectral networks and locally connected networks on graphs. arXiv preprint arXiv:1312.6203 (2013)
8. Cole, J.H., et al.: Predicting brain age with deep learning from raw imaging data results in a reliable and heritable biomarker. NeuroImage **163**, 115–124 (2017)
9. Deprez, M., Wang, S., Ledig, C., Hajnal, J.V., Counsell, S.J., Schnabel, J.A.: Segmentation of myelin-like signals on clinical MR images for age estimation in preterm infants. bioRxiv, p. 357749 (2018)
10. Engle, W.A.: Age terminology during the perinatal period. Pediatrics **114**(5), 1362–1364 (2004)
11. Fetit, A.E., et al.: A deep learning approach to segmentation of the developing cortex in fetal brain mri with minimal manual labeling. In: MIDL (2020)
12. Galdi, P., et al.: Neonatal morphometric similarity mapping for predicting brain age and characterizing neuroanatomic variation associated with preterm birth. NeuroImage Clin. **25**, 102195 (2020)
13. Glorot, X., Bengio, Y.: Understanding the difficulty of training deep feedforward neural networks. In: AISTATS, pp. 249–256 (2010)
14. Gutiérrez-Becker, B., Wachinger, C.: Deep multi-structural shape analysis: application to neuroanatomy. In: Frangi, A.F., Schnabel, J.A., Davatzikos, C., Alberola-López, C., Fichtinger, G. (eds.) MICCAI 2018. LNCS, vol. 11072, pp. 523–531. Springer, Cham (2018). https://doi.org/10.1007/978-3-030-00931-1_60
15. Hanocka, R., Hertz, A., Fish, N., Giryes, R., Fleishman, S., Cohen-Or, D.: MeshCNN: a network with an edge. ACM TOG **38**(4), 1–12 (2019)
16. He, K., Zhang, X., Ren, S., Sun, J.: Delving deep into rectifiers: surpassing human-level performance on imagenet classification. In: Proceedings of the IEEE International Conference on Computer Vision, pp. 1026–1034 (2015)
17. Henaff, M., Bruna, J., LeCun, Y.: Deep convolutional networks on graph-structured data. arXiv preprint arXiv:1506.05163 (2015)
18. Hu, D., Wu, Z., Lin, W., Li, G., Shen, D.: Hierarchical rough-to-fine model for infant age prediction based on cortical features. IEEE J. Biomed. Health Inf. **24**(1), 214–225 (2019)
19. Ioffe, S., Szegedy, C.: Batch normalization: accelerating deep network training by reducing internal covariate shift. arXiv preprint arXiv:1502.03167 (2015)
20. Jiang, H., et al.: Predicting brain age of healthy adults based on structural MRI parcellation using convolutional neural networks. Front. Neurol. **10**, 1346 (2019)
21. Kamnitsas, K., Ledig, C., Newcombe, V.F., Simpson, J.P., Kane, A.D., Menon, D.K., Rueckert, D., Glocker, B.: Efficient multi-scale 3D CNN with fully connected CRF for accurate brain lesion segmentation. Med. Image Anal. **36**, 61–78 (2017)
22. Kipf, T.N., Welling, M.: Semi-supervised classification with graph convolutional networks. arXiv preprint arXiv:1609.02907 (2016)

23. Makropoulos, A.: The developing human connectome project: a minimal processing pipeline for neonatal cortical surface reconstruction. Neuroimage **173**, 88–112 (2018)

24. Masci, J., Boscaini, D., Bronstein, M., Vandergheynst, P.: Geodesic convolutional neural networks on Riemannian manifolds. In: ICCV Workshops, pp. 37–45 (2015)

25. Ouyang, M.: Differential cortical microstructural maturation in the preterm human brain with diffusion kurtosis and tensor imaging. Proc. Nat. Acad. Sci. **116**(10), 4681–4688 (2019)

26. Paladini, D., Malinger, G., Monteagudo, A., Pilu, G., Timor-Tritsch, I., Toi, A.: Sonographic examination of the fetal central nervous system: guidelines for performing the 'basic examination' and the 'fetal neurosonogram'. Ultrasound Obstet. Gynecol. **29**(1), 109–116 (2007)

27. Qi, C.R., Su, H., Mo, K., Guibas, L.J.: PointNet: deep learning on point sets for 3D classification and segmentation. In: CVPR, pp. 652–660 (2017)

28. Qi, C.R., Yi, L., Su, H., Guibas, L.J.: PointNet++: deep hierarchical feature learning on point sets in a metric space. In: NeurIPS, pp. 5099–5108 (2017)

29. Rekik, I., Li, G., Yap, P.-T., Chen, G., Lin, W., Shen, D.: A hybrid multishape learning framework for longitudinal prediction of cortical surfaces and fiber tracts using neonatal data. In: Ourselin, S., Joskowicz, L., Sabuncu, M.R., Unal, G., Wells, W. (eds.) MICCAI 2016. LNCS, vol. 9900, pp. 210–218. Springer, Cham (2016). https://doi.org/10.1007/978-3-319-46720-7_25

30. Schuh, A., et al.: A deformable model for the reconstruction of the neonatal cortex. In: ISBI, pp. 800–803. IEEE (2017)

31. Toews, M., Wells, W.M., Zöllei, L.: A feature-based developmental model of the infant brain in structural MRI. In: Ayache, N., Delingette, H., Golland, P., Mori, K. (eds.) MICCAI 2012. LNCS, pp. 204–211. Springer, Heidelberg (2012). https://doi.org/10.1007/978-3-642-33418-4_26

32. Wu, Z., et al.: 3D shapeNets: a deep representation for volumetric shapes. In: CVPR, pp. 1912–1920 (2015)

The GraphNet Zoo: An All-in-One Graph Based Deep Semi-supervised Framework for Medical Image Classification

Marianne de Vriendt[1], Philip Sellars[2], and Angelica I. Aviles-Rivero[3(✉)]

[1] Nabla Technologies, Paris, France
marianne@nabla.com
[2] DAMPT, University of Cambridge, Cambridge, UK
ps644@cam.ac.uk
[3] DPMMS, University of Cambridge, Cambridge, UK
ai323@cam.ac.uk

Abstract. We consider the problem of classifying a medical image dataset when we have a limited amounts of labels. This is very common yet challenging setting as labelled data is expensive, time consuming to collect and may require expert knowledge. The current classification go-to of deep supervised learning is unable to cope with such a problem setup. However, using semi-supervised learning, one can produce accurate classifications using a significantly reduced amount of labelled data. Therefore, semi-supervised learning is perfectly suited for medical image classification. However, there has almost been no uptake of semi-supervised methods in the medical domain. In this work, we propose an all-in-one framework for deep semi-supervised classification focusing on graph based approaches, which up to our knowledge it is the first time that an approach with minimal labels has been shown to such an unprecedented scale with *medical data*. We introduce the concept of hybrid models by defining a classifier as a combination between an energy-based model and a deep net. Our energy functional is built on the Dirichlet energy based on the graph p-Laplacian. Our framework includes energies based on the ℓ_1 and ℓ_2 norms. We then connected this energy model to a deep net to generate a much richer feature space to construct a stronger graph. Our framework can be set to be adapted to any complex dataset. We demonstrate, through extensive numerical comparisons, that our approach readily compete with fully-supervised state-of-the-art techniques for the applications of Malaria Cells, Mammograms and Chest X-ray classification whilst using only 20% of labels.

Keywords: Deep semi-supervised learning · Image classification · Chest-Xray · Screening mammography · Deep learning

M. de Vriendt, P. Sellars, and A. I. Aviles-Rivero—These three authors contributed equally and hold joint first authorship.

© Springer Nature Switzerland AG 2020
C. H. Sudre et al. (Eds.): UNSURE 2020/GRAIL 2020, LNCS 12443, pp. 187–197, 2020.
https://doi.org/10.1007/978-3-030-60365-6_18

1 Introduction

Deep learning for medical image classification has achieved state-of-the-art results for a variety of medical image classification challenges [2,22,26,29]. However, state-of-the-art deep learning frameworks rely upon the existence of a representative training set, which often requires a large number of manually labelled medical images. Collecting labelled data for medical imaging is a time-consuming, expensive and requires domain expertise from trained physicians. Therefore, obtaining such a representative training set is often a barrier to machine learning in the medical domain.

Semi-supervised learning (SSL) techniques have been growing massively in popularity due to the fact they seek to produce an accurate solution whilst using a minimal size label set. SSL techniques seek to use the information present in a large number of unlabelled examples combined with a small number of labelled examples [5] to obtain a better performance than purely using the labelled samples on their own. There are several different approaches to SSL which can be split into several board families of methods: *low-density separation* [4], *generative models* [10] and graph based approaches [12,31]. In this paper we will narrow our discussion to graphical techniques due to their flexibility in dealing with different data structures, scalability to large problems and their rigorous mathematical definition.

SSL is perfect for any area which produces large quantities of data but also incurs a large cost associated with labelling. Thus making SSL techniques a perfect candidate for use in the field of medical image classification. However, there has been very limited uptake of semi-supervised learning techniques for use in medical image classification. In this paper, we seek to bridge this technical gap and demonstrate, to our knowledge for the first time, the amazing results that can be obtained by using deep SSL for medical large-scale image classification.

The theoretical foundations of SSL has been studied by the community for years. But it is only recently that deep semi-supervised learning has be a focus of great attention. Several techniques has been proposed including [16,23,25]. However, these techniques has been only proven effective for natural images, and the question of how effective they are on complex datasets such as those coming from the medical domain has not been investigated yet. This is not obvious–as there are fundamental differences between natural and medical images [18]. To our knowledge, this paper represented the first major exploration of deep semi-supervised learning for large scale medical datasets.

Our Contributions. We propose an all-in-one framework for Deep Semi-Supervised Medical Image Classification framed into a package called GraphNet Zoo. Our framework works as a hybrid technique that uses an energy model as a core to drive the uncertainty updates through a deep network. Our particular highlights are:

- A generalisable framework which is composed of an energy based model and a deep net. Whilst the embeddings coming from the deep net aim to construct a robust graph, the optimisation model drives the final graph based classifier.

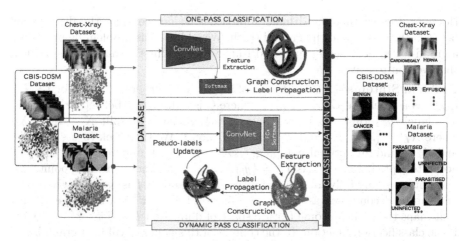

Fig. 1. Visual description of our proposed GraphZoo framework. We split the different graph based models into two different groups, coloured in red and blue, dependent on whether the algorithm is iterative. No update (red) approaches construct the graph only once and immediately perform graph based operations such as label propagation. Update approaches iteratively construct the graphical representation, using the features extracted from the previous epoch to construct an improved graph. (Color figure online)

Our energy model is based on minimising the Dirichlet energy based on the graph p-Laplacian, which we integrate two cases: $p = 2$ and a more robust functional based on the non-local total variation $p = 1$. We also show that our approach can plug-and-play any deep net architecture.

– We demonstrate, through an extensive experiments and for a range of complex medical datasets, that our framework can recreate, and in some cases outperform, the performance of supervised methods whilst using only 20%.

– To the best of our knowledge, this is the first time that a deep semi-supervised framework has been applied and been shown to output fantastic performance to several large-scale *medical datasets*.

2 GraphNet Zoo: An All-in-One Framework

The lack of a large corpus of well-annotated medical data has motivated the developed of new techniques, which need a significantly smaller set of labelled data. Unlike other type of data (e.g. natural images), the complex annotations required in the medical domain advocates for at least a double reading from different experts which is highly subjective and prone to error [15]. At the algorithmic level, this is reflected in greater label uncertainty that negatively affects the classification task. Therefore, how to rely less in annotated data is of a great interest in the medical domain. The body of literature has explored different alternatives including Transfer Learning e.g. [3] and Generative Adversarial Models e.g. [17] to mitigate somehow the lack of well-annotated medical data.

However, the existing algorithmic approaches do not consider the discrepancy between the expert and the ground truth. We address this problem by proposing a graph-based deep semi-supervised framework. We first formalise the problem that we aim to solve.

Problem Statement. Assume a set of inputs $X := \{x_1, x_2, ..., x_n\}$. For $1 \leq i \leq l$, x_i has a label $y_i \in C := \{1, ..., c\}$, where C is a discrete label set for c classes. The labels y_i form a set $Y := \{y_1, y_2, ..., y_l\}$. As such we split $X = X_L \cup X_U$ where $X_L := \{x_1, .., x_l\}$ and $X_U := \{x_{l+1}, .., x_n\}$. We then seek to use X_L, X_U and Y_L to find an optimal mapping $f : \mathcal{X} \rightarrow \mathbb{R}^C$, with minimal error, that can accurately predict the labels $Y_U = \{y_{l+1}, .., y_{u+l}\}$ for the unlabelled points X_U and potential infinitely unseen instances. The mapping f is parameterised by θ and can be decomposed as $f = \phi \circ \psi$, where $\psi : \mathcal{X} \rightarrow \mathbb{R}^P$ is a feature extractor that maps the input to some feature space of dimension P and $\phi : \mathbb{R}^P \rightarrow \{0, 1\}^c$ is the classification function. In the context of this paper ϕ will be a graph based classifier.

How We Represent the Data? For the majority of existing approaches in medical classification, the go-to representation of the the data is thee a standard grid form. In this work, we give a different representation - graphical. Formally, a given dataset can be represented as an undirected weighted graph $\mathcal{G} = (\mathcal{N}, \mathcal{E}, \mathcal{W})$ composed of $\mathcal{N} = \{N_1, ..., N_n\}$ nodes. They are connected by edges $\mathcal{E} = \{N_i - N_j : N_i \rightleftharpoons N_j \in \mathcal{N}\}$ with weights $w_{ij} = \mathcal{F}(i, j) \geq 0$ that represents a similarity measure $\mathcal{F}$ between the nodes $N_i \in \mathcal{N}$ and $N_j \in \mathcal{N}$. If $w_{ij} = 0$ means that $(N_i, N_j) \notin \mathcal{E}$. In this work, a node represent an image in the graph. This representation gives different advantages including strong mathematical properties, the ability to cope with annotation uncertainty and homogeneous space for highly heterogeneous data.

Our All-in-One Framework. Semi-supervised classification has been explored from the model-based perspective in the medical domain e.g. [24,27,30]. Our framework lie in an different category: *hybrid techniques*, which seeks to keep the mathematical guarantees of model-based techniques whilst exploiting the power of deep nets. We remark that we use the term *All-in-One* to describe the ability of our framework to plug-in different architectures and energy functionals without altering either the backbone nor the functionality of our technique.

Our framework has two modes to operate: *One Pass Classification* and *Dynamic Pass Classification*. The key difference lies in the fact that the second option allows the uncertainty in the graph to be updated overtime. The need for having two differing methods is as follows. For more complex datasets, iterative approaches are often needed to extract a rich feature representation. However, for simpler datasets, or those for which the training time is longer, a one-stop construction approach is the only computational feasible approach out of the two. Both modes are composed of two main parts (i.e. hybrid model): i) a deep net, f_θ, that is used to generalise the feature extraction and reduce uncertainty in the labels and ii) a functional that seeks to diffuse the small amount of label data to the unlabelled set.

Our framework uses a given deep net, for example VGG16 or ResNet-18, defined as $f = \phi \circ \psi$, where $\psi : \mathcal{X} \to \mathbb{R}^P$ is a feature extractor and $\phi : \mathbb{R}^P \to \{0, 1\}^c$ is the classification function. Firstly, our approach seek to solve one of the key problems in graph theory, which is – how to construct an accurate embedding. For this, we extract the embeddings from a given deep net to better generalise the feature space to construct a graph.

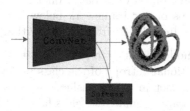

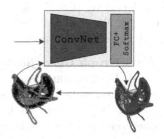

Listing 1.1: One Pass Classification

```
1  Input: Data X = {x₁,..,xₙ},
       Labels Y = {y₁,..,yₗ}
       Architecture
       fθ(.) = ψθ(.) ∘ φθ(.)
2
3  Optimise: Lθ = Σˡᵢ₌ᵢ lₛ(fθ(xᵢ), yᵢ)
4  #Generate features:
5  N = ψ(X)
6  #Construct weighted graph
7  Wᵢⱼ = d(nᵢ, nⱼ)
8  G = (V, E, W)
9  #Compute label diffusion:
10 until convergence:
11 #Hypothesis class H
12 H* = argmin_{H∈H} Q(H)
13 #Extract generated labels:
14 yᵢ = argmax_k h^k_i
15 ---
16 ###energies included Q:
17 ## for the case of p=2
18 S = D^{-1/2}WD^{-1/2}
19 # given labeled set matrix Y
20 H* = (I - αS)^{-1}Y
21 ## for the case of p=1
22 Δ₁(u) = |WD^{-1}u|
23 minimise: Σ_k (Δ₁(u^k))/|u^k|
```

Listing 1.2: Dynamic Pass Classification

```
24 Input: Data X = {x₁,..,xₙ},
       Labels Y = {y₁,..,yₗ}
       Architecture
       fθ(.) = ψθ(.) ∘ φθ(.)
25 Optimise: Lθ = Σˡᵢ₌ᵢ lₛ(fθ(xᵢ), yᵢ)
26 For J epochs:
27 #Generate features:
28 N = ψ(X)
29 #Construct weighted graph
30 Wᵢⱼ = d(nᵢ, nⱼ)
31 G = (V, E, W)
32 #Compute label diffusion:
33 until convergence:
34 #Hypothesis class H
35 H* = argmin_{H∈H} Q(H)
36 #Extract generated labels:
37 Ŷ = (ŷₗ₊₁,..,ŷₙ)
38 #α(t) balance parameter
39 Optimise:
40 Lθ = Σˡᵢ₌ᵢ lₛ(fθ(xᵢ), yᵢ)
       +α(t) Σⁿᵢ₌ₗ₊₁ lₛ(fθ(xᵢ), ((y)ᵢ))
41 #Extract Final Generated
       Labels
42 Ŷ = (ŷₗ₊₁,..,ŷₙ)
```

We emphasise that a node represents an image in the graph. For the second part (i.e. the label diffusion), our setting is focused on the normalised graph p-Laplacian $\Delta_p(u)$. Whilst $p = 2$ has been used extensively in the literature e.g. [6,7] other more robust functionals have not been deeply explored in the medical domain. More recently, authors of that [1] explored a more robust functional based on the case for $p = 1$ $\Delta_1(u) = |WD^{-1}u|$, where W is the weight matrix and D a matrix with the node's degrees. We show in this work, that we can plug-in any functional in our framework. Our GraphNet Zoo includes energies based on $p = 2$ e.g. [31] and more robust ones based on the $p = 1$ case e.g. [1]. We explicitly define the process of our framework below and set explicitly the energies used in this work (see lines 16–23 from the algorithm).

One-Pass Graph Classification: This mode allows us to perform deep semi-supervised classification based on the conditional entropy of the class probabilities for the unlabelled set. To train a deep net in a SSL fashion, we rely on *pseudo-labels* [8,13] where the key idea is to approximate the class label for the unlabelled set from the predictions of a deep net f_θ. This allows to strengthen the graph constructions whilst boosting the classification performance. In short, we extract the embeddings from a deep net trained over the labelled set to build the graph representation of the data and finally apply label diffusion $\mathbf{Q}(H)$. The precise optimisation process is displayed in lines 1:23 on Listing 1.1.

Dynamic Pass Graph Classification: This mode seeks to improve the uncertainty generated by the pseudo-labels overtime. We observe that whilst the first alternative offers good results in terms of classification, there is two ways to further improve it. Firstly the inferred pseudo-labels clearly do not have the same confidence in each example, and secondly the pseudo-labels may be imbalanced over the classes which affect the learning process. We tackle these problems by associating, to each pseudo-label, a weight reflection the inference certainty. We use, as in other works [9,20], an entropy measure $M : \mathbb{R}^C \rightarrow \mathbb{R}$ to assign the certainty $\xi_i = 1 - (M(h_i^*)/log(C))$ to a given example x_i. Note that h_i^* comes from line: 25 of the below algorithm whilst C denotes the classes. The overall procedure is described in Listing 1.2 (lines 17:42).

We detail the implementation of the two approaches in the Listing 1.1 and Listing 1.2, which are displayed next.

3   Experimental Results

This section is devoted to give details of the experiments carried out to validate our proposed framework.

Data Description. We evaluate our approach on three large scale datasets. The first one is *the Malaria Infected Cells* [19] dataset. It is composed of 27,558 cell images of size 224×224 with balance instances of parasitised and uninfected cells. As second dataset, we use the latest version of the very challenging *Digital Database for Screening Mammography (DDSM)* dataset called CBIS-DDSM [14]. It has 2478 mammography images from 1249 women the images size can be as large as $3\,k \times 3\,k$ pixels. It is composed of roughly 40:60 of benign and malignant

Table 1. Performance comparison on the Malaria and Mammogram datasets. For both datasets GraphNet Zoo was able to produce state-of-the-art performance, beating the compared methods, whilst using far fewer labelled data points.

MALARIA CELLS DATASET		
FULLY-SUPERVISED METHODS		
METHOD	ACCURACY (Labelled 70%)	
Xception	0.890	
VGG-16	0.945	
ResNet-50	0.957	
AlexNet	0.937	
DEEP SEMI-SUPERVISED MODELS		
METHOD	10%	20%
GCN [12]	0.865± 0.05	0.895± 0.015
Ours W/[A]	0.877 ±0.006	0.927 ± 0.005
Ours W/[B]	0.930± 0.009	0.943 ±0.005
Ours W/[C]	0.845 ±0.034	0.921± 0.011
Ours W/[A]	0.922 ±0.004	0.928± 0.009
Ours W/[B]	0.94 ±0.0057	0.957± 0.003
Ours W/[C]	0.860 ±0.038	0.929± 0.010

COLOUR CODE AND ARCHITECTURES:

GraphNet Zoo: Model 1; GraphNet Zoo: Model 2

[A]: VGG16; [B]:ResNet-18; [C]: AE

[D]: Custumised CNN; [E]: ResNet-50

CBIS-DDSM DATASET	
FULLY-SUPERVISED METHODS	
METHOD	[% LABELLED] AUC
SHEN [22]	[85%] 0.85 (val) **0.75 (test)**
ZHU [32]	[80%] 0.791
METHOD	20% LABELLED – AUC
Ours W/[D]	0.729
Ours W/[E]	0.717
Ours W/[D]	0.721
Ours W/[E]	0.735
Ours W/[E]	[40%] 0.811

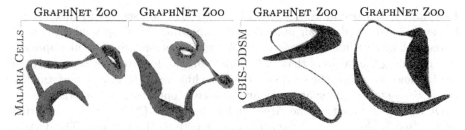

Fig. 2. Feature representation for the Malaria [19] and Mammogram [14] datasets using our graph based approaches using a ResNet18 feature extractor. Red dots denote samples labeled malignant and blue denotes benign samples. (Color figure online)

cases respectively. Finally, we use the ChestX-ray14 dataset [26], which is composed of 112,120 frontal chest view X-ray with size of 1024×1024. The dataset is composed of 14 classes (pathologies).

Parameter Selection. *Architectures:* We set the learning rate to the common value of $r = 0.001$ in all our networks. Additionally, we use the Adam optimiser with early stopping and a dropout rate of 0.2. *Graph:* For the graph based approaches we used k-NN for the graph construction with k=50, α was set with a grid search in $[0, 1]$. Moreover, we used $p = 2$ based energy for the malaria and the mammograms dataset whilst for the chest-xray we used the label diffusion based on minimising our energy based $p = 1$. **Data Pre-processing:** We follow standard pre-processing protocol (e.g. as in [21]) to normalise the images so that the mean of the pixel values is 1 and the standard deviation is 1. For the compared approaches, we used the code provided by each author along with their parameters.

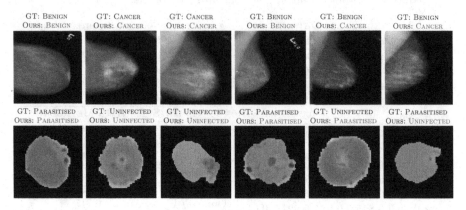

Fig. 3. Example classifications from the Malaria [19] and Mammogram [14] datasets. For each image we give the ground truth class and the predicted classification. Whilst our approach works very well, there are still miss-classifications, as in any algorithmic approach for such applications.

Evaluation Protocol. We use the following evaluation scheme to validate our framework. We validate our approach by comparing our deep semi-supervised framework against fully-supervised SOTA-techniques for each particular application including the works of that [2,22,26,28,29,32]. Moreover, we also compared our framework against the semi-supervised techniques of [1,11]. As performance check we use two metrics: accuracy and a receiver operating characteristic curve (ROC) analysis based on the Area Under the Curve (AUC). In our reported results (see Tables), we use green colour to denote the best results. The darkest green colour denotes the best results whilst the light green colour the second best performance.

Results and Discussion. We begin by analysing the Malaria [19] and Mammography [14] datasets, see Table 1. As our PnP framework is versatile, we can apply any combination of feature extractor and graphical classifier, which can be swapped in and out. To show this ability, we ran our framework using a range of different architectures and graphical propagators. From a closer look at the results, we notice that compared to the other SSL approaches the GCN [12] produces consistently lower results, which suggests that the shallow architecture of GCN's generalise poorly to more complex datasets. However, our framework gives far better results than GCN. We further support our results by running a comparison against fully supervised methods for each particular application. For each dataset we learnt on a very small amount of labelled data but yet managed to obtain a great classification performance which was either comparable to or better than the state-of-the-art supervised approaches which used far more labels. The fact that our approach worked so well for the CBIS-DDSM dataset

Table 2. Classification performance on the ChestXray-14 dataset. When only 20% of the dataset labelled we are able to beat and perform in line with recent methods.

CHESTXRAY-14	
FULLY-SUPERVISED METHODS	
METHOD	70% LABELLED – AUC
WANG [26]	0.745
YAO [29]	0.761
YAN [28]	0.830
BALTRUSCHAT (RESNET-101) [2]	0.785
BALTRUSCHAT (RESNET-38) [2]	0.806
METHOD	20% LABELLED – AUC
GraphXNet [1]	0.788
Ours W/[A1]	0.770
Ours W/[A1]	0.795
Ours W/[A2]	0.815

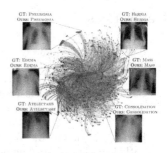

Fig. 4. Visual display of one of our experiments: a graph output in which each colour represent one pathology (class).

is of particular interest as it presents a challenging dataset but yet we were able to get similar performance to SOTA techniques using 20% of the label set but using 40% we were able to surpass all comparison methods using half the label set. This could be explained by uncertainty from the experts, contributing negatively whilst training in a supervised manner but can be regularised against using semi-supervised approaches. Moreover, by decreasing the number of annotated samples one also decreases the labelling error and uncertainty in the classification output.

To test *the generalisability* of our framework we then applied it to the challenging ChestXray-14 dataset [26], and the results are reported in Table 2 and Fig. 4. From the results, one can observe that using far less labels we are able to match or outperform the SOTA-methods. Overall, we underline the message of this paper *we show that our framework is easy applied to a variety of problems and that it reliable produces good performance using fewer labels.*

4 Conclusion

In the field of medical imaging labelled examples are time consuming and expensive to obtain. Supervised approaches often rely upon a large representative training set to achieve acceptable performance. In this paper, we explore the impact that semi-supervised learning (SSL) can have in the domain. We propose a novel framework for SSL algorithms before applying this framework to three large scale medical datasets. Through extensive testing, we clearly show that our graph-based approach can either match or outperform state-of-the-art deep supervised methods whilst requiring a fraction of the labels – only 20%. Overall, *we underline the message of our paper, deep SSL classification is reaching unprecedented performance comparable or better than fully-supervised techniques whilst requiring minimal labelled set.*

References

1. Aviles-Rivero, A.I., et al.: GraphX-^{NET} – chest x-ray classification under extreme minimal supervision. In: Shen, D., et al. (eds.) MICCAI 2019. LNCS, vol. 11769, pp. 504–512. Springer, Cham (2019). https://doi.org/10.1007/978-3-030-32226-7_56
2. Baltruschat, I.M., Nickisch, H., Grass, M., Knopp, T., Saalbach, A.: Comparison of deep learning approaches for multi-label chest x-ray classification. Sci. Rep. **9**(1), 1–10 (2019)
3. Bar, Y., Diamant, I., Wolf, L., Lieberman, S., Konen, E., Greenspan, H.: Chest pathology detection using deep learning with non-medical training. In: 2015 IEEE 12th international symposium on biomedical imaging (ISBI), pp. 294–297. IEEE (2015)
4. Chapelle, O., Zien, A.: Semi-supervised classification by low density separation. In: 10th International Workshop on Artificial Intelligence and Statistics, pp. 57–64 (2005)
5. Chapelle, O., Scholkopf, B., Zien, A.: Semi-supervised learning. IEEE Trans. Neural Networks **20**(3), 542 (2009)
6. Chen, H., et al.: Inferring group-wise consistent multimodal brain networks via multi-view spectral clustering. IEEE Trans. Med. Imaging **32**(9), 1576–1586 (2013)
7. Dodero, L., Gozzi, A., Liska, A., Murino, V., Sona, D.: Group-wise functional community detection through joint Laplacian diagonalization. In: Golland, P., Hata, N., Barillot, C., Hornegger, J., Howe, R. (eds.) MICCAI 2014. LNCS, vol. 8674, pp. 708–715. Springer, Cham (2014). https://doi.org/10.1007/978-3-319-10470-6_88
8. Grandvalet, Y., Bengio, Y.: Semi-supervised learning by entropy minimization. In: Advances in Neural Information Processing Systems, pp. 529–536 (2005)
9. Iscen, A., Tolias, G., Avrithis, Y., Chum, O.: Label propagation for deep semi-supervised learning. In: Proceedings of the IEEE Conference on Computer Vision and Pattern Recognition, pp. 5070–5079 (2019)
10. Kingma, D., Mohamed, S., Rezende, D.J., Welling, M.: Semi-supervised learning with deep generative models. In: Neural Information Processing Systems (2014)
11. Kipf, T.N., Welling, M.: Semi-supervised classification with graph convolutional networks. In: Proceedings of the 6th International Conference on Learning Representations (2017)
12. Kipf, T.N., Welling, M.: Semi-supervised classification with graph convolutional networks (2017)
13. Lee, D.H.: Pseudo-label: the simple and efficient semi-supervised learning method for deep neural networks. In: Workshop on Challenges in Representation Learning, ICML, vol. 3, p. 2 (2013)
14. Lee, R.S., Gimenez, F., Hoogi, A., Miyake, K.K., Gorovoy, M., Rubin, D.L.: A curated mammography data set for use in computer-aided detection and diagnosis research. Sci. Data **4**, 170177 (2017)
15. Lehman, C.D., Wellman, R.D., Buist, D.S., Kerlikowske, K., Tosteson, A.N., Miglioretti, D.L.: Diagnostic accuracy of digital screening mammography with and without computer-aided detection. JAMA Intern. Med. **175**(11), 1828–1837 (2015)
16. Miyato, T., Maeda, S.I., Koyama, M., Ishii, S.: Virtual adversarial training: a regularization method for supervised and semi-supervised learning. IEEE Trans. Pattern Anal. Mach. Intell. **41**(8), 1979–1993 (2018)
17. Moradi, E., et al.: Machine learning framework for early MRI-based Alzheimer's conversion prediction in MCI subjects. Neuroimage **104**, 398–412 (2015)

18. Raghu, M., Zhang, C., Kleinberg, J., Bengio, S.: Transfusion: understanding transfer learning for medical imaging. In: Advances in Neural Information Processing Systems, pp. 3342–3352 (2019)
19. Rajaraman, S., et al.: Pre-trained convolutional neural networks as feature extractors toward improved malaria parasite detection in thin blood smear images. PeerJ (2018)
20. Sellars, P., Aviles-Rivero, A., Schönlieb, C.B.: Two cycle learning: clustering based regularisation for deep semi-supervised classification. arXiv preprint arXiv:2001.05317 (2020)
21. Shen, L.: End-to-end training for whole image breast cancer diagnosis using an all convolutional design. ArXiv arXiv:1708.09427 (2017)
22. Shen, L., Margolies, L.R., Rothstein, J.H., Fluder, E., McBride, R., Sieh, W.: Deep learning to improve breast cancer detection on screening mammography. Sci. Rep. (2019)
23. Tarvainen, A., Valpola, H.: Mean teachers are better role models: Weight-averaged consistency targets improve semi-supervised deep learning results. In: Advances in Neural Information Processing Systems (NIPS), pp. 1195–1204 (2017)
24. Tiwari, P., Kurhanewicz, J., Rosen, M., Madabhushi, A.: Semi supervised multi kernel (SeSMiK) graph embedding: identifying aggressive prostate cancer via magnetic resonance imaging and spectroscopy. In: Jiang, T., Navab, N., Pluim, J.P.W., Viergever, M.A. (eds.) MICCAI 2010. LNCS, vol. 6363, pp. 666–673. Springer, Heidelberg (2010). https://doi.org/10.1007/978-3-642-15711-0_83
25. Verma, V., Lamb, A., Kannala, J., Bengio, Y., Lopez-Paz, D.: Interpolation consistency training for semi-supervised learning. In: International Joint Conference on Artificial Intelligence (IJCAI) (2019)
26. Wang, X., Peng, Y., Lu, L., Lu, Z., Bagheri, M., Summers, R.M.: Chestx-ray8 hospital-scale chest x-ray database and benchmarks on weakly-supervised classification and localization of common thorax diseases. In: IEEE Conference on Computer Vision and Pattern Recognition, pp. 2097–2106 (2017)
27. Wang, Z., et al.: Progressive graph-based transductive learning for multi-modal classification of brain disorder disease. In: Ourselin, S., Joskowicz, L., Sabuncu, M.R., Unal, G., Wells, W. (eds.) MICCAI 2016. LNCS, vol. 9900, pp. 291–299. Springer, Cham (2016). https://doi.org/10.1007/978-3-319-46720-7_34
28. Yan, C., Yao, J., Li, R., Xu, Z., Huang, J.: Weakly supervised deep learning for thoracic disease classification and localization on chest x-rays. In: Proceedings of the 2018 ACM International Conference on Bioinformatics, Computational Biology, and Health Informatics, pp. 103–110 (2018)
29. Yao, L., Prosky, J., Poblenz, E., Covington, B., Lyman, K.: Weakly supervised medical diagnosis and localization from multiple resolutions. arXiv preprint arXiv:1803.07703 (2018)
30. Zhao, M., Chan, R.H., Chow, T.W., Tang, P.: Compact graph based semi-supervised learning for medical diagnosis in Alzheimer's disease. IEEE Signal Process. Lett. $21(10)$, 1192–1196 (2014)
31. Zhou, D., Bousquet, O., Lal, T.N., Weston, J., Schölkopf, B.: Learning with local and global consistency. In: Advances in Neural Information Processing Systems (NIPS), pp. 321–328 (2004)
32. Zhu, W., Lou, Q., Vang, Y.S., Xie, X.: Deep multi-instance networks with sparse label assignment for whole mammogram classification. In: Descoteaux, M., Maier-Hein, L., Franz, A., Jannin, P., Collins, D.L., Duchesne, S. (eds.) MICCAI 2017. LNCS, vol. 10435, pp. 603–611. Springer, Cham (2017). https://doi.org/10.1007/978-3-319-66179-7_69

Intraoperative Liver Surface Completion with Graph Convolutional VAE

Simone Foti[1,2(✉)], Bongjin Koo[1,2], Thomas Dowrick[1,2], João Ramalhinho[1,2], Moustafa Allam[3], Brian Davidson[3], Danail Stoyanov[1,2], and Matthew J. Clarkson[1,2]

[1] Wellcome/EPSRC Centre for Interventional and Surgical Sciences, University College London, London, UK
s.foti@cs.ucl.ac.uk
[2] Centre For Medical Image Computing, University College London, London, UK
[3] Division of Surgery and Interventional Science, University College London, London, UK

Abstract. In this work we propose a method based on geometric deep learning to predict the complete surface of the liver, given a partial point cloud of the organ obtained during the surgical laparoscopic procedure. We introduce a new data augmentation technique that randomly perturbs shapes in their frequency domain to compensate the limited size of our dataset. The core of our method is a variational autoencoder (VAE) that is trained to learn a latent space for complete shapes of the liver. At inference time, the generative part of the model is embedded in an optimisation procedure where the latent representation is iteratively updated to generate a model that matches the intraoperative partial point cloud. The effect of this optimisation is a progressive non-rigid deformation of the initially generated shape. Our method is qualitatively evaluated on real data and quantitatively evaluated on synthetic data. We compared with a state-of-the-art rigid registration algorithm, that our method outperformed in visible areas.

Keywords: Laparascopic liver surgery · Geometric deep learning · Graph convolution · Surface completion · Variational autoencoder

1 Introduction

The loss of direct vision and tactile feedback in laparoscopic procedures introduces an additional level of complexity for surgeons. Augmented reality (AR) is a promising approach to alleviate these limitations and provide guidance during the procedure. However, it remains an open challenge for laparoscopic surgery of the liver, which is one of the largest and most deformable organs. AR is usually achieved by registering a preoperative 3D model to the intraoperative laparoscopic view. Clinically available state-of-the-art commercial systems use manual point-based rigid registration [14], while recent research works focus on either

© Springer Nature Switzerland AG 2020
C. H. Sudre et al. (Eds.): UNSURE 2020/GRAIL 2020, LNCS 12443, pp. 198–207, 2020.
https://doi.org/10.1007/978-3-030-60365-6_19

rigid [12,16] or deformable [3,6,10,13] registration techniques requiring different amounts of manual interactions and computations on the preoperative data. In contrast, we formulate the deformable registration as a shape completion problem that does not rely on patient specific preoperative computations.

Even though the underlying techniques are different, the common application and presence of an optimisation procedure make our method similar to registration. We believe that our method has the potential to become a precursor to a new approach for registration. Thus, we directly compare our method with a rigid registration algorithm (Go-ICP [20]) that aligns two point clouds. This algorithm was successfully used for laparoscopic liver applications in [12], where the preoperative model was registered onto the intraoperative point cloud obtained using an unsupervised neural network for depth estimation. Our method is similar, but relying on a manual interaction it is also able to predict a deformed model that better fits the point cloud. Other methods, such as [10,13] attempt the registration of preoperative models directly on the intraoperative images requiring manual image annotations. Even though they still show high errors in areas not visible from the camera, these methods showed extremely good performances in coping with deformations. Both use biomechanical models to simulate deformations, and [13] requires an additional preoperative step where multiple possible patient-specifc simulations have to be performed.

The most similar works to ours are [1] and [11]. The former leverages a voxel-based conditional variational autoencoder (VAE) to complete missing segments of bone and plan jaw reconstructive surgical procedures. Not only the anatomical structures considered in their work are not deformable and the missing segments are small compared to the complete shape, but also their solution is constrained by the remaining healthy structures. On the other hand, our problem is more ill-posed because the liver is highly deformable and the missing parts are much larger than the partial intraoperative shape. In addition, voxel-based representations of shapes are inefficient volume representations that struggle to achieve high resolutions and to handle deformations. Therefore, we represent 3D shapes as Riemannian manifolds discretised into meshes and use geometric deep learning techniques to process these data. In particular, our work adapts [11] to achieve shape completion in laparoscopic liver surgery by (*i*) overcoming the shortage of data; (*ii*) compensating the lack of point correspondences between partial and complete shapes; (*iii*) redefining the VAE training loss to deal with non-uniformly sampled meshes; and (*iv*) leveraging preoperative data for the initialisation. The optimisation process for shape completion, makes the methodology suitable for registration, but there are a few key steps that need innovating. We believe this is the first attempt to bring geometric deep learning in to computer assisted interventions.

2   Methods

The proposed method (Fig. 1) estimates the complete mesh of a liver given a partial point cloud of its surface. A graph convolutional variational autoencoder is trained to generate complete shapes (Sect. 2.1) and a distinct optimisation procedure non-rigidly deforms them to fit the partial point cloud (Sect. 2.2).

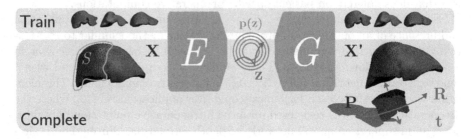

Fig. 1. Schematic Description of the Proposed Method. *Top:* a VAE ($\{E, G\}$) is trained on complete preoperative meshes of the liver. *Bottom:* the shape completion starts with a manual selection S on the preoperative mesh $\mathbf{X}$. The latent representation obtained encoding $\mathbf{X}$ is used to initialise $\mathbf{z}$. The error between the selection on the generated mesh ($\mathbf{X}'_S = S \circ G(\mathbf{z})$) and the partial intraoperative point cloud $\mathbf{P}$ is minimised optimising over $\mathbf{z}, \mathbf{R}, \mathbf{t}$, which control the shape of new generated meshes, the rotation of $\mathbf{P}$ and its translation respectively.

2.1   Shape Generator

A 3D mesh can be represented as a graph $\mathcal{M} = \{\mathbf{X}, \varepsilon\}$, where $\mathbf{X} \in \mathbb{R}^{N \times 3}$ is its vertex embedding and $\varepsilon \in \mathbb{N}^{\epsilon \times 2}$ is the edge connectivity that defines its topology. Traditional convolutional operators, well suited for grid data such as images and voxelizations, are generally incompatible with the non-Euclidean domain of graphs. Following [11], we chose to build our generative model with the Feature-Steered graph convolutions defined in [18]. This operator dynamically assigns filter weights to k-ring neighbourhoods according to the features learned by the network. In particular, given a generic feature vector field where for each vertex i we have a feature vector $\mathbf{x}_i$, we can define the output of the convolutional operator as

$$\mathbf{y}_i = \mathbf{b} + \frac{1}{|\mathcal{N}_i|} \sum_{j \in \mathcal{N}_i} \sum_{m=1}^{M} q_m(\mathbf{x}_i, \mathbf{x}_j) \mathbf{W}_m \mathbf{x}_j \tag{1}$$

where $\mathbf{b}$ is a learnable bias, $q_m(\mathbf{x}_i, \mathbf{x}_j)$ is a translation-invariant assignment operator that, using a soft-max over a linear transformation of the local feature vectors, learns to dynamically assign $\mathbf{x}_j$ to the m-th learnable weight matrix $\mathbf{W}_m$, and $\mathcal{N}_i$ is the neighbour of the i-th vertex with cardinality $|\mathcal{N}_i|$.

Every VAE is made of an encoder-decoder pair, where the decoder is used as a generative model and is usually referred to as generator. Following this convention, we define our architecture as a pair $\{E, G\}$. Let $\mathcal{X}_c$ be the vertex embedding domain of complete shapes and $\mathcal{Z}$ the latent distribution domain. Then, the two networks are defined as two non-linear functions such that $E : \mathcal{X}_c \to \mathcal{Z}$ and $G : \mathcal{Z} \to \mathcal{X}_c$. With $\mathbf{X} \in \mathcal{X}_c$ and $\mathbf{z} \sim \mathcal{Z}$, the generator is described by the likelihood $p(\mathbf{X}|\mathbf{z})$ while the encoder is defined as a variational distribution $q(\mathbf{z}|\mathbf{X})$ that approximates the intractable model posterior distribution. Both E and G are parametrised by neural networks whose building blocks are the Feature-Steered graph convolutions. During training, a reconstruction loss ($\mathcal{L}_{recon}$) encourages the output of the VAE to be as close as possible to its input and a regularisation term ($\mathcal{L}_{KL}$) pushes the variational distribution towards the prior distribution $p(\mathbf{z})$, which is defined as a standard spherical Gaussian distribution. While we set $\mathcal{L}_{KL}$ to be the Kullback–Leibler (KL) divergence, we define $\mathcal{L}_{recon}$ as a vertex-density-weighted mean-squared-errors loss. Let $\mathbf{x}_i$ be the i-th position vector (i.e. a feature vector of size 3) and $\mathbf{x}'_i$ its corresponding point in $\mathbf{X}' = G(E(\mathbf{X}))$. We have:

$$\mathcal{L}_{recon} = \frac{1}{N} \sum_{i=0}^{N-1} \gamma \|\mathbf{x}'_i - \mathbf{x}_i\|_2^2 \quad \text{with } \gamma \propto \frac{1}{\mathcal{N}_i} \sum_{j \in \mathcal{N}_i} \|\mathbf{x}_i - \mathbf{x}_j\|_2^2 \qquad (2)$$

where γ is a vertex-wise weight that increases the contribution of the errors in low vertex-density regions, thus preventing the generated mesh from fitting only densely sampled areas. The total loss is then computed as linear combination of the two terms: $\mathcal{L}_{tot} = \mathcal{L}_{recon} + \alpha \mathcal{L}_{KL}$.

Data Preparation. Though the chosen graph convolution was proven effective also on datasets with different graph topologies [18], we decided to remesh our data in order to have the same topology and known point correspondences across all the preoperative meshes and all the generated shapes. This accelerates and eases the training procedure, allowing us to define a simple and computationally-efficient loss function (Eq. 2). In addition, thanks to the consistent vertex indexing it is possible to easily perform the initial manual selection described in Sect. 2.2.

In order to consistently remesh our dataset, we run an optimisation procedure that iteratively deforms an ico-sphere with a predefined topology and fixed number of vertices. Following [19], the loss function is given by $\mathcal{L}_{remesh} = \lambda_0 \mathcal{L}_{Ch} + \lambda_1 \mathcal{L}_n + \lambda_2 \mathcal{L}_L + \lambda_3 \mathcal{L}_E$. $\mathcal{L}_{Ch}$ is the Chamfer distance that averages the distances between each point in a mesh and the closest point in the other mesh, and vice versa. $\mathcal{L}_n$ is the normal loss that requires the edge between a vertex and its neighbours to be perpendicular to the normal of the closest vertex in the ground truth. $\mathcal{L}_L$ is the mesh Laplacian regularisation loss that avoids self-intersections, acting as a surface smoothness term. $\mathcal{L}_e$ is an edge regularisation that reduces flying vertices by penalising long edges. $\lambda_{0,1,2,3}$ are the weights of each loss term.

Spectral Augmentation. The small size of our dataset makes it difficult to train a generative model that can generalise to new shapes. Simple shape augmentation techniques such as random rotations, translations and scalings can be used to augment the dataset, but shapes are not deformed and the performance gain is therefore limited. Instead of attempting an augmentation in the spatial domain we propose a data augmentation technique that operates in the frequency domain, which is a known concept in the literature [17]. However, we simplify and randomise the spectral deformation making it suitable for data augmentation. We thus compute the un-normalized graph Laplacian operator $\mathbf{L} = \mathbf{D} - \mathbf{A}$, where $\mathbf{A} \in \mathbb{R}^{N \times N}$ is the adjacency matrix and $\mathbf{D} \in \mathbb{R}^{N \times N}$ is the diagonal degree matrix with $D_{ii} = \sum_j A_{ij}$. Computing the eigenvalue decomposition of the Laplacian, $\mathbf{L} = \mathbf{U}\mathbf{\Lambda}\mathbf{U}^T$, we obtain a set of orthonormal eigenvectors (columns of $\mathbf{U}$) which are the Fourier bases of the mesh, and a series of eigenvalues (diagonal values of $\mathbf{\Lambda}$) that are its frequencies. The Fourier transform of the vertices can be computed as $\hat{\mathbf{X}} = \mathbf{U}^T\mathbf{X}$ and the inverse Fourier transform as $\mathbf{X} = \mathbf{U}\hat{\mathbf{X}}$ [5].

Using these operators, each mesh is transformed into its spectral domain, perturbed, and transformed back to the spatial domain. Hence, the spectral augmented mesh $\mathbf{X}^\dagger$ is computed as $\mathbf{X}^\dagger = \mathbf{U}\boldsymbol{\xi}\mathbf{U}^T\mathbf{X}$, where $\boldsymbol{\xi}$ is a vector that randomly perturbs four mesh frequencies. In particular, the first frequency is never modified because, playing the role of a direct current component [2], it would not deform the shape. One of the following three frequencies, responsible for low frequency variations similar to scalings along the three major axes of the mesh, is arbitrarily perturbed. The remaining three perturbations are applied to randomly selected higher frequencies with the effect of affecting the fine details of the shape.

It is worth noting that the remeshed data share the same topology, thus the set of orthonormal eigenvectors used to compute the direct and inverse Fourier transforms can be computed one time and then used for every mesh.

2.2   Shape Completion

This section illustrates how a complete shape is obtained from a partial intraoperative point cloud $\mathbf{P} \in \mathbb{R}^{P \times 3}$. In contrast to [11], we do not have known (or easily computable) point correspondences between intraoperative point clouds and the generated meshes. Therefore, we relax this assumption at the expense of the introduction of a manual step in the procedure. In fact, the surgeon is asked to roughly select from the preoperative 3D model $\mathbf{X} \in \mathcal{X}_c$ a region of interest that corresponds to the visible surface in the intraoperative image. To reduce computational time and increase robustness against the errors in manual region selection and varying vertex density in the region, we sample the selected vertices with an iterative farthest point sampling [15], obtaining a selection operator S that gives sparser and uniformly sampled vertices. Since mesh topology consistency is guaranteed by construction, the selected vertices will always have the same indexing for each mesh $\mathbf{X}' \in \mathcal{X}_c$ generated with the model discussed in Sect. 2.1. The shape completion problem is thus formulated as finding the best latent variable $\mathbf{z}^*$ that generates a complete shape $\mathbf{X}'^*$ plausibly fitting $\mathbf{P}$. Given

$\mathbf{X}'_S = S \circ \mathbf{X}' = S \circ G(\mathbf{z}) \subset \mathbf{X}'$ the subset of selected and sampled vertices from a generated shape, we optimise

$$\min_{\mathbf{z}, \mathbf{R}, \mathbf{t}} \mathcal{L}_{Ch}\Big(S \circ G(\mathbf{z}), \ \mathbf{RP} + \mathbf{t}\Big). \tag{3}$$

It is worth mentioning that not having point correspondences between $\mathbf{P}$ and $\mathbf{X}'_S$ we cannot compute the rotation $\mathbf{R}$ and translation $\mathbf{t}$ in a closed form solution as in [11]. Therefore, they are iteratively updated alongside $\mathbf{z}$ in the same optimisation procedure. The gradient of the loss in Eq. 3 directly influences $\mathbf{R}$ and $\mathbf{t}$, but it needs to be back-propagated through the generator network G, without updating the network's weights, to update $\mathbf{z}$. The completion procedure is initialised by centering $\mathbf{P}$ and $\mathbf{X}'_S$, and by setting an initial $\mathbf{z} = \mathbf{z}_0 = E(\mathbf{X})$, thus using as prior the latent representation of the preoperative mesh. The initialisation $\mathbf{z}_0$ can be further refined to $\mathbf{z}_0^*$ by running a few iterations of a second optimisation $\mathbf{z}_0^* \leftarrow \arg\min_{\mathbf{z}_0} \big(\max_i \|\mathbf{x}_i - \mathbf{x}'_i\|_2^2 \big)$. Finally, by adding to the latent initialisation a small Gaussian noise $\boldsymbol{\eta} \sim \mathcal{G}(\mathbf{0}, \boldsymbol{\Sigma})$ with $\Sigma_{ii} \ll I_{ii}$, we can generate multiple complete shapes conditioned on the preoperative data and that plausibly fit the intraoperative point cloud $\mathbf{P}$.

3   Results

Our dataset consists of 50 meshes of livers which were segmented and reconstructed from preoperative CT scans of different patients. The segmentation and initial mesh generation was performed by Visible Patient. 45 meshes were used to train the VAE, while the remaining 5 meshes were used as a test set to evaluate the network, data augmentation, and shape completion. Given the limited size of the dataset, to not bias results toward the test set, hyperparameters were tuned on the training set. The study was approved by the local research ethics committee (Ref: 14/LO/1264) and written consent obtained from each patient.

The remeshing was performed by deforming an ico-sphere with 2564 vertices. For this, and all the other optimisations described in this paper, we used the ADAM optimiser [9]. We remeshed every model with 500 iterations at a fixed learning rate of $lr = 5e^{-3}$. The weights of the loss function $\mathcal{L}_{remesh}$ were $\lambda_0 = 5$, $\lambda_1 = 0.2$, $\lambda_2 = 0.3$, and $\lambda_3 = 15$.

The VAE was built using $M = 8$ weight matrices, batch size 20 and latent size 128. LeakyReLU and batch normalisation were used after every layer. The network was implemented in PyTorch Geometric [7] and trained for 200 epochs with $lr = 1e^{-3}$ and a KL divergence weight $\alpha = 1e^{-6}$. The training was performed on an NVIDIA Quadro P5000 and took approximately 9 h.

We evaluated the reconstruction performance of the VAE with and without data augmentation while fixing the number of iterations. Applying the spectral augmentation (Fig. 2A) we generated 100 new meshes for each model in the training set, thus obtaining 4500 models. An additional online data augmentation composed of random rotations, scalings, and translations was applied. We obtain

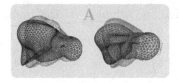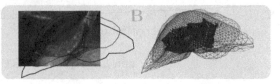

Fig. 2. Augmentation and Qualitative Results A: effects of the spectral augmentation where a real liver (green) is subject to two different random augmentation (black). B: laparoscopic image and comparison between the proposed shape completion (blue) and the Go-ICP registration (black). The intraoperative point cloud is shown in red and the selected point in blue. The contours of the silhouettes are overlaied also on the laparoscopic image. (Color figure online)

a mean-squared testing error of (0.28 ± 0.04) mm when both augmentations are applied, of (0.45 ± 0.18) mm with the online augmentation alone, of (0.50 ± 0.03) mm with the spectral augmentation only, and of (0.92 ± 0.22) mm without any augmentation. We then evaluated the computational cost of the spectral augmentation, finding that when it is performed by computing the Fourier operators for each mesh it takes 0.4532 ± 0.0568 seconds per mesh, while, when the operators are precomputed (Sect. 2.1) the computational time is reduced by one order of magnitude to 0.0487 ± 0.0092 seconds per mesh.

Given the lack of intraoperative 3D ground truths for registration in laparoscopic liver surgery, the evaluation of our method on real data is purely qualitative. In a real operative scenario the computation of a dense and reliable point cloud is still a major challenge. To obtain $\mathbf{P}$ from rectified images of a calibrated laparoscope we used an off-the-shelf depth reconstruction network [4]. Given the predicted depth map and a manual segmentation of the liver, we first compute $\mathbf{P}$ and then estimate the complete shape $\mathbf{X}'^*$ (Fig. 2B).

The quantitative assessment of the shape completion is performed on synthetic data. The five meshes in the test set were manually deformed, trying to reproduce intraoperative liver deformations similar to those expected in a laparoscopic procedure and characterised in [8]. To obtain intraoperative partial point clouds, the surface of the deformed models was sampled with vertex selections on three regions: entire front surface $\mathbf{P}_F$, left lobe $\mathbf{P}_L$, and right lobe $\mathbf{P}_R$. Each deformed model is considered the intraoperative ground truth $\mathbf{X}_{GT}$ that we want to infer given a partial point cloud. To maintain a higher $\mathbf{P}$ density, $\mathbf{X}_{GT}$ was not remeshed. Equation 3 is optimised for 100 iterations using ADAM with a different learning rate for each term. To encourage the optimisation over $\mathbf{z}$ and thus the generation of more diverse, progressively deformed meshes $\mathbf{X}'$, we set $lr_z = 5e^{-2}$. The learning rates for $\mathbf{R}$ and $\mathbf{t}$ are empirically set to $lr_R = 1e^{-2}$ and $lr_t = 5e^{-5}$. Rotations are regressed faster because the two point clouds were initially centred. In case $\mathbf{z}_0$ is further refined to $\mathbf{z}_0^*$, the same learning rate $lr_z = 5e^{-2}$ is used for 20 iterations. In case multiple complete shape proposals are desired, Eq. 3 can be generalised to process batches with a refined initialisation perturbed by $\boldsymbol{\eta}$ with $\Sigma_{ii} = \frac{1}{10}$.

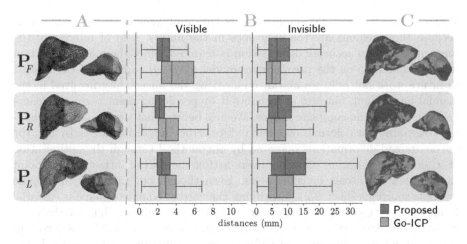

Fig. 3. Quantitative Results. *Rows*: results for intraoperative point clouds of front surface $\mathbf{P}_F$, right lobe $\mathbf{P}_R$, and left lobe $\mathbf{P}_L$. *Columns*: A) front and back view of intraoperative point cloud $\mathbf{P}$ (red), intraoperative ground truth $\mathbf{X}_{GT}$ (green), and prediction $\mathbf{X}'^*$ (blue). B) Comparison of vertex-wise distances (mm) for the proposed method (blue) and Go-ICP (pink). We compute errors separately in the visible and invisible parts of the liver in the camera's field of view. C) Front and back view of $\mathbf{X}'^*$. Colours represent the algorithm with a smaller vertex error. (Color figure online)

The shape completion was evaluated for each partial shape without η perturbation. Since the procedure requires a manual step currently performed with a lasso selection that might affect results, we repeated the evaluation 3 times, for a total of 45 experiments. Selections could be refined and took approximately one minute each. We compared our method with the rigid registration using Go-ICP [12] which has comparable computational time to ours. The lack of point correspondences between $\mathbf{X}_{GT}$ and $\mathbf{X}'^*$ does not allow us to evaluate our method using mean-squared errors. Therefore, we define a variation of $\mathcal{L}_{Ch}$ that allows us to compute vertex-wise errors on $\mathbf{X}'^*$. For each vertex of one mesh we compute the distance to the closest point on the other mesh. All the distances are assigned to the vertices of $\mathbf{X}'^*$ from which they were computed and are locally averaged. Results are reported in Fig. 3.

4   Conclusion

While this work is about shape completion, we believe it could become an alternative to registration or provide a better initialisation for such algorithms. From Fig. 2 we notice that the proposed method seems to fit better the point cloud especially on the left lobe. The lack of a ground truth makes impossible to draw further conclusions from this result. However, observing Fig. 3 (columns B and C), we can conclude that our method outperforms Go-ICP in visible areas, and, despite performing worse in invisible areas, it predicts a realistic looking model of the liver. Of particular importance is the improvement over visible areas, because these regions are the only ones in the narrow field of interest of the surgeon, where an accurate deformation is required. Since the manual selection of the visible area on the preoperative model affects the quality of the results, as future work not only we aim at quantifying the uncertainty involved in the manual interaction, but also at avoiding it by predicting point correspondences between partial and complete shapes. We also believe that the use of biomechanical constraints for deformation could reduce errors in invisible areas. In fact, the unconstrained deformations operated by our method through the optimisation of $\mathbf{z}$, despite generating plausible livers fitting the partial intraoperative point cloud, often downscale invisible areas. Even though our method can propose multiple solutions (Sect. 2.2), identifying the correct complete shape is essential to improve our method and outperform Go-ICP everywhere. Thus, we shall also research the introduction of biomechanical constraints while avoiding any patient specific training or simulation. Finally, we are planning to incorporate the liver's internal structure in our method in order to overlay them on a laparoscopic video during surgery.

Acknowledgments. This work was supported by the Wellcome Trust/EPSRC [203145Z/16/Z], and Wellcome Trust/Department of Health [HICF-T4-317].

References

1. Abdi, A.H., Pesteie, M., Prisman, E., Abolmaesumi, P., Fels, S.: Variational shape completion for virtual planning of jaw reconstructive surgery. In: Shen, D., et al. (eds.) MICCAI 2019. LNCS, vol. 11768, pp. 227–235. Springer, Cham (2019). https://doi.org/10.1007/978-3-030-32254-0_26
2. Bronstein, M.M., Bruna, J., LeCun, Y., Szlam, A., Vandergheynst, P.: Geometric deep learning: going beyond Euclidean data. IEEE Signal Process. Mag. **34**(4), 18–42 (2017)
3. Brunet, J.-N., Mendizabal, A., Petit, A., Golse, N., Vibert, E., Cotin, S.: Physics-based deep neural network for augmented reality during liver surgery. In: Shen, D., et al. (eds.) MICCAI 2019. LNCS, vol. 11768, pp. 137–145. Springer, Cham (2019). https://doi.org/10.1007/978-3-030-32254-0_16
4. Chang, J.R., Chen, Y.S.: Pyramid stereo matching network. In: Proceedings of the IEEE Conference on Computer Vision and Pattern Recognition (CVPR), pp. 5410–5418 (2018)
5. Defferrard, M., Bresson, X., Vandergheynst, P.: Convolutional neural networks on graphs with fast localized spectral filtering. In: Advances in Neural Information Processing Systems (NIPS), pp. 3844–3852 (2016)
6. Espinel, Y., Ozgür, E., Calvet, L., Le Roy, B., Buc, E., Bartoli, A.: Combining visual cues and interactions for 3D–2D registration in liver laparoscopy. Ann. Biomed. Eng. **48**, 1712–1727 (2020). https://doi.org/10.1007/s10439-020-02479-z
7. Fey, M., Lenssen, J.E.: Fast graph representation learning with PyTorch geometric. In: ICLR Workshop on Representation Learning on Graphs and Manifolds (2019)

8. Heiselman, J.S., et al.: Characterization and correction of intraoperative soft tissue deformation in image-guided laparoscopic liver surgery. J. Med. Imaging **5**(2), 021203 (2017)

9. Kingma, D.P., Ba, J.: Adam: a method for stochastic optimization. arXiv preprint arXiv:1412.6980 (2014)

10. Koo, B., Özgür, E., Le Roy, B., Buc, E., Bartoli, A.: Deformable registration of a preoperative 3D liver volume to a laparoscopy image using contour and shading cues. In: Descoteaux, M., Maier-Hein, L., Franz, A., Jannin, P., Collins, D.L., Duchesne, S. (eds.) MICCAI 2017. LNCS, vol. 10433, pp. 326–334. Springer, Cham (2017). https://doi.org/10.1007/978-3-319-66182-7_38

11. Litany, O., Bronstein, A., Bronstein, M., Makadia, A.: Deformable shape completion with graph convolutional autoencoders. In: Proceedings of the IEEE Conference on Computer Vision and Pattern Recognition (CVPR), pp. 1886–1895 (2018)

12. Luo, H., et al.: Augmented reality navigation for liver resection with a stereoscopic laparoscope. Comput. Methods Programs Biomed. **187**, 105099 (2019)

13. Özgür, E., Koo, B., Le Roy, B., Buc, E., Bartoli, A.: Preoperative liver registration for augmented monocular laparoscopy using backward-forward biomechanical simulation. Int. J. Comput. Assist. Radiol. Surg. **13**(10), 1629–1640 (2018)

14. Prevost, G.A., et al.: Efficiency, accuracy and clinical applicability of a new image-guided surgery system in 3D laparoscopic liver surgery. J. Gastrointest. Surg. 1–8 (2019). https://doi.org/10.1007/s11605-019-04395-7

15. Qi, C.R., Yi, L., Su, H., Guibas, L.J.: PointNet++: deep hierarchical feature learning on point sets in a metric space. In: Advances in Neural Information Processing Systems (NIPS), pp. 5099–5108 (2017)

16. Robu, M.R., et al.: Global rigid registration of CT to video in laparoscopic liver surgery. Int. J. Comput. Assist. Radiol. Surg. **13**(6), 947–956 (2018)

17. Rong, G., Cao, Y., Guo, X.: Spectral mesh deformation. Vis. Comput. **24**(7–9), 787–796 (2008). https://doi.org/10.1007/s00371-008-0260-x

18. Verma, N., Boyer, E., Verbeek, J.: FeaStNet: feature-steered graph convolutions for 3D shape analysis. In: Proceedings of the IEEE Conference on Computer Vision and Pattern Recognition (CVPR), pp. 2598–2606 (2018)

19. Wang, N., Zhang, Y., Li, Z., Fu, Y., Liu, W., Jiang, Y.G.: Pixel2Mesh: generating 3D mesh models from single RGB images. In: Proceedings of the European Conference on Computer Vision (ECCV), pp. 52–67 (2018)

20. Yang, J., Li, H., Campbell, D., Jia, Y.: Go-ICP: a globally optimal solution to 3D ICP point-set registration. IEEE Trans. Pattern Anal. Mach. Intell. **38**(11), 2241–2254 (2015)

HACT-Net: A Hierarchical Cell-to-Tissue Graph Neural Network for Histopathological Image Classification

Pushpak Pati[1,2(✉)], Guillaume Jaume[1,3], Lauren Alisha Fernandes[2],
Antonio Foncubierta-Rodríguez[1], Florinda Feroce[4], Anna Maria Anniciello[4],
Giosue Scognamiglio[4], Nadia Brancati[5], Daniel Riccio[5], Maurizio Di Bonito[4],
Giuseppe De Pietro[5], Gerardo Botti[4], Orcun Goksel[2], Jean-Philippe Thiran[3],
Maria Frucci[5], and Maria Gabrani[1]

[1] IBM Zurich Research Lab, Zurich, Switzerland
pus@zurich.ibm.com
[2] Computer-Assisted Applications in Medicine, ETH Zurich, Zurich, Switzerland
[3] Signal Processing Laboratory 5, EPFL, Lausanne, Switzerland
[4] National Cancer Institute- IRCCS-Fondazione Pascale, Naples, Italy
[5] Institute for High Performance Computing and Networking-CNR, Naples, Italy

Abstract. Cancer diagnosis, prognosis, and therapeutic response prediction are heavily influenced by the relationship between the histopathological structures and the function of the tissue. Recent approaches acknowledging the structure-function relationship, have linked the structural and spatial patterns of cell organization in tissue via cell-graphs to tumor grades. Though cell organization is imperative, it is insufficient to entirely represent the histopathological structure. We propose a novel hierarchical cell-to-tissue-graph (HACT) representation to improve the structural depiction of the tissue. It consists of a low-level cell-graph, capturing cell morphology and interactions, a high-level tissue-graph, capturing morphology and spatial distribution of tissue parts, and cells-to-tissue hierarchies, encoding the relative spatial distribution of the cells with respect to the tissue distribution. Further, a hierarchical graph neural network (HACT-Net) is proposed to efficiently map the HACT representations to histopathological breast cancer subtypes. We assess the methodology on a large set of annotated tissue regions of interest from H&E stained breast carcinoma whole-slides. Upon evaluation, the proposed method outperformed recent convolutional neural network and graph neural network approaches for breast cancer multi-class subtyping. The proposed entity-based topological analysis is more in line with the pathological diagnostic procedure of the tissue. It provides more command over the tissue modeling, therefore encourages the further inclusion of pathological priors into task-specific tissue representation.

P. Pati and G. Jaume—The authors contributed equally to this work.

C. H. Sudre et al. (Eds.): UNSURE 2020/GRAIL 2020, LNCS 12443, pp. 208–219, 2020.
https://doi.org/10.1007/978-3-030-60365-6_20

1   Introduction

Breast cancer is the second most common type of cancer with a high mortality rate in women [23]. A majority of breast lesions are diagnosed according to a diagnostic spectrum of cancer classes that ranges from benign to invasive. The classes confer different folds of risk to become invasive. Lesions with atypia or ductal carcinoma in-situ are associated with higher risks of transitioning to invasive carcinoma compared to benign lesions [6,19]. Thus, accurate discrimination of these classes is pivotal to determine the optimal treatment plan. However, distinguishing the classes is not always easy, *e.g.*, in [6] pathologists' concordance rates were as low as 48% for atypia. In a clinical setting, pathologists begin the classification of a tissue biopsy by discerning the morphology and the spatial distribution of tissue parts, such as epithelium, stroma, necrosis, etc. Then, they localize their analysis to specific regions of interest (RoI) on the tissue and evaluate nuclear phenotype, morphology, topology, and tissue distribution among several other criteria for the classification. However, such inspections are tedious, time-consuming, and prone to observer variability, thus increasing the demand for automated systems in cancer diagnosis. Digital pathology has recently motivated innovative research opportunities in machine learning and computer vision to automate cancer diagnosis [16]. The most common technique for classifying RoIs consists of extracting fixed-size patches from an RoI and classifying them using Convolutional Neural Networks (CNN); then, patch-based predictions are aggregated to label the RoI [2,18]. Such approaches are limited to finding the apt patch size and resolution to include context information. It can be achieved by reducing the resolution at the cost of missing cell-level information, or by increasing the resolution at the cost of limiting patch size due to computational challenges. Additionally, patch-based approaches unfairly assume the same label for an RoI and its corresponding patches. Further, the pixel-based analysis by the CNNs does not comprehend the essence of biological entities and their biological context. This inhibits the integration of CNNs and prior pathological knowledge that would require the selective entity-based implementation of CNNs.

To address the above issues, histopathological structures of tissues have been represented by cell-graphs (CG) [10], where cells and cellular interactions are presented as nodes and edges of CG respectively. Then, classical graph learning techniques or graph neural networks (GNNs) learn from CGs to map the structure-function relationship. Recently various CG representations [7,22,26,29] have been proposed by varying the graph building strategies or the node attributes. However, a CG exploits only the cellular morphology and topology and discards the tissue distribution information such as the stromal microenvironment, tumor microenvironment, lumen structure, etc. that are vital for appropriate representation of histopathological structures. Additionally, a CG cannot represent the hierarchical nature of the tissue. For instance, in [29], a hierarchy is defined from the cells with learned pooling layers. However, the tissue hierarchy is inaccessible as the representation does not include high-level tissue features. In [5], the cell-level and tissue-level information are simply concatenated. Thus, the functional representation of the tissue cannot leverage the hierarchy between the levels.

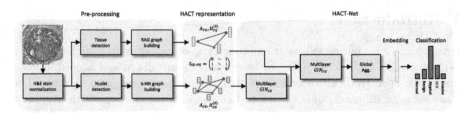

Fig. 1. Block diagram of the proposed methodology including pre-processing module, HACT representation of a RoI and HACT-Net classifying the RoI.

We address the above shortcomings by proposing a novel HierArchical-Cell-to-Tissue (HACT) representation of the RoIs. In HACT representation, a low-level CG captures the cellular morphology and topology; a high-level tissue-graph (TG) captures the attributes of the tissue parts and their spatial distribution, and the hierarchy between the CG and the TG captures the relative distribution of the cells with respect to the tissue distribution. Further, we propose HACT-Net, a hierarchical GNN to learn from the HACT representation and predict cancer types. Similar to the RoI diagnostic procedure by the pathologist's, HACT-Net encodes contextual local and global structural attributes and interactions, thereby allowing for enriched structure-function relation analysis.

2   Methods

We propose a HACT-representation that consists of a low-level CG, a high level TG, and cell-to-tissue hierarchies. This representation is processed by HACT-Net, a hierarchical GNN that employs two GNNs [8,11,14,25,28] to operate at cell and tissue level. The learned cell node embeddings are combined with the corresponding tissue node embedding via the cell-to-tissue hierarchies. Figure 1 summarizes the proposed methodology including the pre-processing for stain normalization [17], HACT-representation building and HACT-Net.

2.1   Representation

We define an undirected graph $G := (V, E)$ as a set of $|V|$ nodes and $|E|$ edges. An edge between the nodes u and v is denoted by e_{uv} or e_{vu}. The graph topology is described by a symmetric adjacency matrix $A \in \mathbb{R}^{|V| \times |V|}$, where an entry $A_{u,v} = 1$ if $e_{uv} \in E$. Each node v is presented by a feature vector $h(v) \in \mathbb{R}^d$. Equivalently, the node features are presented in their matrix form as $H \in \mathbb{R}^{|V| \times d}$. We define the neighborhood of a node v as $\mathcal{N}(v) := \{u \in V \mid v \in V, e_{uv} \in E \}$.

Cell-Graph (CG): In a CG, each node represents a cell and edges encode cellular interactions. We detect nuclei using the Hover-Net model [9], pre-trained on the multi-organ nuclei segmentation dataset [15]. For each detected nucleus at $40\times$ resolution, we extract hand-crafted features representing shape, texture and spatial location following [29]. Shape features include eccentricity, area, maximum and minimum length of axis, perimeter, solidity and orientation. Texture features include average foreground and background difference, standard deviation, skewness and mean entropy of nuclei intensity, and dissimilarity, homogeneity, energy and ASM from Gray-Level Co-occurrence Matrix. Nuclei are spatially encoded by their spatial centroids normalised by the image size. In total, each nucleus is represented by 18 features, noted as f_{CG}. These features serve as the initial node embeddings in CG.

To generate the CG topology, we assume that spatially close cells encode biological interactions and should be connected in CG, and distant cells have weak cellular interactions, so they should remain disconnected in CG. To this end, we use the k-Nearest Neighbors (kNN) algorithm to build the initial topology, and prune the kNN graph by removing edges lengthier than a threshold distance d_{min}. We use $L2$ norm in the image space to quantify the cellular distance. Formally, for each node v, an edge e_{vu} is built if $u \in \{w \mid \text{dist}(v, w) \leq d_k \wedge \text{dist}(v, w) < d_{\min}, \forall w \in V, v \in V, d_k = k\text{-th smallest distance in dist}(v, w)\}$. In our experiments, we set $k = 5$ and $d_{min} = 50$ pixels, i.e. 12.5 μm considering the scanner resolution of 0.25 μm/pixel. Figure 2(a) presents a sample CG elucidating the nodes and edges in the zoomed-in sub-image.

Tissue-Graph (TG): To capture the tissue distribution, we construct a TG by considering interactions among the parts of the tissue. In particular, we consider the SLIC algorithm [1] emphasizing on space proximity to over-segment tissue parts into non-overlapping homogeneous superpixels. Subsequently, to create superpixels capturing meaningful tissue information, we hierarchically merge adjacent similar superpixels. The similarity is measured by texture attributes, i.e., contrast, dissimilarity, homogeneity, energy, entropy, and ASM from Gray-Level Co-occurrence Matrix, and channel-wise color attributes, i.e., 8-bin color histogram, mean, standard deviation, median, energy, and skewness. Initial over-segmentation is performed at 10× magnification to detect more homogeneous superpixels at less computational load. Finally, color and texture features are extracted for the merged superpixels at 40× magnification to capture informative local attributes. A supervised random-forest feature selection is employed and 24 dominant features are selected that classify the superpixels into the epithelium, stroma, necrosis, and background tissue parts. Additionally, spatial centroids of superpixels normalized by the image size are included to construct 26-dimensional representations for the superpixels.

To generate the TG topology, we assume that adjacent tissue parts biologically interact and should be connected. To this end, we construct a region adjacency graph (RAG) [21] using the spatial centroids of the superpixels. The superpixel attributes define the initial node features, noted as f_{TG} and the RAG edges define the TG edges. Figure 2(b) presents a sample TG. The large node at the center represents the centroid of the surrounding stroma that is connected to the parts of epithelium and background. Thus, TG encodes information from the tumor and the stroma microenvironment.

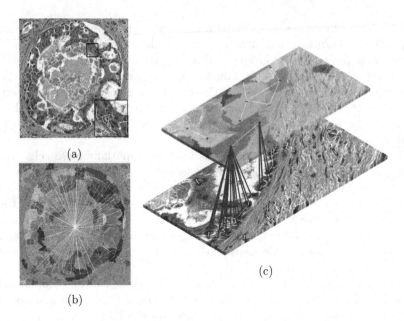

Fig. 2. Visualizing (a) CG, (b) TG, and (c) HACT representations. Nodes are presented in red and edges in yellow. Cell-to-tissue hierarchies are shown in blue in HACT. Note that all hierarchies in HACT are not shown for visual clarity. (Color figure online)

HierArchical-Cell-to-Tissue (HACT) Representation: To jointly represent the low-level CG and high-level TG, we introduce HACT defined as $G_{\text{HACT}} := \{G_{\text{CG}}, G_{\text{TG}}, S_{\text{CG}\rightarrow\text{TG}}\}$. $G_{\text{CG}} = (V_{\text{CG}}, E_{\text{CG}})$ and $G_{\text{TG}} = (V_{\text{TG}}, E_{\text{TG}})$ are CG and TG respectively. We introduce an assignment matrix $S_{\text{CG}\rightarrow\text{TG}} \in \mathbb{R}^{|V_{\text{CG}}|\times|V_{\text{TG}}|}$ that describes a pooling operation to topologically map CG to TG. $S_{\text{CG}\rightarrow\text{TG}}$ is built using the spatial information of nuclei and superpixels, *i.e.*, $S_{\text{CG}\rightarrow\text{TG}}(i,j) = 1$ if the nucleus represented by node i in CG spatially belongs to the superpixel represented by node j in TG. Note that $|V_{\text{CG}}| \gg |V_{\text{TG}}|$. An overview of HACT in Fig. 2(c) displays the multi-level graphs and the hierarchies.

2.2 HACT Graph Neural Networks (HACT-Net)

HACT-Net processes a multi-scale representation of the tissue. Given G_{HACT}, we learn a graph-level embedding $h_{\text{HACT}} \in \mathbb{R}^{d_{\text{HACT}}}$ that is input to a classification neural network to predict the classes. We use the Graph Isomorphism Network (GIN) [28], an instance of message passing neural network [8] with a provably strong expressive power to learn fixed-size discriminative graph embeddings.

First, we apply T_{CG} GIN layers on G_{CG} to build contextualised cell-node embeddings. For a node u, we iteratively update the node embedding as:

$$h_{\text{CG}}^{(t+1)}(u) = \text{MLP}\left(h_{\text{CG}}^{(t)}(u) + \sum_{w \in \mathcal{N}_{\text{CG}}(u))} h_{\text{CG}}^{(t)}(w)\right) \tag{1}$$

where, $t = 0, \ldots, T_{\text{CG}}$, $\mathcal{N}_{\text{CG}}(u)$ denotes the set of neighborhood cell-nodes of u, and MLP is a multi-layer perceptron. At $t = 0$, the initial node embedding is, i.e., $h_{\text{CG}}^{(0)}(u) = f_{\text{CG}}(u)$. After T_{CG} GIN layers, the node embeddings $\{h_{\text{CG}}^{(T_{\text{CG}})}(u) \mid u \in V_{\text{CG}}\}$ are used as additional tissue-node features, i.e.,

$$h_{\text{TG}}^{(0)}(v) = \text{Concat}\left(f_{\text{TG}}(v), \sum_{u \in \mathcal{S}(v)} h_{\text{CG}}^{(T_{\text{CG}})}(u)\right) \tag{2}$$

where, $\mathcal{S}(v) := \{u \in V_{\text{CG}} \mid S_{\text{CG} \rightarrow \text{TG}}(u, v) = 1\}$ denotes the set of nodes in G_{CG} mapping to a node $v \in V_{\text{TG}}$ in G_{TG}. Analogous to Eq. (1), we apply the second graph neural network based on GIN layers to G_{TG} to compute the tissue-node embeddings $\{h_{\text{TG}}^{(t)}(v) \mid v \in V_{\text{TG}}\}$. At $t = T_{\text{TG}}$, each tissue-node embeddings encode the cellular and tissue information up to T_{TG}-hops from v.

Finally, the graph level representation h_{HACT} is built by concatenating the aggregated node embeddings of G_{TG} from all layers [28], i.e.,

$$h_{\text{HACT}} = \text{Concat}\left(\left\{\sum_{v \in G_{\text{TG}}} h_{\text{TG}}^{(t)}(v) \,\middle|\, t = 0, \ldots, T_{\text{TG}}\right\}\right) \tag{3}$$

The graph-level representations are then processed by an MLP classifier to predict the cancer subtype.

3 Experimental Results

3.1 Dataset

We introduce a new dataset for BReAst Carcinoma Subtyping (**BRACS**)[1]. BRACS consists of 2080 RoIs acquired from 106 H&E stained breast carcinoma whole-slide-images (WSI). The WSIs are scanned with Aperio AT2 scanner at 0.25 μm/pixel for 40× resolution. RoIs are selected and annotated independently by three pathologists using QuPath [3] as: Normal, Benign (includes Benign and Usual ductal hyperplasia), Atypical (includes Flat epithelial atypia and Atypical ductal hyperplasia), Ductal carcinoma in situ and Invasive. Disagreed annotations are further discussed and annotated by consensus. BRACS is more than four times the size of the popular BACH dataset [2] and consists of challenging typical and atypical hyperplasia subtypes. Unlike BACH, BRACS exhibits large variability in the RoI dimensions as shown in Table 1. The RoIs represent a more realistic scenario by including single and multiple glandular regions, and comprising of prominent diagnostic challenges such as stain variance, tissue preparation artifacts and tissue marking artifacts. Unlike recent graph-based

---

[1] Currently pending approval for releasing the dataset to the research community.

Table 1. BReAst Carcinoma Subtyping (BRACS) dataset statistics.

	Normal	Benign	Atypical	DCIS	Invasive	Total
# RoI	305	462	387	503	423	2080
Avg. # pixels in a RoI	2.1M	5.8M	1.4M	4.4M	9.6M	4.9M
Avg. # nodes in a Cell-graph	841	2125	584	1740	4176	1974
Avg. # nodes in a Tissue-graph	80	222	70	205	487	223

Fold~Tr/V/Te	Normal	Benign	Atypical	DCIS	Invasive	Total
Fold 1	198/60/47	318/78/66	244/75/68	359/76/68	286/70/67	1405/359/316
Fold 2	202/47/56	304/66/92	245/68/74	355/68/80	283/67/73	1389/316/375
Fold 3	200/56/49	278/92/92	234/74/79	346/80/77	282/73/68	1340/375/365
Fold 4	196/49/60	292/92/78	233/79/75	350/77/76	285/68/70	1356/365/359

approaches on histopathology data [5,26,29] that conduct data splitting at image level, we perform train, validation and test RoI splits at the WSI-level, such that two images from the same slide do not belong to different splits. RoIs from the same WSI can be morphologically and structurally correlated, even if they are non-overlapping. Thus, image-level splitting leads to over-estimated results on the evaluation set, and networks trained in such manner lack generalizability to unseen data. We consider four sets of train, validation and test splits, generated at random at the WSI-level, to evaluate our methodology. The fold-wise number of RoIs for train, validation and test sets are provided in Table 1.

3.2 Implementation

All our experiments are conducted using PyTorch [20] and the DGL library [27]. We benchmark our proposed HACT-Net against several GNN- and CNN-baselines. Comparison with standalone CG-GNN and TG-GNN assess the impact of multi-level information processing. Comparison with Concat-GNN that concatenates CG and TG graph embeddings, $i.e.$, $h_{\text{Concat}} =$ Concat$(h_{\text{CG}}, h_{\text{TG}})$, evaluates the benefit of hierarchical-learning. Note that Concat-GNN is analogous to recently proposed Pathomic Fusion [5]. CNN base-lines include single scale CNNs [24] at three magnifications, and two multi-scale CNNs using late fusion with single stream + LSTM [24]. Multi-scale CNNs use multi-scale patches from $(10\times + 20\times)$ and $(10\times + 20\times + 40\times)$. Considering tumor heterogeneity, CNN approaches are limited to $10\times$ to include only one cancer type in an RoI.

CG-GNN and TG-GNN have four GIN layers with a hidden dimension of 32 in standalone, Concat-GNN and HACT-Net. Each GIN layer uses a 2-layer MLP with ReLU activation. The classifier is composed of a 2-layer MLP with 64 hidden neurons and five output neurons, $i.e.$, the number of classes. The model is trained to minimize the cross-entropy loss between the output logits and the ground truth labels. We set the batch size to 16, the initial learning rate

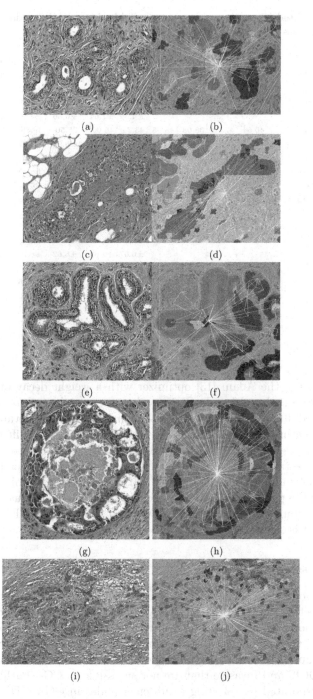

Fig. 3. Cell-graph (left) and tissue-graph (right) examples for four cancer subtypes. (a–b) Normal, (c–d) Benign, (e–f) Atypical, (g–h) DCIS, and (i–j) Invasive. Large central nodes in the tissue-graphs depict the centroids of the surrounding stroma tissues.

Table 2. Weighted F1-scores across four test folds. Mean and standard deviation of fold-wise and class-wise weighted F1-scores. Results expressed in %.

Model/Fold#	1	2	3	4	$\mu \pm \sigma$	Normal	Benign	Atypical	DCIS	Invasive
CNN (10×) [18,24]	49.85	46.86	51.19	54.04	50.49	47.50	46.00	39.25	51.25	69.75
					±2.58	±2.50	±7.45	±3.63	±2.05	±4.21
CNN (20×) [18,24]	52.49	51.88	44.38	56.37	51.28	52.25	47.25	44.50	48.25	62.25
					±4.34	±1.64	±6.80	±4.56	±3.56	±4.44
CNN (40×) [18,24]	40.64	47.30	38.08	48.95	43.74	46.00	35.50	46.75	38.00	56.00
					±4.51	±7.71	±8.96	±5.02	±4.30	±7.12
Multi-scale CNN (10×+20×) [18,24]	56.17	54.41	53.94	55.66	55.04	57.25	51.75	42.25	54.50	72.25
					±0.90	±3.90	±8.78	±8.73	±2.06	±1.92
Multi-scale CNN (10×+20×+40×) [18,24]	58.80	54.64	55.53	53.90	55.72	55.75	52.25	46.75	50.75	71.75
					±1.87	±1.78	±6.38	±2.28	±2.38	±3.34
CGCNet [29]	51.54	58.97	56.70	50.44	54.41	53.00	52.25	42.00	57.00	68.25
					±3.53	±2.55	±4.96	±8.15	±5.52	±2.58
TG-GNN	54.47	55.13	67.84	49.85	56.82	56.78	54.76	48.52	56.53	69.52
					±6.67	±1.89	±6.62	±8.76	±12.78	±11.00
CG-GNN	61.35	53.81	62.00	55.38	58.13	62.66	**64.57**	36.18	59.98	68.12
					±3.59	±5.32	±9.05	±6.85	±1.43	±2.52
Concat-GNN	54.66	54.49	64.59	**63.95**	59.42	57.00	60.31	49.62	60.65	68.94
					±4.85	±4.06	±8.36	±4.71	±4.94	±12.47
HACT-Net	**62.17**	**59.06**	**69.41**	60.92	**62.89**	**65.15**	58.40	**55.45**	**63.15**	**73.78**
					±3.92	±3.64	±10.59	±5.19	±4.08	±7.35

to 10^{-3} and use the Adam [13] optimizer with a weight decay of 5.10^{-4}. For the single-scale and multi-scale CNNs, we extract patches of size 128×128 at 10×, 20× and 40×. Pre-trained ResNet-50 on ImageNet is finetuned to obtain patch-level feature representations after experimenting with different ResNet, VGG-Net and DenseNet architectures. All the CNNs use [18] to derive RoI-level feature representation via aggregate-penultimate technique, and employ a 2-layer MLP with 64 hidden neurons and five output neurons for RoI classification. Considering the per-class data imbalance, weighted F1-score is used to quantify the classification performance. Model with the best weighted F1-score on the validation set is selected as the final model in each approach.

3.3   Discussion

Figure 3 demonstrates CG and TG representations of sample RoIs from BRACS. Visual inspection signifies that the CGs aptly encompass the cellular distribution and interactions. Similarly, the TGs aptly encode the tissue microenvironment by including the topological distribution of tissue components, such as lumen in Benign, apical snouts in Atypical, necrosis in DCIS, and tumor-associated stroma in DCIS and Invasive that are not accessible to CGs. Pathological prior can be incorporated by selecting a subset of nodes in CG or TG to construct task-specific representations.

Table 3. Confusion matrix for the HACT-model on the test samples of Fold 1.

	Normal	Benign	Atypical	DCIS	Invasive
Normal	33	7	6	1	0
Benign	16	39	8	3	0
Atypical	1	7	36	24	0
DCIS	0	1	8	50	9
Invasive	1	3	4	7	52

Table 2 presents the weighted F1-score on four test folds and their average statistics for the networks. Standalone CNNs perform better at lower magnification by capturing larger context. Multi-scale CNNs perform better by including context information from multiple magnifications. The CG-GNN and TG-GNN results signify that topological entity-based paradigm is superior to pixel-based CNNs. Further, they indicate that tissue distribution information is inferior to nuclei distribution information for breast cancer subtyping. Our CG-GNN baseline outperforms CGCNet [29] justifying the use of expressive backbone GNNs like GIN [28]. Also concatenating the updated node representation at each layer as shown in Eq. 3 brings a performance boost without additional parameters. Concat-GNN outperforms TG-GNN and CG-GNN indicating that CG and TG provide valuable complementary information. Further, HACT-Net outperforms Concat-GNN confirming that the relationship between the low and high-level information must be modeled at the local node-level rather than at the graph-level for better structure-function mapping.

Class-wise performance analysis in Table 2 shows that the invasive category is the best detected due to the topologically discernible patterns with scattered nodes and edges in CG and TG. Atypical cases are the hardest to model due to high intra-class variability and high ambiguity with benign and DCIS. Large drops in performance in the CGCNet and CG-GNN for Atypical convey that standalone cell information is not adequate enough to identify these patterns. Tissue information such as apical snouts in FEA, necrosis in DCIS, stroma microenvironment in Benign, etc. bolster the discriminability for Atypical. Thus, all the networks including TG perform better than CG-GNN for the Atypical. The CG-GNN and TG-GNN performances for the Normal, Benign, and DCIS indicate that nuclei information is more informative for these categories. HACT-Net utilizes both nuclei and tissue distribution properties, thus performing superior to CG-GNN and TG-GNN for almost all subtypes. Unlike CG-GNN, HACT-Net utilizes stromal microenvironment around the tumor regions which is a pivotal factor in breast cancer development [4]. The class-wise comparison between HACT-Net and Concat-GNN establishes the positive impact of hierarchical learning. The gain in class-wise performances of HACT-Net substantiates that the network does not get biased towards one particular class. The confusion matrix in Table 3 depicts the expected inter-class ambiguities. The per-class accuracies from Table 3 for Benign without atypia, Atypical, DCIS and Invasive are 83%, 53%, 74% and 78% respectively compared to 87%, 48%, 84% and 96% in [6]. HACT-Net accuracies are promising and can potentially be improved.

Moreover, the paradigm shift from pixel-based to entity-based analysis can potentially yield interpretability of the deep learning techniques in digital pathology. For instance, [29] analyzes the cluster assignment of each node in CG to group cells according to their appearance and tissue types. [12] introduces a post-hoc interpretability module for CG-GNN to identify decisive cells and interactions. However, both approaches are limited to CG analysis. Considering the pathologically aligned multi-level hierarchical tissue attributes in HACT, the interpretability of HACT can reveal pathologically crucial entities, such as nuclei, tissue parts and interactions, to imitate the pathologist's assessment.

4   Conclusion

In this work, we have proposed a novel hierarchical tissue representation in combination with a hierarchical GNN to map the histopathological structure to function relationship. We have extensively compared the proposed methodology with the state-of-the-art CNNs and GNNs for breast cancer subtyping. The enriched multi-level HACT-representation and hierarchical learning strengthen our methodology to result in superior classification. HACT-representation can seamlessly scale to any RoI size to incorporate vital local and global context for subtyping. The entity-based graphical representation yields better control for pathologically inspired tissue encoding and modeling. The success of our methodology motivates to explore the inclusion of task-specific pathological prior knowledge. Further, our hierarchical modeling paves way for recent interpretability techniques in digital pathology to decipher the hierarchical nature of the tissue.

References

1. Achanta, R., et al.: Slic superpixels compared to state-of-the-art superpixel methods. IEEE Trans. Pattern Anal. Mach. Intell. **34**, 2274–2282 (2012)
2. Aresta, G., et al.: BACH: grand challenge on breast cancer histology images. Med. Image Anal. **56**, 122–139 (2019)
3. Bankhead, P., et al.: QuPath: open source software for digital pathology image analysis. Sci. Rep. **7**, 1–7 (2017)
4. Bejnordi, B., et al.: Using deep convolutional neural networks to identify and classify tumor-associated stroma in diagnostic breast biopsies. Mod. Pathol. **31**, 1502–1512 (2018)
5. Chen, R.J., et al.: Pathomic fusion: an integrated framework for fusing histopathology and genomic features for cancer diagnosis and prognosis. arXiv preprint arXiv:1912.08937 (2019)
6. Elmore, J.G., et al.: Diagnostic concordance among pathologists interpreting breast biopsy specimens. JAMA **313**, 1122–1132 (2015)
7. Gadiya, S., et al.: Histographs: graphs in histopathology. arXiv preprint arXiv:1908.05020 (2019)

8. Gilmer, J., et al.: Neural message passing for quantum chemistry. ICML **70**, 1263–1272 (2017)
9. Graham, S., et al.: Hover-Net: simultaneous segmentation and classification of nuclei in multi-tissue histology images. Med. Image Anal. **58**, 101563 (2019)
10. Gunduz, C., et al.: The cell graphs of cancer. Bioinformatics **20**(Suppl 1), i145–i151 (2004)
11. Hamilton, W., et al.: Inductive representation learning on large graphs. In: NeurIPS, pp. 1024–1034 (2017)
12. Jaume, G., et al.: Towards explainable graph representations in digital pathology. In: ICML, Workshop on Computational Biology (2020)
13. Kingma, D., Ba, J.: Adam: a method for stochastic optimization. In: ICLR (2015)
14. Kipf, T., Welling, M.: Semi-supervised classification with graph convolutional networks. In: ICLR (2017)
15. Kumar, N., et al.: A dataset and a technique for generalized nuclear segmentation for computational pathology. IEEE Trans. Med. Imaging **36**, 1550–1560 (2017)
16. Litjens, G., et al.: A survey on deep learning in medical image analysis. Med. Image Anal. **42**, 60–88 (2017)
17. Macenko, M., et al.: A method for normalizing histology slides for quantitative analysis. In: IEEE ISBI, pp. 1107–1110 (2009)
18. Mercan, C., et al.: From patch-level to ROI-level deep feature representations for breast histopathology classification. In: SPIE 10956 Medical Imaging: Digital Pathology, vol. 109560H (2019)
19. Myers, D.J., Walls, A.L.: Atypical breast hyperplasia. In: StatPearls (2019)
20. Paszke, A., et al.: PyTorch: an imperative style, high-performance deep learning library. In: NeurIPS, pp. 8024–8035 (2019)
21. Potjer, F.: Region adjacency graphs and connected morphological operators. In: Maragos, P., Schafer, R.W., Butt, M.A. (eds.) Mathematical Morphology and its Applications to Image and Signal Processing. Computational Imaging and Vision, vol. 5, pp. 111–118. Springer, Heidelberg (1996). https://doi.org/10.1007/978-1-4613-0469-2_13
22. Sharma, H., et al.: Cell nuclei attributed relational graphs for efficient representation and classification of gastric cancer in digital histopathology. In: SPIE 9791 Medical Imaging: Digital Pathology, vol. 97910X (2016)
23. Siegel, R.L., et al.: Cancer statistics, 2016. CA Cancer J. Clin. **66**, 7–30 (2016)
24. Sirinukunwattana, K., Alham, N.K., Verrill, C., Rittscher, J.: Improving whole slide segmentation through visual context - a systematic study. In: Frangi, A.F., Schnabel, J.A., Davatzikos, C., Alberola-López, C., Fichtinger, G. (eds.) MICCAI 2018. LNCS, vol. 11071, pp. 192–200. Springer, Cham (2018). https://doi.org/10.1007/978-3-030-00934-2_22
25. Velickovic, P., et al.: Graph attention networks. In: International Conference on Learning Representations, ICLR (2018)
26. Wang, J.O.: Weakly supervised prostate TMA classification via graph convolutional networks. arXiv preprint arXiv:1910.13328 (2019)
27. Wang, M., et al.: Deep graph library: towards efficient and scalable deep learning on graphs. CoRR, vol. abs/1909.01315 (2019)
28. Xu, K., et al.: How powerful are graph neural networks? In: ICLR (2019)
29. Zhou, Y., et al.: CGC-net: cell graph convolutional network for grading of colorectal cancer histology images. In: Proceedings of the IEEE ICCV Workshops (2019)

Correction to: Graph Matching Based Connectomic Biomarker with Learning for Brain Disorders

Rui Sherry Shen, Jacob A. Alappatt, Drew Parker, Junghoon Kim, Ragini Verma, and Yusuf Osmanlıoğlu

Correction to:
Chapter "Graph Matching Based Connectomic Biomarker with Learning for Brain Disorders" in: C. H. Sudre et al. (Eds.): *Uncertainty for Safe Utilization of Machine Learning in Medical Imaging, and Graphs in Biomedical Image Analysis*, **LNCS 12443, https://doi.org/10.1007/978-3-030-60365-6_13**

The original version of this chapter was revised. Figure 2 was updated with the correct numbers.

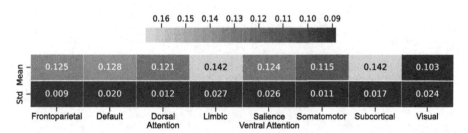

Fig. 2. Dysfunction coefficients at functional systems level, with larger dysfunction coefficients indicating a dominant pathology effect at the associated functional systems. We observe large coefficient values for limbic and subcortical networks, which highlights their vulnerability to injury. Note that, dysfunction coefficients are normalized by the total sum of coefficients to show the relative vulnerability of the systems.

The updated version of this chapter can be found at
https://doi.org/10.1007/978-3-030-60365-6_13

© Springer Nature Switzerland AG 2020
C. H. Sudre et al. (Eds.): UNSURE 2020/GRAIL 2020, LNCS 12443, p. C1, 2020.
https://doi.org/10.1007/978-3-030-60365-6_21

Author Index

Alansary, Amir 174
Alappatt, Jacob A. 131
Allam, Moustafa 198
Anniciello, Anna Maria 208
Aviles-Rivero, Angelica I. 187

Bischof, Horst 42
Bos, Daniel 32
Botti, Gerardo 208
Brancati, Nadia 208

Camarasa, Robin 32
Cardoso, M. Jorge 23
Chen, Lei 121
Clarkson, Matthew J. 198
Cupitt, John 174

Davidson, Brian 198
de Bruijne, Marleen 32
De Pietro, Giuseppe 208
de Vriendt, Marianne 187
Demir, Uğur 109
Desrosiers, Christian 152
Di Bonito, Maurizio 208
Dowrick, Thomas 198

Erdil, Ertunc 13

Fernandes, Lauren Alisha 208
Feroce, Florinda 208
Fidon, Lucas 164
Foncubierta-Rodríguez, Antonio 208
Foti, Simone 198
Frucci, Maria 208

Gabrani, Maria 208
Gantenbein, Marc 13
Garbi, Rafeef 97
Garifullin, Azat 52
Gharsallaoui, Mohammed Amine 109
Glocker, Ben 3
Goksel, Orcun 208
Gopinath, Karthik 152

Graham, Mark S. 23
Grzech, Daniel 3

Hendrikse, Jeroen 32
Hodgson, Antony 97

Irzan, Hassna 164

Jaume, Guillaume 208
Jin, Lili 121

Kainz, Bernhard 3
Kaisar, Maria 61
Kannan, Arunkumar 97
Kim, Junghoon 131
Konukoglu, Ender 13
Koo, Bongjin 198
Kooi, Eline 32

Laves, Max-Heinrich 81
Le Folgoc, Loic 174
le Folgoc, Loïc 3
Lensu, Lasse 52
Li, Qinfeng 121
Lindén, Markus 52
Lombaert, Herve 152

Makropoulos, Antonios 174
Marlow, Neil 164
Melbourne, Andrew 164
Mulpuri, Kishore 97

Nachev, Parashkev 23
Nederkoorn, Paul 32

Ortmaier, Tobias 81
Osmanlıoğlu, Yusuf 131
Ourselin, Sebastien 23, 164

Parker, Drew 131
Pati, Pushpak 208
Payer, Christian 42
Peng, Ziwen 121
Ploeg, Rutger 61

Rajan, Deepta   71
Ramalhinho, João   198
Rekik, Islem   109, 142
Riccio, Daniel   208
Rittscher, Jens   61
Rueckert, Daniel   174

Sağlam, Mustafa   142
Sattigeri, Prasanna   71
Schuh, Andreas   174
Scognamiglio, Giosue   208
Sellars, Philip   187
Shen, Dinggang   121
Shen, Rui Sherry   131
Shi, Feng   121
Sirinukunwattana, Korsuk   61
Soares, Maria F.   61
Štern, Darko   42
Stoyanov, Danail   198
Sudre, Carole H.   23

Tam, Ka Ho   61
Thiagarajan, Jayaraman J.   71

Thiran, Jean-Philippe   208
Tölle, Malte   81
Tudosiu, Petru-Daniel   23

Urschler, Martin   42

van der Lugt, Aad   32
Varsavsky, Thomas   23
Venkatesh, Bindya   71
Vercauteren, Tom   164
Verma, Ragini   131
Vosylius, Vitalis   174

Wang, Andy   174
Ward, Francis   174
Waters, Cemlyn   174

Xing, Xiaodan   121
Xue, Zhong   121

Zakharov, Alexey   174

Printed in the United States
By Bookmasters